The View
from Nebo

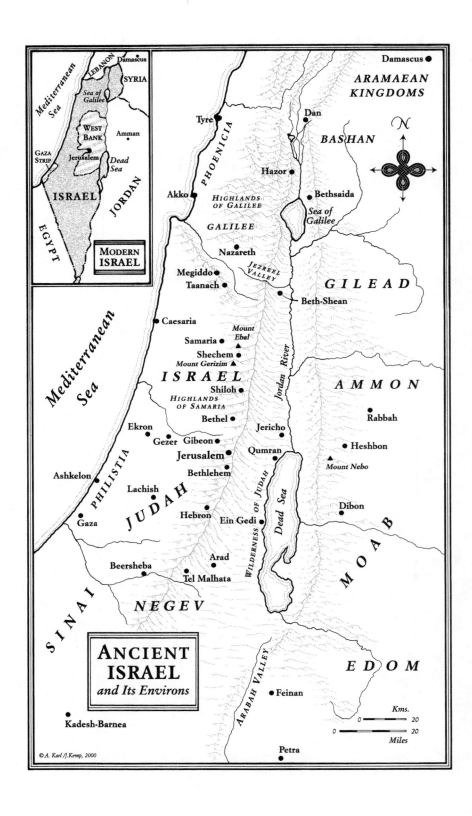

MODERN
ISRAEL

ANCIENT
ISRAEL
and Its Environs

© A. Karl /J. Kemp, 2000

The View from Nebo

How Archaeology Is

Rewriting the Bible and

Reshaping the Middle East

Amy Dockser Marcus

Little, Brown and Company

Boston New York London

First Edition

Library of Congress Cataloging-in-Publication Data

Marcus, Amy Dockser.
    The view from Nebo : how archaeology is rewriting the Bible and
reshaping the Middle East / by Amy Dockser Marcus.
        p.   cm.
    ISBN 0-316-56167-3
    1. Bible. O.T. — Antiquities. 2. Palestine — Antiquities. 3. Middle
East — Antiquities. 4. Jews — History — To 70 A.D. I. Title

BS621.M36   2000
221.9'5 — dc21   99-087911

10 9 8 7 6 5 4 3 2 1

Q-FG

Text design by Chris Welch

Printed in the United States of America

For Ronen, who shared the view

and to my parents, Bob and Golda Dockser,
with love and gratitude

Contents

Acknowledgments

❧

This book is the result of seven years I spent living and working in the Middle East, from 1991 to 1998. I am grateful to Paul Steiger, the managing editor of the *Wall Street Journal,* who sent me there in the first place and granted me a year's leave of absence from the newspaper to write this book. Other *Journal* friends and colleagues helped make my journey so rewarding and my copy so much better. John Brecher and Bill Grueskin on Page One ran the articles that led to this book. John Bussey and Michael Williams on the Foreign Page let me wander around the Middle East and write about what caught my eye. I was fortunate to have met Steve Adler, an assistant managing editor at the *Journal,* early in my career; much of what I know about journalism I learned from him. My deepest thanks for his many years of friendship, support, and wise counsel.

My agent, Kris Dahl, believed in this book when it was still a conversation and got others to believe in it too. Rick Kot, my editor at Little, Brown, made this book better in every way. I'm grateful for his instructive insights and artful editing. His assistant, Michael Liss, was helpful throughout the process. My thanks also to Judy Clain, who took over at the end and oversaw the final stages of the book's publication with enthusiasm and good cheer. Peggy Leith Anderson's meticulous copyediting and rigorous standards were greatly appreciated.

Ann Killebrew, archaeologist and friend, introduced me to the world of Middle Eastern archaeology and was a wonderful companion on many road trips to visit digs. She also read several chapters of an early draft of the manuscript with care. Piotr Bienkowski read large portions of this work and offered helpful criticism. I'm also grateful to Jane Cahill, Steven Fine, and Ronald Hendel for reading and commenting on chapters.

This book could not have been written without the help of the many archaeologists who let me visit their excavations, shared their research, and sat through endless interviews. For their generosity and openness, my thanks and appreciation to: Israel Finkelstein and David Ussishkin at Megiddo; Amnon Ben-Tor at Hazor; Adam Zertal at Har Eval; Itzhaq Beit-Arieh in Tel Malhata; Gabriel Barkay, Dan Bahat, Jane Cahill, and Ronny Reich in the City of David; Amihai Mazar at Rehov; Jeffrey Zorn at Mizpah; Shlomo Bunimovitz at Beit Shemesh; Motti Aviam at Yodfat; Yizhar Hirschfeld at Ein Gedi; Shimon Gibson at Modiin; Eliezer Oren and Steve Rosen in Beersheba; Khaled Nashef at Khirbet Bir Zeit; Jalal Kazzouh in Nablus; Zahi Hawass, Mansour Radwan, and Kent Weeks in Cairo; and Larry Herr, Douglas Clark, Larry Gerarty, and Oystein LaBianca from the Madaba Plains Project. Avi Ofer, Rami Arav, Randall Younker, R. Thomas Schaub, and David Ilan shared their research, theories, and excavation reports. William Dever, Richard Elliot Friedman, Nadav Na'aman, Oded Lipschits, Marwan Abu Khalaf, Neil Asher Silberman, Philip Davies, Niels Lemche, and Thomas Thompson helped illuminate some of the political controversies that surround archaeology in this region. Rami Khouri generously shared his reports about archaeology and excavations in Jordan. Charles Carter arranged for me to receive an advance copy of his fascinating study about Yehud's fate under the Persians. Ornit Ilan gave me a private tour of the Rockefeller Museum that vividly illustrated the complex intertwining of archaeology and nationalism in the Middle East.

Nancy Shekter-Porat in Jerusalem managed to track down even the most unusual requests for information. My thanks also to Khaled Abu Toameh for his help in Hebron and to Ghadeer Taher for her reporting assistance from Amman. Ranya Khader in Amman, Wassim Wagdi in Cairo, and Ahmad Mashal in Ramallah made my work in those cities successful and interesting over the years.

My parents, Bob and Golda Dockser, have supported my career at every turn, even when it took me 10,000 miles away. This book has been no exception. They did everything possible to ensure that I would have the time and freedom to write, from spending the hottest summer on record in the Middle East baby-sitting my daughter to tracking down and photocopying articles in obscure journals and cooking meals during the final push to finish the book. They read and commented on each chapter, and their thoughts about what worked and what didn't were invaluable. Their love, wisdom, and selflessness inform my life and every page of this book. My love and gratitude also to my sister, Lynne, whose moral support and enthusiasm were constant throughout this project.

As always, my husband, Ronen, shared this adventure with me from the beginning. We visited many of the sites together, and each chapter reminds me of happy times spent in far-off desert places. His love of the Bible and the lands it describes helped sharpen my own thinking. And finally, to our children, Eden and Yuval, my love and thanks for being themselves; more than anything else, they have made all the difference.

A Time Line of Key Events in
Ancient Israel's History

❦

Establishing a reliable chronology for ancient Israel's history seems, on the face of it, a straightforward task. The Bible purports to be a history of Israel from its beginning and as such is filled not only with psalms, stories, and songs, but with numbers. The writers were sticklers for recording every generation that descended from Abraham, with names of fathers and whom they begat sometimes running on for pages. We learn that Abraham, the patriarch of the Israelites, was seventy-five years old when he left his father's home in Ur and set out for Canaan, and one hundred when his son Isaac was born. The Book of Exodus, which describes the Israelites' miraculous delivery from Pharaoh's bondage in Egypt, states that the period of their enslavement lasted 430 years. King David reigned 40 years and his son and successor, King Solomon, 40 more, the Bible says. Using various clues like these, scholars have estimated that the period that is known as the patriarchal age, from the birth of Abraham to the death of his grandson Jacob, lasted a little more than 300 years, until 1876 B.C.E., and that the exodus from Egypt occurred in 1446 B.C.E.

But this chronology has a number of serious problems. First of all, it does not correspond with the other evidence we have, such as extrabiblical historical records and archaeological material. It requires accepting the idea that the patriarchs' life spans were incredibly long. The biblical texts themselves do not always agree on the duration of key events. One book might state that the sojourn in Egypt lasted "four generations"; another reference states 400 years; and a third, 430 years. Furthermore, many numbers in the Bible are symbolic, not literal. Biblical writers often say that significant events lasted 40 years, for example.

Over the years, though, scholars have weighed biblical texts, archaeological finds, and historical records discovered in sites located in ancient Israel's neighbors and have created a generally accepted structure of Israelite history. The dating of some events, such as the patriarchal age, is based on the similarities between biblical accounts and the archaeological evidence; the dates of others, like the exodus and the reigns of the later Israelite kings, are based on historical assumptions or correlation with outside sources such as Egyptian or Assyrian texts. The time line thus established has enjoyed widespread consensus among scholars for more than a hundred years. Lately, new archaeological evidence and textual analysis of the Bible have prompted some archaeologists, Bible historians, and scholars to suggest various changes to this chronology. Some argue that certain events should be dated earlier or later or, in a number of cases, that an event did not occur at all. Many of these debates are recounted in the chapters that follow. But this book uses what is still considered the standard dating for key events in the Bible, the sequence against which all new ideas must measure themselves, and makes note of any deviations and outstanding controversies in the text.

The designations B.C.E. (before the Common Era) and C.E. (Common Era) are the equivalent of B.C. and A.D.

2000–1500 B.C.E.	The time when Abraham, Isaac, and Jacob are most likely to have lived.
1260 or 1250 B.C.E.	The exodus of the Israelites from Egypt, under the leadership of Moses.
1200–1000 B.C.E.	The settlement of Canaan by Israelite tribes led by Moses' successor, Joshua.
1001–969 B.C.E.	The Israelite monarchy is founded under King David. At its peak, it encompasses roughly the area from Dan to Beersheba.
970/969–931 B.C.E.	David's son Solomon takes over as king and expands the united monarchy.
931 B.C.E.	Solomon dies and his son Rehoboam takes over. Rehoboam is unable to keep his father's kingdom together and it splits into two separate entities, the northern kingdom of Israel and the southern kingdom of Judah.
931–913 B.C.E.	King Rehoboam rules over Judah.
931–910 B.C.E.	Jeroboam is proclaimed king and rules over Israel.
885–874 B.C.E.	After years of instability, Omri becomes king of Israel and founds a dynasty of four kings who will sit on the throne for forty-four years.
874–853 B.C.E.	Ahab, Omri's son, is king of Israel. Under him, Israel becomes a military and economic power.
723/722 B.C.E.	The Assyrians, the regional power, conquer Samaria, Israel's capital, and the kingdom of Israel comes to an end after some two hundred years. (The ten tribes of Israel are deported and become known as "the lost tribes.") The Assyrian army is unable to conquer Jerusalem and the kingdom of Judah is saved.
605–587/586 B.C.E.	Assyria's empire crumbles and Babylonia takes over as the regional power. Nebuchadnezzar, king of Babylonia, plunders Jerusalem in 597.

After Judah's king forms an alliance with Egypt, the Babylonians besiege and destroy the city. The First Temple is burned (587/586) and the Judeans are exiled.

587/586–538 B.C.E.   The Babylonian Captivity. Babylonians rule Judah. Gedaliah is appointed governor and Judah's capital is moved from Jerusalem to Mizpah.

538 B.C.E.   Cyrus the Great, the ruler of Persia, conquers Babylonia and issues a decree that the Judeans may return to their ancestral homeland.

538–332 B.C.E.   Persia controls Judah. Ezra, a scribe, and Nehemiah, an administrator, are among the Babylonian exiles who return to Judah. They become leaders of Jerusalem's physical resurgence and religious revival. The walls of the city are rebuilt and the Second Temple is built and dedicated (538–515).

336 B.C.E.   Alexander the Great becomes king of the Greek city-states; in 332 B.C.E. he conquers Judea. After his death, the Ptolemies and then the Seleucids rule Judea.

141 B.C.E.   After a twenty-five-year civil war against the Seleucids, the Hasmoneans (or Maccabees) establish a monarchy and Jewish sovereignty of Judea. During this period, the writing of the works that are now known as the Dead Sea Scrolls begins.

63 B.C.E.   Pompey, ruler of Rome, conquers Judea and the Jewish state ends. The Romans take over and install the Herodian dynasty, named after its most famous member, Herod the Great.

37–4 B.C.E.   Herod the Great rules Judea, building Masada and Herodium, and rebuilding the Second Temple area.

4 B.C.E.	Herod dies and a series of Roman-appointed prefects govern Judea, the most famous of whom is Pontius Pilate (governed 26–36 C.E.), who orders that Jesus be crucified.
66 C.E.	Under the Roman military leader Vespasian, soon to become emperor, the Romans fight to suppress the First Jewish Revolt, the Judean uprising. Vespasian's son, Titus, commands the Roman army's attack on Jerusalem.
70 C.E.	A besieged Jerusalem cannot hold out any longer and falls. The Second Temple is destroyed.
73/74 C.E.	The Romans succeed in breaching the walls of Masada, the desert fortress that serves as headquarters for the remaining Jewish resistance. The first-century Jewish historian Josephus records that the Jewish rebels decide to commit suicide rather than surrender to Rome.
132–135 C.E.	The Second Jewish Revolt, under Simon bar Kochba, is brutally put down. Jerusalem is destroyed, Judea is razed, and Judaism is banned.

The View
from Nebo

Introduction

The View from Nebo

And Moses went up from the plains of Moab unto Mount Nebo,
to the top of Pisgah, that is over against Jericho. . . . And the Lord
said unto him: "This is the land which I swore unto Abraham,
unto Isaac, and unto Jacob, saying: I will give it unto thy seed; I
have caused thee to see it with thine eyes, but thou shalt not go
over thither." *(Deuteronomy 34:1–4)*

It takes half a day to travel to Mount Nebo from Jerusalem. The
two sites are so close that, when the haze that is typical of summer
days in this region lifts for a moment, it is possible to see from the
top of the mountain the hills of Judea that surround Jerusalem, the
same view that the Bible says Moses had right before he died. To
journey to Nebo, one first has to cross the Allenby Bridge, which
connects Israel and the West Bank to Jordan. The waiting areas at
both ends of the bridge are always crowded with people, youth with
backpacks hiking their way through the Middle East, elderly women
holding bags of fruits and vegetables on expansive laps or clutching a
chicken in a sack, families laden with their shopping returning from
visiting relatives in the West Bank. On the Israeli side, the area is air-
conditioned, but in Jordan, visitors still jostle for space on the bench
directly in front of the huge fans that churn the humid air. On both

sides of the border, the procedure is the same. A bus arrives, some-times after a wait of thirty minutes, sometimes after three or four hours. There are many times when, for one reason or another, the vehicle never appears, and everyone is turned back for the day, silently resigned to the mysteries of bureaucracy. The police search the travelers' belongings, opening parcels and checking packages. After asking a series of perfunctory questions, they loudly stamp the proper visa into the passports that pile up in front of them. Then everyone climbs on board and takes a seat.

The bus rumbles out to the bridge, and from its windows it's pos-sible to see the Jordan River flowing below, but only for a brief moment. Described in the Bible as a mighty stream that God miracu-lously stopped so that Joshua could lead the Israelites into the land of Canaan after Moses died, today it is merely a bubbling brook and, during a particularly dry summer, only a trickle of water. It is hard to believe this is the same river that has inspired songs and gospels. The ride is so short that it takes only a minute or two for the bus to lum-ber across the bridge. Pilgrims don't have enough time to finish a song before the gate on the other side swings open. There are more security checks, and then the travelers are finally allowed outside, where a line of taxicabs waits to ferry them to their destinations.

Those journeying to Nebo travel along a flat road through a desert landscape of brown patches that rise and fall gently alongside the highway. Bedouin tribes set up camp here according to the season and the location of the best springs. Then, suddenly, Nebo rises in the desert. The mountain's plateau runs westward, stretching far across the horizon, until with an abrupt drop it falls away, and the valley below comes rushing in. All year round, a number of streams flow down the sides of the mountain, leaving in their wake a trail of vegetation, small shrubs, and greenery. The walls on the edge of Nebo's summit form strange patterns and create an unusual perch from which to view the valley. Tourists climb to the top, then clamber on the roughly hewn rocks, standing amid the ruins for a better vista. The hills in the distance stretch until, in the words of one traveler who journeyed here in the 1800s, the last summit "lifts itself against the Dead Sea" and after a final embrace settles in the valley opening like the palm of a hand outside the city of Jericho.

Nebo actually has several peaks, the highest of which rises 800 meters above the surrounding hills. Even lower ones are all 700 meters or more, including the most famous, Siyagha, which stands on the western side of the mountain. This is the peak where it is believed Moses had his first sight of the land that he had struggled so long to reach, only to be told at the end by God that he would not be allowed to cross over into Canaan. That honor would be granted to Moses' successor, the military commander Joshua.

The visitors who come here are drawn to Nebo by the power of this story. In one of the most moving episodes in the Old Testament, after forty years of wandering in the desert following their liberation from slavery in Egypt, the Israelites have come to the end of the road. They arrive in Moab, now in modern Jordan, directly at the entrance to the promised land of Canaan. But even as Moses readies the people for the final leg of their long journey, he informs them that he will not be accompanying them across the river Jordan. "I am a hundred and twenty years old this day," he tells the Israelites after gathering them together to hear his final words. "I can no more go out and come in, and the Lord hath said unto me: Thou shalt not go over the Jordan."

It is a heartbreaking moment. After so many years of self-sacrifice, of suffering the problems and complaints of the people he calls "stiff-necked," Moses is finally within view of achieving his lifelong ambition. But the ultimate prize is withheld from him. God's decision is not arbitrary; He explains to Moses that he will not cross over the Jordan because of a transgression. God reminds him of a brief moment back in the desert, at the waters of Meribah-kadesh, where Moses disobeyed God's instructions. Told to strike the rock there once in order to bring forth water for his thirsty followers, Moses in a moment of frustration — at the Israelites' constant complaining, or perhaps at God's rigid orders — hit the rock twice. For most modern readers of the Bible, it is hard to understand why so harsh a sentence was passed for so apparently minor an infraction. Didn't the many years of loyal service merit a lesser punishment for one moment of disobedience? Despite the fact that, according to the Bible, Moses actually sees God face to face, he does not try to plead his case or ask for a lesser punishment. After forbidding him entry to the Promised Land, God instructs Moses to climb to the top of Nebo and look at the land of Canaan that stretches out before him, and tells him that he will "die in the mount whither thou goest up, and be gathered unto thy people."

Moses' death perplexes and compels contemporary readers because it is difficult to decide whether God is taunting Moses with that final view of the Promised Land from atop Nebo, or giving him comfort. In Moses' final speech to the people of Israel, it is clear that he is bitter about his fate. He blames the Israelites and their rebellious nature for his harsh sentence. As consolation, however, Moses is spared from ever discovering if reality falls short of his dreams. Barred from actually entering Canaan, he will always have that wonderful view from Nebo and the promise that something better awaits.

This incident has made Nebo perhaps the most famous mountain in the Bible after Mount Sinai, the site where Moses was given the Torah, God's set of laws and commandments, to bring down to his people. And yet there is very little information contained in the Bible about what Nebo or the surrounding area looks like. The Bible's writers considered their work a history, but they were more interested in why the nation of Israel was created, not where. Their lack of specificity, though, helps give the story its metaphorical power. They instinctively understood that their readers could stand on their own Nebos anywhere, and at any time of their lives. Only Bible scholars are likely to notice and appreciate details like the fact that the Scriptures refer to Nebo and its various peaks by three different designations and that the mountain also appears as a backdrop in several other stories. Nebo is the setting for the famous story in the Book of Numbers about Balak, the king of Moab, who asks the seer Balaam to curse Israel, whose army at the time is encamped in the plains of Moab. The king brings Balaam up to three different mountains, including Nebo's summit. Even after many sacrifices to his own deity, each time that Balaam tries to curse Israel, God intervenes and the chastened Balaam ends up uttering instead a blessing on Israel.

The most detail we are given about Nebo comes elsewhere in Numbers, in a story about the tribes of Reuben, the eldest son of Jacob, and his brother Gad. The tribes own a large number of cattle, the Bible records, and when they see the richness of the land around Nebo they decide that they don't want to enter Canaan with the other Israelites after all. They are willing to forsake the prospect of a divine promise for the certainty of the present and go to Moses to discuss matters. "If we have found favor in thy sight, let this land be given unto thy servants for a possession," they petition him. "Bring us not over the Jordan."

Moses, aghast, reprimands them, and first tries to appeal to their sense of loyalty, reminding them that the Israelites are about to embark on a crucial battle to conquer the land. "Shall your brethren go to war, and shall ye sit here?" he argues. More important, Moses fears that if the others see these two tribes remaining behind, they will lose heart and also refuse to leave. Such an event would surely anger God. "Will ye turn away the heart of the children of Israel from going over into the land which the Lord hath given them?" he worries aloud. Moses even goes so far as to recall for them what happened previously when some of the Israelites neglected to show God sufficient gratitude for the land He had promised them: God in response swore that those above the age of twenty when they left Egypt would not be allowed to go to Canaan, and instead condemned the Israelites to wander in the desert for the next forty years, until a new, more courageous generation could be born and come of age. Moses definitely does not wish his people to suffer a similar misfortune now.

So the men try to reach a compromise. Reuben's and Gad's kinsmen agree that if they are promised the parcels they want, they will first go to Canaan and fight alongside the other tribes until the Israelites have triumphed. "We will build sheepfolds here for our cattle, and cities for our little ones," they tell Moses, "but we ourselves will be ready, armed to go before the children of Israel until we have brought them unto their place. . . . We will not return to our houses, until the children of Israel have inherited every man his inheritance." And with that promise, Moses relents and apportions them the land.

From this context, we can assume that the land around Nebo is fertile with ample supplies of water and hence attractive to cattle owners. And yet, just as in the story of Moses' death at the mountain, it seems that it is the larger message, rather than the precise details of place and time, that most concerns the Bible's writers. The descendants of Reuben and Gad are familiar characters to us. We don't really have to know exactly what property they desired to understand why they don't want to leave Nebo. It is easy to share in their unwillingness to take a risk on the unknown, even if it might offer a better future, when one is standing on Nebo and the familiar beckons.

One of the central paradoxes of the Bible is that while it tells readers everything they need to know, they always want to know more. They want to see Nebo for themselves, to climb to the top of the mountain, look out at Canaan, and see what Moses saw. The earliest biblical interpreters were scholars, men like the sage Ben Sira, of the second century B.C.E., and Philo, a Greek-speaking Jew who lived in Alexandria until around 40 C.E. and whose work influenced generations of biblical historians. In their books, they would often recast stories from the Scriptures. They recognized what many of the most ardent pilgrims to Nebo do not: whether one is interpreting a biblical passage or an archaeological artifact, the story invariably shifts. The view from the summit of Nebo is never the same. It is always changing as new possibilities that weren't considered before suddenly open up.

This has never been more true than it is today. As visitors climb up the steep hill, they pass a sign erected by the Franciscan order, which has run the site since the 1930s. At the top of Siyagha is a large stone monastery that has been painstakingly restored. Its floors are decorated with several mosaics dating from the Byzantine era, the color on the tiles fading but still beautiful. Upon closer examination it is clear that many of the animal and human figures in the mosaics have been defaced by Christian iconoclasts during a period of religious schism. Over the course of hundreds of years, an entire complex of churches, chapels, and small places of worship have sprung up in the shadow of this main monastery.

The first major archaeological excavations of this area were undertaken in 1933, when the mountain was definitively identified as Mount Nebo. This conclusion was based on records left by Christian pilgrims of the fourth century C.E., who had traveled there to visit a sanctuary set up to Moses' memory. Since then, with only brief hiatuses during times of political crisis or war, the digging has never stopped. Initially the goal of the archaeologists working on the mountain and in the valley was to uncover the various layers of structures that had been built throughout the centuries to honor Moses and the Bible. But as the excavations continued, something amazing occurred. The archaeologists started turning up artifacts and remains that significantly predated the period during which most scholars believed that the stories of Moses were set. Suddenly Nebo took on significance outside the pages of the Bible as well; here was an entire history that probably hadn't been known during the biblical age. Eventually, more than six hundred sites of archaeological interest were located. Among the finds were six hand axes, as well as arrowheads and scrapers, dating back some eighteen thousand years to the Paleolithic prehistoric period.

But the most fascinating artifacts were from the fourth millennium B.C.E., the era archaeologists call the Late Chalcolithic and Early Bronze Ages. All around Nebo, on top of the hills and mounds that represent the ruins of ancient settlements, the archaeologists unearthed a series of huge dolmens. Dolmens are manmade structures, usually used as tombs, composed of huge stones that form a kind of circle, with an opening to the east, and a circular rock serving as a capstone. At Nebo, the dolmens sometimes covered entire fields, appearing individually or in large groups. The remains of the structures are still visible in the hills east and southeast of Siyagha. In one area alone, there are close to two hundred such structures, sometimes interconnected with other standing stones. The archaeologists even found the tools used to make the dolmens lying next to some of them, along with thin scrapers made of flint used to etch out carvings, and fragments of basalt jars possibly connected to the burial rituals. Nearby was another group of tombs, dating more than two thousand years later than the first set. They too had been erected on high ground, overlooking the Nebo plateau. In the middle of each tomb was a burial chamber, surrounded by one or two circles of stones. These discoveries indicated that more than six thousand years ago, long before Moses received word of his fate from God, people had come to this mountain to bury their dead. The archaeologists who made the discoveries have speculated that Nebo was used as a burial site not because it was already considered a sacred mountain, but rather because the presence of cool springs there continually drew nomadic groups searching for water.

The Bible never reveals exactly how Moses dies. As with so many of its accounts, it offers a very spare narrative that leaves many of the details vague. We learn merely that "Moses the servant of the Lord died there in the land of Moab, according to the word of the Lord. And he was buried in the valley in the land of Moab over against Beth-peor, and no man knoweth of his sepulchre unto this day." The archaeological digs that have taken place in the last few years at Mount Nebo indicate that, wherever Moses' grave might be, he was buried in what was already a vast field of dolmens. In this valley of lost hopes, Moses was neither the first nor the last to be halted at the edge of the Jordan.

———

The first known visitors to Nebo in the postbiblical era were a group of pilgrims in the fourth century C.E. who came with the express purpose of looking from the top of the mountain to see the landscape Moses saw before he died. The Roman emperor Constantine recently had declared Christianity to be a lawful religion, and his mother, Helena, set out shortly afterward in an effort to retrace Jesus' footsteps and visit the most famous landmarks mentioned in the Bible. Queen Helena has been called the world's most successful archaeologist. Relying primarily on religious visions to guide her, she always found what she went looking for, and Constantine had basilicas erected around the Middle East to mark each of her discoveries. In this manner she determined the location of both Mount Sinai and Mount Nebo, and a Christian sanctuary dedicated to the memory of Moses was established on top of the latter mountain shortly afterward. Scholars and pilgrims were regular visitors to Nebo during the Byzantine era (roughly 324–640 C.E.); and the Roman pilgrim Egeria and the bishop of Maiumas of Gaza, Peter the Iberian, both kept detailed records of their visits to the Memorial Church of Moses, relating what they saw there to the biblical narratives. The pilgrim Theodosius, who came to Nebo in the first half of the sixth century C.E., wrote that close to the city of Livias and east of the Jordan River, one could see "the water made to flow from the rock, the place of Moses' death and the hot springs of Moses where lepers come to be cured." Over the course of centuries these records and the knowledge of the location of Nebo would be lost.

So in 1838, when two Americans named Edward Robinson and Eli Smith set out to try to match sites mentioned in the Bible to their actual locations in Palestine, they embarked on a difficult task. The pair employed a number of strategies in their quest, including talking to the area Bedouins to see if any of the names of the places had been preserved in the Arabic words for the various locales. It was this tactic that eventually led the intrepid pair to Nebo, when they had pointed out to them a mountain that was known to the locals as Mount Nabo or Mount Musa (Moses in Arabic). They also recorded the presence of a spring, called Moses' Spring, situated on the northern slope of the mountain.

Descriptions of the topography of Nebo in earlier records, as well as the local legends that had developed over the years around the site, helped lead to an identification of the ruins at Siyagha as the place where the Memorial Church of Moses once stood. Over the succeeding centuries, the main memorial church had become the centerpiece of an entire group of places of worship, all devoted to Moses, that sprang up literally in its shadow. One notable example was a three-nave basilica with a chapel that contained both wall and floor mosaics. By the seventh century C.E., another sanctuary was added. Its Chapel of the Theotokos, or Mother of God, featured an especially beautiful mosaic scene whose artist had sought to depict his vision of the altar in the temple in Jerusalem, with a rectangular panel of flowers, gazelles, and two bulls. All these various chapels and sanctuaries were separate, and yet interrelated in their common devotion. There were also small, one-person cells that had been carved out on the top of the mountain and around its sides, where some of the monks lived. The ruins of these structures were first discovered by the Duke of Luynes, a Frenchman, who photographed the remains of the churches during an 1864 trip and drew an accurate but partial rendering of the surrounding area. The duke's party also descended the mountain to visit Moses' Spring, which they likewise photographed.

It is not easy to pinpoint the date when religious tourism ends and the field of biblical archaeology begins in earnest. Many of the earliest travelers came as pilgrims, but they often had an eye for archaeological and historical detail and left behind travelogues that provided geographical information for later explorers. But scholars generally agree that biblical archaeology as we understand it today first came into its own in the nineteenth century. What drove the early biblical archaeologists to Nebo was an impulse similar to that of the pilgrims: the desire to prove the historicity of the story of Moses' presence there and his death. Henry B. Tristram, an explorer who had climbed all the peaks on the mountain, wrote in 1872 that he and his group had visited Nebo three times because they were "anxious to verify exactly the view of Moses." Tristram was enough a man of the modern age to approach his goal with some skepticism. In his journals before reaching Nebo, he questioned whether the mountain was truly connected to the biblical story, or was in fact part of some elaborate hoax mounted by the local sheikh hoping to capitalize on the religious interest of wealthy and gullible Westerners eager to see the spot where Moses supposedly died. Tristram also acknowledged that his party could never hope to determine exactly where Moses actually last stood. Still, once he arrived at Nebo, his allegiance to skepticism and science gave way to religious inspiration. He wrote that, standing on the mountain, "the first feeling is that of admiration at the divine power which drew Israel from the wondrously fertile country eastward and northward determinedly to force the rugged hills of Palestine, not richer than the Gilead they had already won."

Soon after Tristram made his expeditions, the most intensive exploration of Nebo to date was conducted by the American Palestine Exploration Society. The organization had been founded in 1870 in New York, soon after a similar group was established in London called the Palestine Exploration Fund of England. The leader of the American group's 1873 expedition, John A. Paine, set out his aims in his journal, which was a manifesto of a biblical archaeology on the cusp of change. Merely obtaining scientific data about Nebo and the nearby area was not sufficient, Paine argued. He wanted, he wrote, to "collect all references in the Scriptures to these sites . . . so as to show [how] the chain, its heights, headlands, valleys, springs, ruins, even in minutest particulars fulfills and confirms the Bible."

Paine's expedition would be among the last to concern itself only with the pursuit of the biblical past. Over the ensuing years, it became increasingly difficult to separate archaeological goals from the strategic aims of groups like the American Palestine Exploration Society and the Palestine Exploration Fund of England, whose officials often had close ties to their governments. By the early 1870s, Napoleon III's empire was in ruins and France's influence in Egypt coming to an end. The British War Office wanted to insure that the recently completed Suez Canal would remain open to British trade with India and the Orient. Around this time it also became clear that the Ottoman Empire, which had dominated the entire Middle East, was close to falling. The European powers were eager to establish footholds in the region in anticipation of the not so far off time when they would be able to divide up among themselves the empire's former territories. The search for antiquities and biblical sites became the main arena of these burgeoning territorial ambitions. By 1913 the Turks had aligned themselves with Germany and against Britain, France, and Russia, and the world lurched ever closer to outright war. In December of that year, the Palestine Exploration Fund decided to conduct an archaeological survey of the Wilderness of Zin in southern Palestine, which the Bible says the Israelites passed through on the way to Canaan. One of the archaeologists the group hired was a young man named T. E. Lawrence, later famous as the leader of the Arab revolt during World War I. Lawrence was eager for the chance to explore his passion for the Bible, but his participation in the dig also afforded him a unique opportunity to view the Ottoman line of defense in the desert. He duly recorded what he saw. General Edmund Allenby, who led the British forces to final victory in Jerusalem in 1917, studied the publications of the Palestine Exploration Fund in preparation for the war. After one battle, British forces had to clear German positions that had been set up in the remains of the archaeologists' trenches at Tel Gezer, the site where the Bible says one of the fortresses of King Solomon was located.

Even after World War I ended, it would still take most of the remainder of the twentieth century for biblical archaeology to move sharply away from proving the historicity of the Bible's narratives and toward a broader investigation of Middle Eastern culture, a shift that has only gained force in the last decade. But a discipline that from its inception was tied so closely to the competition for influence in the region among the imperial powers has never been able to completely cut loose from politics. In most countries of the Middle East today, archaeology is still a national undertaking, and excavation results have political consequences. When the Palestinians began to take power from the Israelis in the West Bank and the Gaza Strip following the signing of the 1993 peace accords, one of the first acts of the Palestinian government was to establish a department of archaeology. And yet, even peace has not stopped the conflict but merely shifted it in a different direction. One of the sticking points between the two sides is that Israel wants the Palestinians to control only Muslim and Arab archaeology sites on the West Bank. The Palestinians insist on the right to dig at, and hence interpret, all the sites that fall in the territories under their political jurisdiction. Moreover, they want artifacts found at the sites over the years returned to them in order to be placed in their own museums, including the Dead Sea Scrolls. This fight has still not been resolved completely, and it is clear that sharing the past is proving to be as difficult a prospect as splitting the land.

The following chapters of this book chronicle the work of a new generation of archaeologists, and how their excavations at key biblical sites such as Megiddo, Jerusalem, and Hazor are reshaping the biblical narrative as well as the map of the Middle East. For the most part, these are not officially sponsored activities, even in the financial sense, since few Middle Eastern governments can afford to grant the large sums of money needed to keep complex digs running for years. But this is the very reason they are so important. Freed from the need to advance a government's territorial ambitions or to come up with proof for a religious or ethnic group's claims of superiority, these digs offer alternative visions of where the area's peoples came from and who they are now. Sometimes the results subvert the conventional wisdom, whether biblical or nationalistic. But mainly today's archaeologists are doing what readers of the Bible and even its original writers have always done: interpret the text in light of changing circumstances. In this way, every generation makes the stories its own.

The evolution of the Franciscan dig at Nebo is a useful gauge of these shifts in attitudes. The Franciscan order originally managed to get an exclusive license to dig at Nebo mainly through the efforts of one of its monks, the resourceful Brother Jerome Mihaic. On his many trips from Jerusalem to Nebo, he would arrive laden with fruits and vegetables and other gifts that helped insure a safe passage along dangerous routes. He provided manpower and money to build a road that joined the peak of Siyagha with the main road from the town of Madaba, opening the way to tourism. He came up with the funds and materials to build a small house for the monks to use as base camp for the group's expeditions, and restored the large Byzantine cistern situated on the southern slope of the mountain in order to supply clean drinking water.

Brother Mihaic recorded in his journal that the first thing his party did when it reached the top of Siyagha during a pilgrimage to the site in 1931 was to open copies of the Bible and read the last chapter of Deuteronomy, which describes Moses' death. Soon after they officially began digging in 1933, the monks discovered there the basilica and the large monastery around the main sanctuary. On these expeditions and on ones carried out in succeeding decades by new groups of archaeologists, most of the work was concentrated on uncovering and restoring this complex. Because the main churches had been built during the Byzantine period, a time of Christian rule in the Middle East, it's hardly surprising that a group of Franciscan monks would focus its attention on excavating these remains. But over the years, the Franciscans eventually joined forces with other archaeologists working in the area, and the scope of their work expanded far beyond the Christian period. Michele Piccirillo, the Franciscan monk who now runs the Nebo digs, says that at least a few of the finds that the groups were recording already had been noted by the earliest explorers of Nebo. But Brother Piccirillo distinguishes himself from his predecessors in his steadfast reluctance to enter into any discussion about Moses and what he may or may not have seen from atop Nebo. That isn't to say that the topic is of no interest to the Franciscans. In a monumental 1998 volume detailing their archaeological finds and interpretations, they also include a number of articles about the biblical traditions surrounding Nebo, among them a chapter on the grave of Moses in Jewish literature and Nebo's significance in biblical tradition. Every year in early September, the local Christian community celebrates the liturgical feast of Saint Moses at the church, which is also a way to mark the progress of the restoration and archaeological work at the site, and Piccirillo and many of the other members of his archaeological team are enthusiastic participants.

The initial focus on the site's biblical connections and the Christian era had, as later groups discovered, resulted in a skewed picture. The early archaeology had centered on excavating artifacts that had the strongest connection to the traditions surrounding Moses' death at the site. The discovery of the Paleolithic artifacts and other additional data during a 1993 survey pushed Nebo's history back six thousand years, and the focus turned to reconstructing the history of human occupation at the site from its inception. But even with this expansion of research, there are still gaps in Nebo's history and some will be difficult to fill. Locals have looted archaeological sites over decades and taken stones to use for construction. A fortress called Rujm al-Mukhayyat, which dates to the Iron Age, was noticed by archaeologists as early as the 1930s but subsequently ignored. The results from an excavation at the structure undertaken in the 1960s have never been published, and even worse, no one knows any longer where the material and artifacts found during the excavations are stored. By the time a new study of the site was drawn up by the Franciscans in 1993, the edifice was in such a state of ruin that they concluded it would be almost impossible to reconstruct it. To protect the Nebo complex from further losses, the monks are lobbying the king of Jordan to turn the area into an archaeological park, a proposal complicated by the fact that some of the lands are privately owned. "We are less interested in Moses," Piccirillo told me in an interview, "and more interested in archaeology."

The change in focus from biblical historicity to a more general investigation of the material culture of the entire Middle East, and one that looks back to prebiblical periods, has been brought about in part by scientific advances made over the last fifty years. In the days when Nebo was first excavated, archaeology was still largely an amateurs' pursuit, dominated mainly by those drawn by the stories they read in the Bible or heard preached in church. Now archaeology is practiced in the laboratory as well as in the field. Its basic methodology has not changed substantially: archaeologists still use picks and shovels for excavating. They cut out squares in the earth, and the dirt they remove is piled up neatly at the sides of their work area or carted away to another spot on the site in wheelbarrows. But in other ways, the discipline has been dramatically transformed. At some digs, archaeologists employ a machine called an electronic distance meter, which uses a laser beam to automatically measure the various heights and widths of the trenches they dig and send it to a computer for recording. Other devices can detect the smallest variations in the magnetic sensitivity at any spot on a site, pinpointing the most likely places to dig. Radar and sonar help locate previously undetected sites and structures. When the first major excavations took place in the Middle East in the early 1900s, archaeologists had used a quarter-inch-mesh screen to sift through the earth and isolate faunal remains or small pieces of pottery. Now the meshes are half a millimeter wide — about 0.02 inch — allowing for the recovery of bones belonging to animals as small as mice or shrews. In excavations conducted recently in Jericho, the meshes were invaluable in the study of the origins of wheat and barley cultivation, as well as seeds and pollen in order to pinpoint changes in climate.

One of the most significant technological advances, which has only recently begun to be employed in a widespread manner in digs in Israel and other Middle Eastern countries, is the practice of using radiocarbon remains to date finds. Radiocarbon dating first emerged after World War II, the work of a chemist who had spent the war years studying cosmic radiation and realized that it was possible to date the age of organic materials by analyzing the amount of a residual isotope, carbon-14, that they contained. Unfortunately, the first attempts to apply radiocarbon dating to archaeology used wood samples, which provided imprecise and often inaccurate results. This was due primarily to the fact that sections taken from different parts of a tree yielded widely divergent dates, depending on when the tree started growing and when it was cut. It also wasn't possible to determine how long the wood might have been in storage before it was used in building. Recently the process has been fine-tuned, and archaeologists have also used it to test the remains of seeds, such as olive pits, which don't present the same problems as wood and have supplied more precise dates. Some archaeologists also have begun to explore the idea of studying the DNA in bones and mummies in the hope of determining when new ethnic groups immigrated to various countries, information that has simply been unavailable to previous generations of scientists.

This is not to say that the individuals most closely associated with the traditional agenda of biblical archaeology — scholars such as the Americans William Foxwell Albright, who helped establish Palestinian pottery chronology with his 1926–1932 work at Tel Beit Mirsim, and Nelson Glueck, a rabbi and archaeologist who also visited Nebo — chose not to implement new methods in their excavations. Glueck, in fact, was one of the early pioneers in archaeological surveys, a technique that involves collecting pottery shards on the ground that is still used today. But the fact remains that, whatever their methodology, the Bible, and finding a way to make archaeological discoveries correlate with the Bible, remained at the heart of their work. "Discovery after discovery has established the accuracy of innumerable details, and has brought increased recognition of the Bible as a source of history," wrote Albright in his 1932 classic work, *Archaeology of Palestine and the Bible.* Albright, Glueck, and a small group of other archaeologists and Bible scholars dominated the world of Middle East archaeology from 1920 up until the 1970s.

For more progressive archaeologists, however, these radically new research tools have led to the re-creation of an entire world, and not just the world described in the Bible. Discoveries made in one country are now compared as a matter of course to others from around the region, and even outside the borders of Canaan, in areas that generally did not interest the Bible's writers. Although archaeologists have certainly not abandoned the idea of the value of studying the Bible and the biblical world, they now take an approach far different from that of their predecessors. "If you want to learn more about the Bible," Bruce Routledge, an archaeologist who is directing an excavation in Jordan, said at a 1998 conference about ancient Israel organized at the University of Pennsylvania, "stop looking at the Bible. If you want to learn more about ancient Israel, stop looking at ancient Israel." What Routledge meant was that the Bible could be better understood against the canvas of broader regional trends. "There were probably many Davids and Solomons operating around the Middle East during the tenth century B.C.E.," he added. The idea that Israel's history was unique has gradually been giving way to the notion that Israel's past can be best understood in the context of the general history of the ancient Near East.

This is not an uncontroversial notion. In 1998 the Israel Exploration Society celebrated its fiftieth anniversary at its annual meeting at the Israel Museum in Jerusalem. The national organization of archaeologists came into existence soon after the creation of the state of Israel, and the timing was no accident. In Israel, the heart of the biblical landscape, archaeological finds have been the source of virtually every national symbol, from the state seal to government-issued medallions. Postage stamps use archaeological motifs, and Israeli coins are stamped with images taken from Jewish silver coins of the first century C.E. Even the name of the country's currency — the shekel — remains the same as it did in ancient times. For years, Israeli tank troops were sworn in on the top of Masada, the mountain fortress where, according to the first-century historian Josephus, the last remaining Jewish rebels against Roman rule chose to commit suicide rather than surrender to the besieging army.

During the first decades of its existence, the Israel Exploration Society's annual meetings attracted large crowds. But over the years, the ranks of amateurs willing to travel to Jerusalem for a day of lectures and discussions had thinned, as fewer and fewer people seemed interested in listening to archaeologists talk and give slide-show presentations about their digs. By 1998 most of the members of the audience were archaeologists who came to listen politely to colleagues repeat the traditional theories about the sites they were excavating. But this year would be different. Israel Finkelstein, the head of the Tel Aviv University Institute of Archaeology, delivered an opening speech in which he proceeded to dismiss virtually every accepted belief about the emergence of ancient Israel that the Israel Exploration Society as a national institution upheld.

Finkelstein's speech was the most forceful articulation yet of the seismic shift that was under way in archaeology. He wasn't the first to argue that the Israelites had not, as had long been believed, actually introduced any great technological breakthroughs in agriculture, pottery, or architecture. For several years, archaeologists had been turning up so-called four-room houses, once considered a hallmark of Israelite construction, across the Jordan River in sites in ancient Ammon. Similarly, other archaeologists had suggested that collar-rimmed jars — considered an Israelite innovation and so named because the rim of the jar turned down like a shirt collar at the neck — had been in use as far back as the thirteenth century B.C.E., long before the Israelites existed as a distinct group. The jars were also unearthed in later periods at sites not associated with the Israelites. "The material culture all existed before the Israelites," Finkelstein told the audience, "and you can't say who made it, whether it was Israelites or Ammonites or someone else."

The Israel Exploration Society, which represented the consensus view in archaeology, saw itself as the keeper of the archaeological faith. Yet the society's top officials had known what line Finkelstein would take when they selected him to give the opening remarks. It is hard to imagine anyone at the society fifty years ago agreeing with

Finkelstein's major point that there weren't significant differences between what was happening culturally in Canaan thousands of years ago and what was taking place in the larger Levant area.

"We are emerging from a huge mistake that both biblical scholars and, to some extent, though perhaps less, archaeologists have been making," said Philip Davies, a Bible scholar at the University of Sheffield in England, when we met one afternoon in Tel Aviv. "That mistake is simply to assume that a literary collection like the Bible and the data unearthed by archaeology can possibly be made to tell the same kind of story. To try to combine them into a single story is precisely where we have been going wrong. Why should we seek to make one story out of two?"

To the Bible's writers, Israel and everything that had happened to it throughout its history were unique phenomena. But the archaeological record that is now emerging demonstrates that, overall, the country was in fact subject to the same kinds of historical and environmental forces as its neighbors in the region. Israelites by and large lived very much like their contemporaries in the Middle East, an idea that biblical scribes, with their relentless focus on the creation of Israelite identity, tended either to profess disinterest in or ridicule.

As revelatory as it has proven to be, this new approach stressing the common elements that linked the Israelites to their neighbors has vulnerabilities as well as strengths. The truth about the past, the ability to determine what really happened, has, as always, remained elusive. Brian Hesse and Paula Wapnish, zooarchaeologists based in the Department of Anthropology at the University of Alabama in Birmingham, have spent their careers studying the remains of animal bones at sites around the Middle East. In the past few years, they have focused their attention in particular on pig remains, and on discovering how avoidance of the animal became a signal part of Jewish, and later Muslim, ethnic identity. Many archaeologists, particularly the Israelis, have been eagerly following their work, hoping that it might help ascertain when the Israelites emerged as a distinct ethnic group. Israel Finkelstein had led the charge on this issue, enthusiastically declaring in one article that "food taboos, more precisely pig taboos, are emerging as the main, if not the only avenue that can shed light on ethnic boundaries in the [Iron Age I period]. Specifically, this may be the most valuable tool for the study of ethnicity of a given, single Iron I site."

Many archaeologists have assumed that the presence or absence of pig bones at different sites might be a useful index of ethnic identity in a given region. In many respects, this line of reasoning makes eminent sense. Food laws are one of the central and most visible expressions of Jewish religious community, and none is better known than the prohibition against eating pork. It is mentioned in Deuteronomy, which declares, "And the pig, because it divides the hoof but does not chew the cud, is unclean for you. You shall not eat their meat, and you shall not touch their carcasses." A similar prohibition is reiterated in Leviticus. For years, as Hesse and Wapnish recount in one of their studies, archaeologists, sociologists, and historians all had been searching for the "one 'true' rationale that lies behind the origin of pig disdain as expressed in the Bible." The debate had grown contentious, and there were numerous theories from which to choose. For instance, some scholars had posited that the Israelites hadn't eaten swine as a matter of hygiene, and the dietary rule therefore contributed to better health. Others suggested that their avoidance was a reaction to swine behavior and the animal's unattractive physical appearance; a response to the loss of forest cover where the pigs thrived; an element borrowed from Egyptian theology; or even a kind of superstitious ritual to insure the Israelites' successful migration to the Promised Land. Hesse and Wapnish rejected all these explanations and proposed a different approach. They wanted to look beyond ideology and instead try to identify the myriad of forces — including economic, political, and ecological — that might have influenced the use or rejection of pigs.

When their research was completed, they reached a startling conclusion, one at odds with the conclusive results that Finkelstein optimistically had predicted in his paper. After studying bone remains at archaeology sites throughout the Middle East, they determined that during the biblical period virtually no one in the region was eating pig. Similarly, the refusal to use pigs as sacrifices in official religious rituals hadn't been limited to the Israelites, but was a common feature of religions throughout the Middle East. Hesse and Wapnish developed a set of what they called "pig principles" to try to explain why this might be the case.

Pigs require larger amounts of water than other kinds of livestock, which means that they can be raised only in areas that receive substantial rainfall. Pigs are also quite difficult to herd, requiring that a group who chooses to raise them be willing to give up its nomadic ways and settle down. Changes in a community's agricultural patterns would also affect whether or not pigs were raised. Studies done on pig production in ancient Egypt indicated that when more grain was grown, cattle and goats were raised instead of pigs, because of the specific demands of land use. And in every part of the region, production and consumption of pork were far more typical of lower- or working-class people than of the elite. At urban sites in Mesopotamia, archaeologists had learned that refuse associated with labor gangs was filled with pig bones, but that the garbage of residential sectors from the same periods was not. Searching for a way to feed workers economically, the local administration apparently had served pork.

These various factors had resulted in a significant, long-term, historical decline in the use of the animal. The peak of pig consumption, according to Hesse and Wapnish's study, had been in the prehistoric era. The low point was in the early Iron Age period, from the twelfth to the tenth centuries B.C.E., the time when, according to the Bible, King David and King Solomon reigned. Israelites weren't eating pigs then, Hesse and Wapnish concluded, but neither was anyone else.

As a result, it was difficult to propose any valid generalizations about who used pigs and why. Some archaeologists had assumed early on that pig bones, which were found in southern coastal cities in

Palestine known to have been conquered by the Philistines, a seafaring people from the Aegean region who arrived in Canaan in the twelfth century B.C.E., might be a key to determining the presence of Philistines at other sites. However, the study by Hesse and Wapnish showed that, while pig use was found in some Philistine cities in Canaan, such as the port of Ashkelon and the more mountainous cities Ekron and Timna, not all the Philistine sites had pig bones. The most interesting finding was that pig use by the Philistines took place only within the first century or two after their arrival in Canaan. By the time the Babylonian ruler Nebuchadnezzar destroyed Ashkelon in 604 B.C.E. during one of his campaigns in Palestine, the Philistines had generally stopped eating pork, just like their neighbors. "Rigorously applied, such a procedure of equating the absence of pigs with cultural identity would lead to a remarkable (and preposterous) expansion of early Israelite hegemony," Hesse and Wapnish wrote.

In this sense, the debate over pigs vividly illustrates both the potential and the limitations of the new approach to biblical archaeology. The search for the ancient Israelites has been going on since the beginning of biblical archaeology. But critical interpretation is needed just as much for the latest finds as for the old technique of reading every Bible verse literally. The study of pig bones tempted many scholars to think they would soon be able to look at a bone and know who had lived there, Israelite, Ammonite, or Philistine. The past is too messy, the social interactions and material finds too complex and overlapping, to allow for such a simplistic correlation. In this arena, there are many truths, not one.

Still, techniques such as the study of pig bones get us closer than we have ever been before to the ancient Israelites, as well as to their neighbors, and this is no small achievement. Over the years, many scholars had read the biblical injunctions against pork consumption and assumed that they were among the earliest rules of the Israelites. But by focusing so narrowly on the biblical text, they missed the larger picture. Pig prohibitions were a widespread phenomenon at this time, one the Israelites shared with their neighbors. Eventually this changed. During the Hellenistic period, when the Greeks ruled the Middle East, for example, abstaining from eating or raising pigs became an important avenue of political, social, and religious protest among Jews. Stories, traditions, and both Jewish and Greek texts describe Jews of this time as refusing to eat pork despite torture or threat of death. In his 1993 *History of Ancient Palestine,* Bible scholar Gösta Ahlström sums up the various prohibitions found in the biblical texts by arguing that they resulted in a situation whereby "the term 'Israel' took on a new and narrower meaning. . . . It was based on a religious ideology that excluded other worshippers of Yahweh." Under Hesse and Wapnish's reconstruction of pig use in the ancient Near East, Israel has taken on its broadest meaning yet. Their work is a reminder that even the things that eventually made Israel unique had their roots in the wider world.

By examining what was happening historically not just to Israel but to its neighbors the Ammonites, Edomites, Moabites, and Canaanites, archaeologists have not only expanded the borders of the biblical world but also made it possible to understand the Bible in a new way. The last time I visited Nebo it was in mid-July, a time of year when few tourists are willing to brave the intense heat to undertake the climb up the mountain. At the summit, candles were lit in the main altar of the large stone monastery but flickered in the damp church. The building was tranquil, its stone benches cool. The stained glass windows behind the main altar provided the only burst of color. A guard on the church steps dozed quietly in the heat, his gun across his knees, until he wakened to guide me to the edge of the mountain. He pointed out the Dead Sea, the desert, the hills of Judea and Samaria. "There is Jerusalem," he said, his finger hovering for a moment on the horizon. Then he returned to his perch on the church steps and lay down, not saying another word.

If the Book of Deuteronomy is any indication, the view that Moses saw from atop the mountain shortly before his death must have been stunning. "And Moses went up from the plains of Moab unto Mount Nebo, to the top of Pisgah, that is over against Jericho," the verses read. "And the Lord showed him all the land, even Gilead as far as Dan, and all Naphtali, and the land of Ephraim and Manasseh, and all the land of Judah as far as the hinder sea; and the South, and the Plain, even the valley of Jericho, the city of palm-trees, as far as Zoar."

The Bible says that Moses was shown "all the land" — that he was able to stand on top of Nebo and cast his eye from Dan, located some 90 miles to the north on what is now Israel's border with Lebanon, all the way down to the desert town of Beersheba, about 65 miles to the southwest. The improbability of being able to see such a distance has been debated over the years by Bible scholars, archaeologists, and armchair travelers. Was it a miracle, a final gift to Moses to assuage him for what he had lost? Some of the earliest explorers of the mountain fiercely debated about precisely where Moses might have stood to obtain, on a clear day, such a spectacular vista. Even now the speculation continues. One historian in Jordan, Kamal Salibi, has published an entire book arguing that Nebo was probably located somewhere else — he proposes perhaps in Saudi Arabia — because it is physically impossible to see from Dan to Beersheba from a mountaintop in Jordan.

There is another possibility. It is more modest than a miracle, and it circumvents the debate over the Bible's historicity, as it cannot be proven and would not really matter to the faithful in any case. Whatever Moses saw from Nebo, for the Bible's writers, and for so many others who have followed them and read their work with devotion and fervor, it surely belonged to the Israelites. Today from the edge of the summit, the view is more expansive. There are the hills of Amman, Jordan's capital city and capital of the ancient Ammonites, the Israelites' rivals and neighbors. There is Jericho, where the Canaanites lived, and the valley of Moab, home of the Moabites, close kin to the Israelites and yet their longtime enemies. On the edge of the desert is the Dead Sea and near its northern shore the ancient ruins of Qumran, where the Dead Sea Scrolls were found and where an ancient sect of ascetics known as the Essenes may have lived. The outline of Bethlehem appears, the great builder King Herod's ancient fortress Herodium visible directly next to it. And there, shimmering elusively in the distance, is the beautiful and mysterious Jerusalem, the city that King David made his capital after moving from Hebron. The valley below this mountain contains the histories of peoples who didn't always make it into the pages of the Bible — lost tribes, overlooked lives. Each group beckons with a different story, and looks out with longing on a Promised Land that remains just out of reach.

Chapter 1

❧

Genesis

Abraham's Odyssey

Now the Lord said to Avram, "Get thee out of thy country, and
from thy kindred and from thy father's house, unto the land that I
will show thee. And I will make of thee a great nation, and I will
bless thee, and make thy name great; and be thou a blessing. And I
will bless them that bless thee, and him that curseth thee I will
curse; and in thee shall all the families of the earth be blessed."
(Genesis 12:1–3)

The history of the Israelites begins with the story of a family, the
personal odyssey of Abraham, his wife Sarah, their son Isaac
and his wife Rebecca, their grandson Jacob, and Jacob's twelve
sons. Throughout the Bible, but especially in its first five books —
Genesis, Exodus, Leviticus, Numbers, and Deuteronomy — we follow every detail of their increasingly complex lives, sharing their
betrayals, deceptions, and multitude of sins. Only much later, after a
miraculous escape from slavery in Egypt, a forty-year sojourn in the
desert, and their conquest of Canaan, is it clear that somewhere along
the way this family has become a dynasty and, finally, a nation.

Many of the most widely known stories in the Bible, including the
story of Abraham's journey from his father's house in Ur, in
Mesopotamia, to the Promised Land in Canaan, date to ancient
times, some as far back as three thousand years ago. Despite the

chronological gap that exists between Abraham's life and days and our own, part of the Bible's power throughout the centuries has been the writers' ability to convince us that these events are as real as those that occurred only recently.

More than any other patriarchal figure, Abraham remains a vivid, living presence, a familiar part of the daily life — and daily politics — of the Middle East. Virtually every country through which Abraham passed en route to Canaan has its own holy site and legend associated with him, and a tourism industry eager to promote it. In Urfa, a city near the border between Turkey and Syria, locals venerate and regularly visit a cave where the infant Abraham and his mother are popularly believed to have hidden for three years after the king of Ur decreed that all newborn males were to be killed. Another tradition in Urfa says that when this same king heard of the young Abraham's refusal to pray to idols he ordered him thrown into a fiery furnace on a mountain summit. Water from a pool below the mountain miraculously rose up and extinguished the fire, and the fish living in it carried Abraham away to safety. To this day, no one will touch the carp swimming in the site designated as Abraham's pool out of the conviction that they are the descendants of the fish that rescued Abraham. Anyone who harms the fish, it is said, will go blind.

In downtown Baghdad, in Iraq, a mosque stands in the place where Iraqis believe Abraham's childhood was spent, and the faithful gather there five times a day to pray to him. On the Israeli-Syrian border, Druze Arabs maintain a site they hold sacred as the place where God and Abraham established their covenant, and where today barren women of all religions make pilgrimage with prayers for a child. On the outskirts of Hebron, in the West Bank, members of a Russian hospice carefully tend an oak tree in their courtyard garden. They believe that it was here that Abraham rushed out to greet and offer hospitality to the three angels of God who came to visit him and tell him that his wife Sarah soon would give birth. In the coffee shops of downtown Hebron, the waiters still serve steaming bowls of a lentil dish called Abraham's soup, and in Damascus, street vendors hawk Abraham's juice, made from the fruit of the tamarisk tree, which the Bible records was planted by Abraham in Beersheba. At the Cave of the Patriarchs in Hebron, where the Bible says Abraham and Sarah are buried, Israelis and Palestinians still battle over Abraham's legacy, praying in separate sections of the divided sanctuary at the cave both claim to own.

Despite Abraham's continuing hold on the lives of so many people, a vastly different situation exists among Bible scholars, archaeologists, and historians where Abraham is concerned. They still debate vociferously the extent of David's empire and argue passionately about whether Solomon built a certain building. They mine historical texts searching for additional clues about Omri and Ahab in order to reconstruct the lives and reigns of these lesser-known kings of Israel, and parse the later books of the Old Testament in order to determine whether the writings of Ezra and Nehemiah jibe with Persian records of the same events. In their many acrimonious disagreements exists the conviction that biblical history remains open to interpretation and is a worthy subject of vigorous academic debate and scholarship. The one glaring exception to this breadth of inquiry is Abraham and his times. There is virtually no interest at all in investigating what used to be called the patriarchal age. "Most Bible scholars and archaeologists have abandoned the question of the patriarchs altogether," says Ronald Hendel, himself a Bible scholar. "They don't regard Abraham as having anything historical to say."

Until the 1970s archaeologists were bent on proving the historical accuracy of the patriarchal narratives. But the belief that it was possible for archaeology to validate such an ancient religious story instead led to serious mistakes. In 1975 Italian archaeologists digging at Tell Mardikh, the site of the ancient city of Ebla, about 34 miles south of Aleppo, Syria, stumbled upon sixteen thousand cuneiform tablets, a spectacular find. Most of the tablets seemed to be routine administrative records of the palace, including receipts for purchases and ledgers of income and expenditures. But the Ebla tablets, as they soon came to be called, caused a sensation after an Italian Assyriologist began translating them and announced that they contained the names of biblical sites such as Hazor, Megiddo, Gaza, and Sodom and Gomorrah. They even featured a creation story that read very much like the one in Genesis, at least according to a translation that was soon published. Not everyone was thrilled with the discoveries. Syrian officials asked the archaeologists to downplay the tablets' possible biblical connections, particularly the growing suggestion that the Eblaites might have been ancient Hebrews. But the major backlash came later, and from a more scholarly quarter, when more careful translations revealed that the tablets did not in fact mention biblical cities; the translation of the creation poem was also rejected.

During the same period two influential books were published by American bible scholars, *The Historicity of the Patriarchal Narratives,* by Thomas L. Thompson, and *Abraham in History and Tradition,* by John van Seters. Both works examined the biblical text and concluded by questioning the historical validity of the patriarchal narratives. These scholars suggested that the stories surrounding Abraham and the other patriarchs had been invented as late as the fifth century B.C.E., a thousand years after the patriarchal age, when the Bible's writers wanted to explain the origins of the emerging Israelite nation-state.

Before the 1970s scholars and archaeologists had argued for the patriarchal narratives' historical accuracy based on the fact that many of their details appeared to correspond to practices recorded in cuneiform archives found in the ancient city of Nuzi, in Mesopotamia, which dated from the second millennium B.C.E. But this theory met the same fate as the Ebla tablets when it turned out that some of the putative parallels between the biblical stories and the Nuzi archives, such as personal names and family law customs, were the result of scholarly misinterpretations of the documents, or would have been equally true of later historical periods. "By the time the dust cleared from the academic battle," Hendel recalls, "people had moved on. They never looked back."

But for the first time, we now have the ability to piece together with a reasonable degree of certainty at least parts of Abraham's world. From archaeological excavations and surveys in the Judean hills of Israel, a richer reconstruction has emerged of the economic, social, and agricultural development of Hebron over a period of thousands of years, illustrating how the current political conflict over Abraham has its roots in the biblical era. New research being conducted on the Middle Bronze Age (2000–1550 B.C.E.), the period of time to which scholars still date traditions about a figure named Abraham, reveals that Abraham's actions can be best understood in the context of the changing conditions in the Middle East. Textual criticism of the patriarchal narratives further illuminates the way much of Abraham's story evolved over time.

The significance of this cannot be overestimated, especially in an area of the world where the past still has such a hold on people. Archaeology helps us understand not just the Bible, but what the Bible left out. Biblical interpretation is an ancient phenomenon, something that occurred almost simultaneously with the writing of the narratives. The scribes responsible for insuring the survival of the stories, histories, psalms, and regulations that we read today, the ones who painstakingly copied the texts as parchments aged and disintegrated, didn't simply transfer the texts word for word, comma for comma. The stories were changed, their meanings shifting slightly, or sometimes more dramatically. "By omitting some things and adding others, [an] author reshaped the past and so made it into a more perfect model of what he himself wished to prescribe for the future," writes the prominent Bible scholar James L. Kugel about the ancient biblical interpreters. He might as well be talking about the modern interpreters too. Archaeology recovers what was omitted and adds things that were never considered; in the process, it reshapes history and its consequences.

Yehuda Yaniv, an Israeli documentary filmmaker, is one of these new interpreters. He has followed the progress of the latest research and its implications for the patriarchal narratives, visiting the sites of a few digs in Israel and Jordan. In 1994, firmly believing that the

Abraham who was slowly emerging from the work could be used as a bridge between Jews and Muslims, Yaniv decided he wanted to make a film about Abraham. "I was looking for a way to explore what links us, rather than what separates us," he says.

This wouldn't be an easy task, he recognized, despite the fact that both faiths venerate Abraham as a prophet. The narratives concerning Abraham that developed over the years and now appear in both the Bible and the Koran seem virtually irreconcilable. There is the famous Bible story of the sacrifice of Isaac. After years of their praying for a child, a son, Isaac, is born to Abraham and Sarah. One day God orders Abraham to sacrifice his son as an offering, proof of his ultimate fealty to his faith. Abraham is strangely silent in the face of this demand — he doesn't even plead for his son's life. He silently sharpens his knife and sets out with Isaac to the place God shows him. When they arrive at the designated spot, Abraham methodically binds Isaac, then in a chilling scene, raises his knife. At the very last moment, God stays his hand, sparing the boy and providing a ram for a sacrifice instead. In the Koran's version of this story, it is Ishmael, Abraham's older son, the child of his wife's handmaid Hagar, who is commanded to be sacrificed and then saved. After Ishmael's miraculous deliverance, he and Abraham build the Kaaba, the Islamic holy shrine at Mecca to which millions of Muslims go on pilgrimage every year. Muslims praying there walk around the Kaaba seven times, in remembrance of Hagar's circling in the desert seven times in order to find water for her child after she and Ishmael are banished by Abraham at the insistence of the jealous Sarah. The Koran says that Muhammad developed the faith that Abraham initiated, and Abraham is considered Islam's first prophet, the first Muslim.

Despite this divergence in tradition, Yaniv persisted in the notion of establishing a common religious ground. Shortly after the signing of the peace treaty between Israel and Jordan in 1994, he teamed up with a Jordanian film company and set out to retrace the route Abraham takes in the Bible. Unlike scholars who preceded him, the filmmaker wasn't interested in determining if Abraham actually stopped at every single place on the biblical itinerary. Instead, his intention was to search for Abraham the man. He wanted people to understand what it might have been like to live in Abraham's time. Yaniv hired two actors to be the narrators, a famous Jordanian comedian and stage performer named Hisham Younis, and an Israeli radio and television personality, Alex Ansky. At the Allenby Bridge, the main crossing point between Jordan and Israel, the two men greeted each other warmly, calling each other Isaac and Ishmael. They read passages related to Abraham's story from both the Koran and the Bible. For the most part, however, it wasn't easy making the film. Very few Muslim religious leaders wished to appear on camera in a joint Israeli-Jordanian project. No Jordanian professors or religious leaders took part, and only one Palestinian lecturer working in the West Bank agreed to be filmed. The majority of contributors were Israeli Jews or Israeli Arabs. Yaniv followed Abraham's route at great expense, journeying as far as Haran, on the Turkish-Syrian border, in order to visit the village from which Abraham sets out for the Promised Land after leaving his home in Ur. It was difficult for Yaniv to obtain permission from the Turks for the trip, due to the tensions with the Kurdish resistance groups that opposed the Turkish government, and government officials feared he might be kidnapped or killed. On his way to the village, Yaniv's driver fell asleep at the wheel of the jeep, just as a man was driving a tractor across the treacherous road. The driver was killed, the jeep went off the road and flipped over, and Yaniv and his wife were both injured. Still, he persisted, filming mosques, caves, tombs, and synagogues all over the Middle East, filming anywhere the Bible or other traditions and legends said Abraham had stopped along the way to Canaan.

The movie he ultimately prepared, called *Abraham's Odyssey,* is a fascinating document, though perhaps even more interesting is what Yaniv ended up having to leave on the cutting-room floor. The original film featured one scene in which Younis and Ansky stood together on Mount Nebo in Jordan, where the Bible says Moses viewed the land promised to Abraham. The two men began to argue, Ansky insisting that the promise was most important to the Jewish people. Younis protested that it had been made to all the children of Abraham, Ishmael as well as Isaac. "The expression Promised Land was too charged, and we had to throw the whole scene out," says Yaniv.

Other scenes had to be cut as well. The Jordanian producer insisted that a picture of Younis, a Muslim, wearing a traditional Jewish head covering at the Western Wall in Jerusalem be left out in order not to offend Islamic fundamentalists. A visit to a mosque in Amman that ended when a group of Islamic fundamentalists gathered and started shouting, "Kill the Jews!" was likewise dropped.

Yaniv professes to be uninterested in politics, and he gave an interview to a French newspaper after the Abraham movie was shown at the 1998 Cannes Film Festival. In the interview the reporter described him as an atheist. Members of the Islamic movement in the Jordanian parliament cited the interview during a debate calling for the Jordanian film company that participated in the project to back out of the coproduction deal and the plans to translate the film into Arabic in order to widely distribute it in the Arab world. Since then, Yaniv has been reluctant to try to characterize his religious views. Today he admits he is not certain whether Abraham really lived. But after working on the film, he came to the conclusion that answering that question didn't matter, and could produce no fruitful avenue of scholarly inquiry. "If Abraham was historical or he wasn't historical is really no longer relevant," says Yaniv. "The important fact is that Abraham lives today."

Abraham lives, but it still remains extraordinarily difficult to determine conclusively the origins of such an ancient religious figure based on archaeological evidence. In 1975, around the same time of the Ebla discoveries and the publication of the books questioning the patriarchal narratives, two American professors, R. Thomas Schaub and Dr. Walter Rast, led an expedition to the southeastern section of the Dead Sea in Jordan in the hope of finding the lost cities of Sodom and Gomorrah. These are probably two of the most famous biblical cities, destroyed by God because of the hedonism and abominations of the people living there. Abraham's nephew Lot lives there, and Abraham pleads with God to spare the cities if ten righteous men can be found. God saves Lot, largely on the strength of his kinship tie to Abraham, but decides to destroy the cities. "Then the Lord rained on Sodom and Gomorrah brimstone and fire from the Lord out of heaven. And he overthrew those cities. . . . And Abraham went early in the morning where he had stood before the Lord and he looked down toward Sodom and Gomorrah and toward all the land of the valley, and beheld, and lo, the smoke of the land went up like the smoke of a furnace," the Bible says in Genesis 19.

Over the course of the next fifteen years, Schaub and Rast outlasted all the academic disputes, managing to excavate and identify over thirty sites, from walled towns to huge cemeteries, dating from the earliest historical period through the Islamic era. The two cities that they speculate might be Sodom and Gomorrah are Bab edh-Dhra', the largest of the towns that grew up along the southeastern shore of the Dead Sea, and its neighbor, Numeira.

Both date to the Early Bronze Age, around 3300–2100 B.C.E. This dating places them far earlier than the traditionally accepted time period for when Abraham might have lived. At an earlier time, the archaeologists probably would have insisted that despite the chronological discrepancy, the sites were the Bible's Sodom and Gomorrah. In fact, in their report about the early work at the sites, Schaub and Rast had made just such an argument. Over the years they tempered their initial enthusiasm and became much more cautious about drawing conclusions.

The digs at Bab edh-Dhra' and Numeira offered an unprecedented look at the life and demise of villages thousands of years ago. The two had similar layouts, and both were built on top of hills overlooking the sea, close to freshwater sources. Although Bab edh-Dhra' had already been inhabited for a thousand years, it wasn't until the Early Bronze Age period that its citizens began burying their dead in tombs in a cemetery located at its outskirts. The cemetery has been the source of some of the richest finds, with many objects found surrounding the bones, including pots, clay figurines and beads, wooden tools, and food offerings. Most of the skeletons that have been unearthed there are incomplete, and archaeologists have speculated that the deceased were buried elsewhere at the time of their death, then brought to Bab edh-Dhra's cemetery for reburial in what was probably a family or clan tomb. At first the cemetery was used only seasonally, probably by nomads who came to take advantage of the water there and buried any that had died during their trips. But the settlement nearby gradually developed into a permanent village. The residents built simple homes from mud bricks atop stone foundations. These structures were the first indication to archaeologists that there was eventually a continual presence at the site. A variety of crops were raised there, including wheat, barley, grapes, olives, lentils, and chickpeas. Bone remains indicate that there were also sheep and goats, lizards, donkeys, and camels. Then, around 2350 B.C.E., the city came to a sudden and violent end. No one is certain what precipitated the community's demise — it could have been an earthquake, a military attack from outsiders, or some sort of natural disaster or plague. The Numeira site contained even more dramatic evidence of destruction. The archaeologists found thick ash layers all around the city, burned roof timbers, and walls that had collapsed. There were even freshly picked grapes with their skins still intact. These had been carbonized by the conflagration that destroyed the town, and helped establish that it had come to an end in the late summer or early autumn. The doorways in Numeira were blocked with stones, which was interpreted as possible evidence that its inhabitants might have anticipated some kind of earthquake or natural disaster and evacuated, perhaps expecting to return at a later date. Indeed most of the homes had none of the small items that are typically found at a dig, such as jewelry, and no human remains were located in the debris.

There was nothing in the sites themselves that might conclusively link them to the biblical traditions, but Schaub points out that Bab edh-Dhra' and Numeira had not been inhabited again after they were destroyed. The ruins were right there on the surface. "People passing by could have seen it, the desolation would have been evident to all," says Schaub. He says it is not hard to imagine the kind of history the Bible's authors could infer from such dramatic wreckage. The valley must have seemed cursed by God. The tradition of Sodom and Gomorrah "probably does go back to some historical event," says Schaub. "But at this stage we will never know what it was."

Still, in the shadow of this doubt, some progress is slowly being made. David Ilan, an archaeologist who digs at Tel Dan, a huge site that sits on the border of modern Israel and Lebanon, specializes in the Middle Bronze Age. He calls this period "the dawn of internationalism" in the Middle East, because it marks the first time when encountering a stranger outside one's tent was the normal course of events. People were on the move in great waves throughout the region, and their mobility led to the creation of intricate trading networks that stretched from one city to another. Throughout Tel Dan, there was evidence that people who came from cities in Mesopotamia, including Abraham's birthplace, Ur, really did have an important impact on both the settlement pattern and the character of the area.

During a tour he gave me of the Jerusalem-based Skirball Museum, which houses artifacts from a number of important digs in Israel, Ilan pointed to a replica of the Tel Dan mud-brick gate, the only complete Bronze Age arched structure that has survived intact in the southern Levant. According to Ilan's research, the gate hadn't been used for very long, and apparently had been filled in intentionally with soil soon after its construction. The reason for its abandonment was clear: evidence revealed that soon after its completion the gate had started falling apart. Its north tower began to detach from the base, and an attempt to put up a stone buttress as a support for the collapsing mud bricks had failed. Inside the gate the damage was even worse, as the earthern rampart collapsed into the street leading to the town. Every time it rained, mud and debris would break off and pile up in the main passageway. "If Abraham came riding through that gate on his donkey, he would have had to detour a huge pile of debris." Ilan laughed. He speculated that the townspeople had probably tried to clear the debris away initially but eventually conceded defeat to the elements and filled in the whole structure before building another gate at a different site in the city. In fact, archaeologists had found a stone gate just a short distance from the mud-brick one.

The question that concerned Ilan was the reason for the failure of the gate. "Didn't its engineers realize that in an area that receives relatively large amounts of rain, that gate was going to collapse?" he asked. It puzzled him too that they hadn't used local stone and timber, in ample supply in the surrounding countryside, an oversight that was especially glaring given that these materials had been employed successfully in constructing stone gates during the same time periods at nearby sites like Megiddo and Hazor. Ilan's explanation for these anomalies was that the engineers came from Mesopotamia. "Mud brick was really the only material easily available in Mesopotamia," he explained. "The same kind of vaulting technique at Dan was commonly used in places like Ur for spanning gateways, where precipitation was much lower than in northern Canaan. The architects at Dan simply maladapted the technique they knew from home to this region. Once they saw it wasn't working, they quickly abandoned it."

Ilan made his way around the museum's display cases, past stone coffins, pottery, and other material. Following the finds from Dan was like traveling along the trail the migrants from Mesopotamia had taken into Canaan, bringing their own habits and customs with them as they moved. At Dan and in a small number of northern Canaanite cities, they introduced new burial practices that supplemented traditional practices. Studies of human skeletal remains from the period also showed significant changes in the demographics of the cities that could not be explained by environmental or evolutionary factors, but indicated that new groups of people had lived and died there. At Dan, Ilan and some of his colleagues had also unearthed a particular kind of painted pottery whose style and technique seemed to originate far to the north.

The new research has led to other tantalizing clues about the Middle Bronze Age. In the few cuneiform tablets found dating from this period in Palestine, including in Hebron, are names believed to be of Hurrian origin — the Hurrians were a shadowy ethnic group that dominated northern Mesopotamia and parts of Syria and Anatolia during the second millennium B.C.E. — yet another indication that northern groups mixed with the local population. Other archaeologists are examining food remains, like those of a legume called the Spanish vetchling, consumed in the Aegean but not native to the eastern Mediterranean or to the Near East. The legume contains toxins that can cause paralysis and nerve disorders if not removed through cooking before it is consumed. The people who brought the plant to Canaan or ate it, the archaeologists argue, would have had to know about this preventive treatment. None of this explains how or why immigration took place, Ilan points out, or confirms the historical accuracy of Abraham's journey. But in archaeology's ability to suggest the history of forgotten cities and nomadic peoples, the biblical record is slowly being transformed.

In this past lie the beginnings of the modern political conflict. According to the account in Genesis, it was in Hebron that Abraham was living, across the Dead Sea from his nephew Lot, when his wife Sarah died at the age of 127. Abraham goes to speak to the townspeople about buying a burial place, having already set his eye on the cave of Machpelah (known in English as the Cave of the Patriarchs), at the end of a field owned by Ephron, who is described as a Hittite who lives in the city. Ephron first offers to give the cave and land to Abraham, then states a price when Abraham insists. The price is steep, 400 shekels of silver, but Abraham weighs out the coins and takes possession of not only the cave but the entire field. Eventually he will be buried here too, by his two sons, Isaac and Ishmael, in one of the few recorded acts that they perform together.

It is hard to imagine this event occurring in modern Hebron, where some of the most extremist elements on both sides of the Arab-Israeli conflict live. In 1929 Arabs in Hebron turned on their Jewish neighbors during nationalistic riots and massacred 67 Jewish inhabitants, many of whom they had known all their lives. In a small museum set up by the current Jewish residents of Hebron, there are photographs showing a woman's cut-off hand and people with gashes in their backs. The city's Muslim community has its own suffering and memorials stemming from the 1994 massacre by Baruch Goldstein, an Israeli Jew who burst into the Cave of the Patriarchs during prayers in Ramadan, Islam's holiest month, and shot and killed at least 29 men worshipping there, wounding about 150 others. Since then, the sanctuary to Abraham's memory has been divided by a wall, and the Israeli soldiers who control the site have set up a more stringent praying schedule so that the two sides are never together.

Hebron's history has emerged largely through the efforts of an Israeli archaeologist named Avi Ofer, and it turns out that Hebron has always been a city of radicals, a refuge for those who disdain compromise. As part of his graduate work in archaeology in the early 1980s, Ofer had begun the most comprehensive and important survey yet conducted of the entire Judean highlands area, about 800 square kilometers of territory comprising the heartland of Judah (including Hebron) and extending all the way down to Beersheba in the south. The survey had involved combing the hills, collecting pottery shards, and examining the remains of houses and other architecture in the hope of creating a settlement history of the area through every possible historical period, starting in the fourth millennium B.C.E. and ending in the Ottoman age directly before the founding of the modern state of Israel. As an outgrowth of that work, Ofer decided to spend several years digging at Hebron. He was interested mainly in the biblical period there, the Bronze and Iron Ages, particularly the city's association with the patriarchs and its role as King David's capital for seven years before David conquered Jerusalem from the Jebusites and moved the center of his growing kingdom there. Ofer's preliminary investigation indicated that during these periods Hebron was a key center in the area for trading and commerce, but perhaps more interesting, that it had always been a self-contained community, distinct socially, economically, and politically from Judah's larger centers like Jerusalem, even when it was formally considered a subdistrict.

Despite Hebron's historical significance, it wasn't easy for Ofer to obtain funds to dig there. Hebron had been a political hot spot since shortly after the 1967 Arab-Israeli war, which had left Jordan's West Bank in Israel's control. A group of Jewish settlers had moved into a hotel in its downtown area, ostensibly to spend Passover in the city of the patriarchs. But after the holiday they refused to leave, and eventually the government backed down from a confrontation and approved the establishment of a small Jewish settlement there. When Ofer began his excavations, political tensions between Israelis and Palestinians in the West Bank and Gaza Strip were even worse than usual, eventually culminating in the 1987 outbreak of the Palestinian uprising, or intifada, against Israel's continued military presence.

Ofer was finally able to get the financial support he needed to dig largely due to a political stroke of fortune. The Jewish settlers of Hebron had recently decided to expand their foothold there and set up a neighborhood in Tel Romeideh, a hilly section of the city. Ofer's investigations confirmed that Tel Romeideh was the center of biblical Hebron, and so he, along with his advisers and colleagues, the prominent Israeli archaeologists Benjamin Mazar and Moshe Kochavi, approached the minister of defense — at that time, Yitzhak Rabin — and argued that they urgently needed funding to dig before the settlers established an entire neighborhood on the mound and destroyed the archaeological materials located below. In fact, temporary caravans had already been set up on a small section of the mound, and Ofer was ultimately never able to excavate there. But with the 20,000 shekels Rabin authorized for the dig, Ofer was able to study other areas of Tel Romeideh.

Throughout its history, Hebron had been relatively poor compared to other cities in Judah. Situated in a remote and hard-to-reach location, the settlement was in an agricultural frontier zone, bordering the desert. Hebron's fortunes changed for the better in the tenth century B.C.E., when a new wave of settlement began. There is evidence of more impressive construction, and as time passed, fortresses were built and the city expanded, until it eventually became the most important and largest center in southern Judah. Ofer believes that King David's coronation in Hebron, as recounted in the Bible, and the seven years the town served as his capital before he moved to Jerusalem, took place during the period that the archaeological record shows Hebron at its peak. But he is quick to point out that even at that time, it remained the richest city in an impoverished, distant section of Judah. Although Hebron was David's capital, it was the capital of a very circumscribed region. "According to the Bible, David left for Jerusalem as soon as he could, and you can't blame him," said Ofer in a 1999 interview. "You can't control any significant part of Judah from Hebron, it's not in the center. And after David leaves, the Bible hardly mentions Hebron again."

The city continued to haunt David, though. David's plans to expand his holdings were almost derailed by his rebellious son, Absalom, who chose Hebron as the place to attempt a coup. There is a story in Second Book of Samuel in which Absalom comes to his father and asks for permission to go to pray in Hebron. David gives him his blessing, telling him, "Go in peace." But Absalom has other plans and once in Hebron foments rebellion against his own father. "As soon as ye hear the sound of the horn, then ye shall say: 'Absalom is king in Hebron,'" he tells his followers, whom he places as spies throughout David's kingdom. Absalom's rebellion is eventually defeated and Absalom killed, but not before he forces David out of Jerusalem and nearly takes over the kingdom. Ofer thought it likely that Hebron's economic and demographic decline after the capital moved to Jerusalem had led to bitterness and resentment among many of the city's residents, who gave Absalom the support he needed to oppose Jerusalem politically.

From the biblical texts as well as administrative records, it became apparent that Hebron had been treated differently by the central authorities. Its tax and population records were listed separately from those of Jerusalem, under whose jurisdictional umbrella it technically fell. To Ofer, this fact seemed to indicate that Hebron had a unique character, that its people saw themselves as both part of the larger Judean entity and somehow separate from it. Ofer could speculate about why that was the case. The cultic material he found indicated Hebron was a self-contained religious center, with its people not dependent on traveling to Jerusalem to worship. That meant that they did not have to pay tribute to the priests in Jerusalem or follow their line of preaching. The lack of any sort of flourishing local agriculture, combined with the city's remote location, must also have resulted in a particular kind of personality being able to thrive there, Ofer theorized.

Little seems to have changed in modern Hebron, with its hardscrabble existence and residents bent on conflict rather than compromise. Its sad, difficult history hangs over the city. And yet within the city's past lies also potential salvation. Unlike in Jerusalem, where David managed to establish a strong political dynasty that continued for many generations after his death, no one group in Hebron has ever been able to control the city for any length of time. Life there was difficult and the winds of fortune were particularly capricious. "Its residents would stay as long as they could," said Ofer. Then they would move on, relocating to nearby communities when ecological or political circumstances changed, waiting for a chance to return.

Archaeology has enabled a more complete reconstruction of Hebron's development, but textual criticism of the patriarchal narratives reveals something unexpected: Abraham's association with Hebron is not an original part of the patriarchal tradition, but was added at a later date in order to reflect changing political circumstances inside Judah. It is widely accepted among Bible scholars that the composition of the

Bible was an ongoing process that took place over the course of several centuries, and many of its stories underwent considerable alteration from the time they were first written down to the time the editing of the Old Testament works was under way, probably in the fifth century B.C.E. Many examples of this abound. The Bible scholar Kyle McCarter Jr. has argued that the twelve tribes of Israel who appear in the stories about Jacob and Joseph that we now read in the Bible represent the tribal list as it stood at a later point in the editing process. As proof, he cites a passage recorded in the Book of Judges describing the victory of the Israelite tribes over a Canaanite foe. This passage contains a different list, one that doesn't mention the southern tribes of Judah and Simeon. McCarter speculates that this discrepancy indicates that when this text was written southern Canaan, which later writers would associate with Abraham himself, was not yet considered part of the territories of Israel and therefore remained outside the list.

In the earlier versions of the stories, Abraham is reported to have settled in the Jezreel Valley, in north-central Israel, and his nephew Lot in Transjordan, while Hagar, Sarah's handmaid and the mother of Abraham's son Ishmael, is associated with a tribe located in northern Arabia. But when the tribe of Judah under David later became the dominant force in Israel, its scribes assumed responsibility for the editing of the Scriptures. They subsequently revised these traditions, McCarter argues, so that in later versions Abraham, along with the rest of the family, was relocated south, to the Judean hills. When Abraham parts from Lot he settles not in the central highlands area, but near the oaks of Mamre in Hebron. He pays the 400 shekels to Ephron in order to buy the family burial plot there too.

Although there is a fairly broad consensus that Abraham's association with Hebron was a later addition to Scripture, exactly how late is still a matter for debate. McCarter suggests that the stories were modified in part out of political motivations, in order to reflect the way the writers viewed matters when King David was in power, in the tenth century B.C.E. But other Bible scholars have staked out even later dates for the final shape of the Abraham traditions, perhaps after the fall of Israel to the Assyrian army in 722 B.C.E. and the subsequent rise of the Judean monarchy and its attempt to create a pan-Israelite national identity. One of the most interesting theories about the dating of the Abraham story has been proposed by Oded Lipschits, a young historian working at Tel Aviv University and specializing in the so-called Babylonian Captivity, the fifty-year period of Babylonian rule in Palestine, beginning with the destruction of the temple in Jerusalem in 587/586 B.C.E.

Lipschits believes that many of the geographic and other references in the Abraham narrative argue for its having been composed during the Babylonian period, and that the story of Abraham's buying a burial plot and land in Hebron had a specific political function. "Hebron had been a traditional center of the Judeans, one of the capitals of Judah, and an important city. But at the time the Judeans started to move back to Jerusalem from the exile in Babylonia, Hebron was no longer part of Judah," he says. "The Babylonians had changed the borders when they took over, and the Persians retained these same borders when they took over from the Babylonians. So the Bible's writers and editors shaped the story to show that Hebron belonged to the Judeans, despite the fact that they didn't control it anymore. They were establishing a claim in case political circumstances changed in the future."

The folk traditions associated with the cave continued to evolve even into the Second Temple period. Jewish sages of the second century B.C.E. wrote that not just Abraham, Isaac, Jacob, and their wives Sarah, Rebecca, and Leah were buried in Abraham's tomb, but all of Jacob's sons as well. The sages also added some biblical characters whose tombs were not associated with Hebron by earlier tradition, including Moses and his brother Aaron, according to research by historian Steven Fine. One rabbi reported having seen Adam wandering in Abraham's tomb during a visit to the site. Eventually, Fine argues, the cave became a kind of national burial ground for all biblical heroes.

These legends are of little interest to Hebron's mayor, Mustafa

Abdel Nabi Natsheh. "This has always been an Arab city," he says, dismissing the subject. Just as Jewish ties to the city are ignored by Hebron's Muslim community, so is the last seven hundred years of Muslim rule there by the Jewish settlers. "And the title to the field and the cave in it was made over to Abraham," David Wilder, the spokesman for the Jewish community living in Hebron counters. The biblical quotation, stamped on the back of commemorative coins the settlers sell along with other Abraham-related products to support the Jewish community, is often cited to explain why fifty or so families who depend on the protection of Israeli soldiers in order to live amidst 120,000 Arabs will never leave the city. But even the architectural changes at the Tomb of the Patriarchs over the centuries make a mockery of both sides' claims. Each of Hebron's conquerors and religions has added to the structure, which has become a reflection of the competing traditions that have grown up around Abraham over the years. No one is certain who built the original monument that now houses the tomb, although it is usually attributed to the Jewish king Herod the Great (ruled 37–4 B.C.E.) himself. The building was constructed at some point during the thirty- or forty-year period when the Herodian style of architecture was prevalent, most likely on top of some earlier structure traditionally associated with the site of Abraham's burial.

Today the site is a crazy quilt of different styles. There are huge Herodian-style walls, with the well-carved ashlar masonry common in Jerusalem. The Romans built a church over the cave, and when the Arabs conquered Hebron in 638 C.E., they converted the church into a mosque. In the twelfth century, Crusaders captured the city and turned the mosque back into a church, until the Mamluks, who were Muslims, retook Hebron, made the church a mosque, and for good measure prohibited Jews and Christians from entering either the sanctuary or the cave. Non-Muslim worshippers were prohibited from ascending any higher than the seventh step on the external staircase leading to the tomb, from where they could look through a hole in the wall over the entrance to the cave.

Jutting out from the enclosure below one of several minarets erected on the building by Saladin is a domed mosque. The Bible records that Joseph's remains were taken from Egypt when Moses and the Israelites escaped and then buried in Shechem (contemporary Nablus), but later Muslim and Jewish legends state that the bones were buried in the tomb in Hebron. In the tenth century c.e., one story goes, the Muslim caliph sent workers to the tomb to try to clear up the mystery. The workers found a huge boulder, cracked it open, and discovered therein the body of Joseph. The caliph promptly built the domed mosque to mark the site. Saladin, the Muslim conqueror who took the tomb in 1188 c.e. after fighting the Christian Crusaders, added the minarets and the crenellations that can still be seen along the building's rooftop. A Crusader column remains standing next to a marble one erected by the Mamluks, who ruled from the thirteenth to the sixteenth centuries c.e. The Israelis have also made changes. When they took over Hebron after the 1967 Israeli-Arab war, the stairway to the tomb was partly removed and the hole through which Jews and Christians used to stare into the sanctuary since the days of the Mamluks was cemented over. Despite the best efforts of all these competing groups, no one has ever succeeded in completely obliterating the contributions of his predecessors.

The biblical text and the city's recently recovered archaeological history belie the idea that Hebron — or Abraham — can ever belong exclusively to one group. Abraham for one seems to have recognized this and acted accordingly. God gives him a divine promise that all the land of Canaan will be his and that the obligation to obtain this land is absolutely critical. But when Abraham and his nephew Lot realize they can no longer live together in peace, it is Abraham who suggests that they divide the land between them, even offering Lot the chance to choose first which portion he wants. "Let there be no strife, I pray thee. . . . Is not the whole land before thee? Separate thyself, I pray thee, from me; if thou wilt take the left hand then I will go to the right; or if thou take the right hand, then I will go to the left," Abraham tells Lot in Genesis 13, hardly the words of a man willing to conquer at any cost. Later, when Abraham wants to buy the Cave of the Patriarchs in which to bury Sarah, he presents himself as a sojourner, humbling himself before the locals rather than citing God's promise to him or brandishing his historical and divine rights in the city like a weapon. The Bible records his gesture of humility with these simple words: "Abraham bowed down before the people of the land." It would take another four hundred years or so, much of it spent as slaves in Egypt according to the Bible, before Abraham's descendants would improve their circumstances.

Chapter 2

⚭

Exodus

Pharaoh Speaks

I am the Lord your God who brought you out of the land of Egypt, the house of bondage. *(Exodus 20:2)*

To the Bible's authors, the critical event in the history of the Israelite people is their escape from a life of servitude in Egypt under the leadership of Moses. Complete with plagues, the parting of waters, and other assorted miracles, their exodus provides a vivid stage for Yahweh to flex some divine muscle. During the subsequent forty-year trek through the desert, the Israelites finally become a nation. They form a lasting covenant with Yahweh; receive the Ten Commandments, which become the basis of the Judeo-Christian tradition as we know it today; and eventually enter the Promised Land. Over the years, the exodus has become a cornerstone of both Jewish and Christian liturgy and tradition, as well as the inspiration for any number of liberation movements, including the struggle for black civil rights in the United States. But although Moses is also considered a key prophet in the Koran, ancient Egypt's view of the critical events that took place within its borders has not been recorded.

In some ways, Egypt's absence is to be expected. Its role in this great story has always been to serve as a foil, the backdrop against which the Israelites' relationship to God was defined, and the traditional focus of scholarship has therefore been almost exclusively on the biblical narrative itself. But over time this approach has seemed to raise more questions than it has answered. First there were the many confusions and ambiguities in the biblical text itself. Moses' father-in-law had various names; the fact that Moses had an older brother and sister was not mentioned in the account of his birth and rescue; and in Exodus 34, in one of the different versions of the giving of the laws, the Ten Commandments turned out to number twelve. Other sundry chronological discrepancies and contradictions were supported by archaeological discoveries, which eventually led many scholars to accept an indigenous origin for the Israelites — that is, within Canaan rather than in Egypt.

And yet it has been impossible to completely abandon the search for the historical legitimacy of the exodus. There is a great human need for the story, which is simply too compelling to abandon exclusively to the realm of theology. What would be the rationale for inventing such a narrative, and assuming the mantle of slavery in Egypt, if there wasn't at least some basis in historical reality? Even those who doubt that the events occurred exactly as the Bible recounts them have offered no satisfactory answer to that question.

Over the years a number of creative theories have arisen attempting to explain the events of the early history of the Israelites. Some Bible scholars have suggested that there wasn't one exodus but a series of them that took place over time. They support their argument by noting that certain details in the story do seem to have an authentic basis in Egyptian reality, such as the personal names of characters like the Egyptian midwives who disobey Pharaoh's order to kill all the Hebrew male babies at birth. Another view holds that a number of the phenomena described in Exodus, including the parting of the

"Sea of Reeds" (mistranslated as the "Red Sea" in some versions of the Bible), could be linked with the volcanic eruption of Thera on the Mediterranean island of Santorini, which most scholars date to around 1500 B.C.E. Such a proposal presupposes a much earlier exodus than traditionally assumed.

Other scholars have advocated an even more dramatic shift in focus and have proposed returning to the source of much of the mystery, to Egypt. This new strategy has come about at a time when the Egyptians themselves have made some new discoveries, including uncovering more information about the lives of the people who built the huge monuments, temples, and pyramids celebrating the pharaohs. Egyptian archaeologists aren't specifically searching for the truth about Exodus; even if they were interested, there is no Egyptian text that even mentions the events described in the Hebrew Bible, no artifact that records the Israelite sojourn in Egypt. In the early days of archaeological research in the Middle East, Egypt's shrines and tombs were almost exclusively the focus. Researchers, many of whom worked for big museums in London, Paris, and Berlin, were eager to bring treasures back home to be put on display. The Egyptians, working both alone and with foreign excavators, are trying to take a different approach, studying the lives of workers and slaves for information about ancient Egypt's broader society rather than concentrating only on the pharaohs and kings who led it. During this search they have encountered the Egypt of the Bible; and what they have found challenges Exodus's version not just of the Israelites' very presence in Egypt, but of the kind of country from which they putatively fled.

The Egypt portrayed in the Exodus story is a land of despotism and idolatry, arrogance and oppression. But the Bible actually offers a far more textured, and in some places even flattering, portrait of Egypt. The Book of Genesis, for instance, is a veritable hymn to its glories. Egypt is the perennial refuge for those seeking to escape the frequent bouts of famine in the Middle East. Abraham, who journeys there in search of food during one such period, notices that the pharaoh casts a covetous eye on Sarah and, fearing he will be killed if Pharaoh learns they are married, says Sarah is his sister. Believing she is unmarried, Pharaoh installs her in his harem. When Pharaoh discovers his mistake, he rewards Abraham with cattle, silver, and gold in order to make amends, generous with his country's bounty, and Abraham returns to Canaan a wealthy man. Egypt is even more of a land of opportunity for Joseph, Abraham's great-grandson and Jacob's favorite son, who manages to rise from enslavement and false imprisonment to become Pharaoh's confidant.

Famine eventually brings Joseph's family and other Israelites to Egypt, where, the Bible says, life for a time was good. But after Joseph dies and a new pharaoh comes to power, the Israelites are left without a protector and their lives become more difficult. Indeed, it is these later stories of the Israelites' bitter toil and of the hard-hearted pharaoh who refuses to let them go free that dominate our impressions of the country. This is equally true in Muslim tradition. In the Koran, Pharaoh is described as an evil tyrant, the oppressor of Musa and Harun (Moses and Aaron), and stories present pharaohs both before and after Moses as equally unsavory characters. For religious Muslims, the age of the rule of the pharaohs has come to symbolize what life was like before the coming of Islam, a time of sinfulness and despair.

Seeking to redress this balance, recent Egyptian governments have used the country's pharaonic past as a way to glorify both the pharaohs and, by extension, themselves as their modern incarnation. Anwar el-Sadat, Egypt's president from 1970 to 1981, insisted that the body of Ramses II, considered by many the most likely candidate for the pharaoh of the Exodus story, be treated with the respect due a visiting head of state, including a twenty-one-gun-salute, when the mummy was flown to France for restoration work. In the summer of 1998, President Hosni Mubarak threw a huge party celebrating the completion of an international effort to preserve the Sphinx in Giza, featuring people dressed as high priests and a re-creation of the days of the pharaohs. At the same time, Egyptian authorities are less enthusiastic when it comes to Exodus. In the Cairo Museum, the bastion of Egypt's official version of its past, Exodus is a taboo subject.

The Cairo Museum is located in one of the busiest intersections in downtown Cairo, Liberation Square, where buses, taxis, and cars generate a constant buzz of noise. Tourist vehicles let out a steady stream of passengers eager to visit the museum, next to which looms the Hilton hotel, gray and squat and looking like something out of the 1950s Soviet Union. In the garden outside the museum entrance are a reflecting pool and statues of pharaohs, ancient gods, and even the stone sarcophagus of Auguste-Ferdinand-François Mariette, the French Egyptologist who established the museum in 1863. It is designed to be an island of tranquillity amidst the commotion of downtown Cairo, but recently visitors have not been lingering for too long outside. In 1998 two Islamic militants opposed to the secular regime of President Mubarak attacked tourists as they sat on a bus waiting to enter the museum.

Indoors, the museum director's office is small and cluttered. The government press agency, which must formally approve all interview requests with officials at the museum, has arranged for me to meet with the assistant director in order to discuss the museum's presentation of the past. But the assistant director, a religious Muslim woman whose white head covering obscures any view of her hair and falls well past her shoulders, is decidedly uncomfortable with the idea.

"What is the message about Egypt that you would like tourists to take home after seeing the artifacts?" she is asked. She pauses a moment, rearranges the cup of pencils on her desk, and finally replies, "I really couldn't say."

"Do you feel that any artifacts here shed light on the biblical stories about Moses and the Israelite sojourn in Egypt?" This time the response is quick, but the same: "I really couldn't say." Each subsequent question is met with this answer until she lifts the phone, barks out an order, and turns to her visitors. "Your questions are embarassing me," she announces. "Would you like a tour of the museum?"

Almost simultaneously, a young man in a light shirt and dark pants knocks and enters the office. This is Muhammad, the English-speaking tour guide, who offers to show the visitors around. He claims to be fluent in English and adds that he knows much about the museum's Exodus-related treasures, since most Western tourists request to see something related to the story. It quickly turns out that Muhammad has overstated the case on both counts. After a few minutes he abandons the pretense of speaking English, claiming he finds American accents difficult to understand though he never has trouble with the English spoken by Australian visitors. Likewise, his knowledge of the museum's holdings seems a little out-of-date. He starts with the Merneptah Stela, a huge, black, granite slab that was found in Thebes at the end of the last century. The stela recounts the exploits of the pharaoh Merneptah, thirteenth son and successor to Ramses II, during a military campaign in Libya as well as his earlier victories during battles in Canaan. Dated to 1207 B.C.E., the stela contains the earliest extrabiblical mention of Israel. "Canaan has been plundered into every sort of woe," it boasts. "Ashkelon has been overcome, Gezer has been captured, Yanoam was made nonexistent; Israel is laid waste, his seed is not." The hieroglyphics on the stone indicate that the term "Israel" is used to refer to a people, not a place. Muhammad points out the sign for "Israel" on the lower part of the stela. "You see how it is a slightly different color than the rest of the stone?" he asks. "This is how it was found, the name Israel jumping out at your eyes!"

He walks by rows of display cases without a glance. "We will skip the Hyksos period," he declares by way of explanation, dismissing as unimportant and distasteful the conquest of Egypt by foreigners around 1670 B.C.E., and one of the events that many scholars believe may be the basis of the Joseph tale. "The Hyksos were bad, bad, very bad people. There is nothing to see here, they created nothing beautiful." He races upstairs to the mummy room, where the bodies of the pharaohs are kept in glass cases, and stands next to the remains of Ramses II and Merneptah. Ramses II still has tufts of hair on his head — he was a redhead, tests have shown — and his skin has the texture and nut-brown color of one of those children's dolls made from a shriveled apple. Merneptah somehow seems smaller and more delicate, his complexion a chalky white color. This last detail is what leads Muhammad to conclude that Merneptah, and not his long-ruling and powerful father, Ramses II, is the pharaoh of the Bible: "His skin is white from the salt from the sea where he drowned when God parted the sea for Musa to allow him to escape and then closed it back up on Pharaoh," he enthusiastically offers. A small circle of Egyptians begins to form around him as he spins out his theory, which was popular among nineteenth-century scholars but was later discounted when tests on the mummy revealed that a saltlike substance that leaves a chalky white residue was frequently used in the mummification process. As the crowd grows larger, people begin to shout out questions with great enthusiasm and press eagerly around the mummy cases, trying to get a look at what Muhammad, ending his talk with an inspired flourish, describes as "the man who saw the face of Musa."

Zahi Hawass, the official keeper of the pyramids, is the modern-day pharaoh of Giza. His office, not too far from the Sphinx, looks like a former army barracks, and the sand and dust from the pyramids constantly blows inside. A cat with green eyes hisses as my translator and I enter the waiting area. Hawass's own room is cramped, his desk piled with faxes and manila folders, but he rules here with the imperiousness of one who is accustomed to power and giving orders. The walls are decorated with pictures of him showing famous guests around the pyramids: Zahi with Chelsea and Hillary Clinton, Zahi with the actor Omar Sharif, Zahi with King Juan Carlos of Spain and Princess Diana of England. As he seats us, he directs an aide to bring a television set into the room so he can watch a match of the Egyptian national soccer team. He shouts orders into two phones simultaneously, one on each ear. His remarks punctuated by the cheers of the crowd at the soccer game, which fill the tiny office with noise, Hawass discusses his major complaint.

"No one wants to acknowledge that we built the pyramids," Hawass says. In his years in charge, he has heard every possible explanation accounting for them, including aliens from outer space. But one theory that disturbs him even more is the suggestion that the Israelites were responsible for their construction. The Bible never actually mentions the word "pyramid." It reports that the Israelites were slaves in Egypt, and that they built for Pharaoh granaries in the royal cities of Pithom and Ramses. It is true that forced laborers, including foreigners, were in fact conscripted by Ramses II for work on the construction of his capital city, Pi Ramesse, and other massive building projects that he undertook during his reign. But Ramses didn't actually build the Giza pyramids, which were completed more than a thousand years before his rule, although he did sponsor a major restoration effort there for which he also needed large numbers of conscripted workers.

It was actually the work of later historians, such as the Greek Herodotus (fifth century B.C.E.) and the Jewish Josephus, and then again nineteenth-century biblical scholarship, that reinforced the image later immortalized by Hollywood of slaves cringing under the Egyptian whip. Until recently, virtually nothing was known about the people who built what are among the best-known sights in the world, the three pyramids raised to house the tombs of the pharaohs Khufu, Khafre, and Menkaure, and the Sphinx. These monuments were erected in around 2500 B.C.E., and the combined time it took to build the pyramids alone is estimated at about seventy years. From hieroglyphic inscriptions, ancient graffiti, and mason marks left by the laborers, scholars assumed that skilled craftsmen probably lived and worked all year round at the pyramid construction site. Still, most research focused primarily on the treasures found inside royal tombs — such as the one belonging to Tutankhamen in the Valley of the Kings — rather than on the workforce that might have constructed them.

Then in 1990 an American tourist riding a horse at Giza was

thrown from the animal when its hoof plunged through a previously undiscovered mud-brick wall. The wall later turned out to be part of a tomb, with a long vaulted chamber and two false doors through which the builders thought the dead could make contact with the living and receive gifts and offerings. In the months that followed, Hawass and his staff found hundreds of additional graves in the same area, only a few miles south of the Sphinx. It was determined that this was the cemetery of the workers who built the pyramids.

The cemetery is divided into two main sections, 60 large tombs for overseers and about 650 smaller graves, which were further divided by rank. The lowest level of the cemetery was for the poorest workmen, the ones who moved the giant limestone blocks that make up the pyramids and who ended up buried in small graves. The next level was for the higher class of artists and craftsmen. The overseers' tombs featured carved hieroglyphic inscriptions that preserve their official titles: the director of building tombs, the inspector of building tombs, director for the king's work, along with many others. Their final resting places were filled with small statues, engravings, and elaborate hieroglyphic decorations on the walls — all of which were indications of their high status, Hawass contends. Inscriptions on the tombs revealed that one worker at Giza, named Mehi, had served as a witness for the sales contract of a house, a role slaves were barred from fulfilling. From such details Hawass has concluded that the workers weren't slaves but rather skilled craftsmen helped seasonally by peasants who labored as a corvée when flooding made agricultural work impossible.

From the construction of the pyramids emerged one of the world's most powerful bureaucracies. Workers came from all over Egypt, meeting and living together for the first time at the site of the pyramids. Villages throughout the country had to supply either food and wine for the workers' sites or laborers to work for the king's building projects as part of what was evolving into a widespread national tax system. Some sent food from as far away as southern Egypt, in burnished bowls once thought to have been reserved only for the upper class. "Without the building of the pyramids, there probably wouldn't be an Egyptian nation. The pyramids built Egypt," Hawass says. Then he turns back to the television for a moment and gives a quick shout out loud. The national team has finally scored a goal.

Mansour Radwan has overall responsibility for all the digs under way at Giza, but he decided to personally run the cemetery excavation out of curiosity about what kind of life the ancient Egyptians had led. For him, the most interesting point is how closely the workers attempted to imitate the official burial ground of the kings when they were building their own graves. They constructed their tombs of dried brick and leftover building materials from the royal temples and pyramids, including pieces of granite, limestone, and basalt. The tombs came in varied styles — a small pyramid, a dome, an egg — and were complete with tiny courtyards, stone false doors, and curses to discourage thieves. Many workers were buried with finely crafted stone figurines, often representing entire households, or statuettes to protect them as they journeyed to the next world.

Radwan met me in 1998 at his small office in Giza. It perches on a hill that gives him a view of the workers' tombs, the tops of the pyramids in the background, and further on in the distance, the city that the archaeologists believe arose to support the workers' community, the downtown Cairo of the ancient world. In 1984 a team of American archaeologists led by Mark Lehner embarked on a project to map the entire area of the Giza plateau. During excavations of one section they turned up thousands and thousands of baking pans, the remnants of what they believe was the site's bakery, one of the first dating from the Old Kingdom period found intact. The bread molds were incredibly heavy, each weighing as much as twenty-two pounds. They also found huge vats for mixing batter. The bakers worked in smoke-filled rooms, the ash accumulating day after day as they produced sufficient bread to feed thirty thousand people.

According to tomb reliefs, the bread pans were stacked and heated over an open fire, then placed in baking pits in the ground, filled with dough from a nearby vat, and covered with another pot and hot embers and ashes for baking. At one point, Lehner and a team from the National Geographic Society tried to re-create the bakery and actually prepared bread. Based on the remains of grains found at the site, the Egyptians apparently baked with barley, which has no gluten, as well as emmer, which contains only a small amount. Gluten is the part of wheat that gives bread dough its elasticity and allows the air pockets within it to expand during baking, resulting in a loaf with a crispy crust and a soft center. Based on the size of the molds, Lehner believed the bread would be so heavy it would be inedible. After much experimentation, the team did manage to come up with a combination of barley and emmer that produced an edible loaf, although Lehner admitted it was "a bit too sour even for most fans of sourdough."

Radwan shared Hawass's idea that the men were not slaves, but he brought to it a different perspective. The skeletal remains in the cemetery were sent for forensic examination to Egypt's National Research Centre, and the results revealed the costs to lives spent performing backbreaking labor. Many of the men had died between the ages of thirty and thirty-five and showed signs of degenerative arthritis in their vertebral column and knees. The skeletons of both men and women, particularly those from the cemeteries reserved for lower-class workers, had multiple fractures, most frequently in the upper arms and lower leg bones. Evidently, though, the workers had received high-quality medical treatment: most of the fractures had healed completely, having been set with splints; there were even two cases that suggested a limb had been amputated.

On a table outside his office, Radwan opened up containers and showed me some of the smaller finds from the site, things, he said, that moved him even more than the pyramids. There was a stone, split in two, with graffiti marks written in black, probably the plan for a grave. There was a clay statuette found in a small niche in one of the tombs, used in the hope of warding off thieves and evil spirits.

Radwan held up a flint knife, a stone that fit perfectly in the groove of his hand and was probably used for polishing, and small tufts of rope.

At the far edge of the site, barely discernible from Radwan's office with the sand blowing in huge waves, was a passageway leading from the workers' community to the site of the pyramids and through which the archaeologists had driven to work every day without giving its design much thought. Later digging revealed that most of the structure was still buried in the sand, and that it was part of a huge wall that once stood thirty feet above the desert. Radwan and the other archaeologists speculate that this wall is what separated the sacred area from the secular, the pyramids and tombs built for the afterlife from the mud-brick structures of everyday life in the workers' community. Many of the people who worked here probably did believe that they were laboring to build the tombs of gods. Hawass had mused that it must have been inspiring to walk out from the dim passageway, through the mammoth gate, and into the alabaster luminous light of the pyramids. While it wasn't unreasonable to argue that the workers hadn't been slaves, the huge gateway was placed there for a reason, and it almost certainly functioned as more than just a religious marker. It also served as a reminder to the workers not to question their place in a system where a small group enjoyed unparalleled wealth while the rest built their own graves from the scraps of their daily toils.

In the heart of the graveyard, a worker at the dig had uncovered a skeleton that was going to be removed after lunch. Others, wearing long white robes and head coverings twisted like turbans, sat inside the tombs, eating a meal of cucumbers and bread in the cool shadows. Wandering around the cemetery, Radwan stopped for a moment in front of a tomb shaped like a giant mud beehive, one of his favorites. While in so many ways the workers had strived to copy the upper classes in their funerary design, this structure was unique. The archaeologists had searched but had found no parallels for this tomb on the other side of the gate. Here from beyond the grave was finally the still, hushed voice of individuality, an echo against the power and might of the pyramids that loomed above. "They labored for what?" mused Radwan, his hand briefly touching the tomb. "To protect the bodies of kings. And then what they had left to protect themselves was these poor small graves." For Radwan, the lives of the ancient Egyptians were in many respects as familiar as those of his neighbors in the village where he grew up. The distance that separated them was as short yet as vast as that walk through the imposing gateway and up to the pyramids. "I deal with what we find as if I am one of them," said Radwan, allowing himself a slight smile. "I know I'd be out here with them, and not with the kings."

The Bible never specifically names the pharaoh who figures so prominently in Exodus; he is called simply "Pharaoh" throughout. And yet, even nameless, he is vivid in his arrogance and in his confidence in his own might. When Moses tries to impress him by turning his staff into a serpent, Pharaoh merely laughs, calls in his court magicians, and declares he can match any such feat. Subsequent events prove him wrong, and after Egypt is overrun with frogs, devoured by locusts, and has suffered the loss of all its firstborn sons, Pharaoh finally relents. But then he changes his mind and sends his army out to bring back the newly freed slaves. At the Sea of Reeds, Pharaoh watches as his entire army races headlong into the passage that Moses has opened with God's help, only to stand by helplessly as the waters swallow up what remains of Egypt's power.

That image of Pharaoh as misguided tyrant has survived throughout the millennia, and these days many archaeologists and historians even put a name to him. If the exodus was in fact a historical event, the consensus is that the pharaoh in question was Ramses II. Part of the presumption about his identity is based on chronology. Ramses II ruled Egypt from around 1304 to 1237 B.C.E., an unprecedented sixty-seven-year reign during a time period that would correspond with the subsequent emergence of the Israelites in the central highlands of Canaan. He was also one of ancient Egypt's most prolific builders, whose tastes ran to the monumental. The projects that bear his name are not always Egypt's most beautiful — in fact, Ramses tended to build quickly but not to a high quality — but they are spectacular in their enormity: huge statues carved out of the cliffs at Abu Simbel, where Egypt meets the Sudan; the mortuary temple Ramesseum; the city of Pi Ramesse. Ramses' rule was also the time when pyramids and tombs from more than a millennium earlier, like the ones that Hawass and Radwan are excavating in Giza, were restored to their former glory. These sorts of projects also supported the notion that Ramses might be the pharaoh who made the lives of the Israelite slaves so bitter.

In recent years, however, Egyptologists have promoted the idea that Ramses has been maligned by biblical history. Among Egyptians, Ramses has always had a completely different reputation than the one popularized by the Bible. Streets, parks, and buildings are named after him. His statue stands in the middle of one of Cairo's busiest intersections, serenely watching over the cars that race around him at breakneck speed. Rather than a tyrant who had to force his subjects to build monuments to his glory, as the Bible portrays, he is popularly viewed by Egyptians as the architect of a system of government that profoundly changed the world.

Egyptologists have recently helped support that characterization. Excavations at Deir el-Medineh, a village a few miles south of the Valley of Kings where the workers who dug out the royal tombs lived, have contributed many details of the daily life of an ancient Egyptian working for Ramses II. The people left behind thousands of ostraca (pieces of pottery with writing on them) and other artifacts that give a rich picture of life in the village from 1550 to around 1050 B.C.E. The village was constructed along the lines of a modern suburb, with row houses off a central street. The interiors of the homes all had similar floor plans: three rooms laid out one behind the other. A loom usually stood at the front of the house, the middle room was the place for eating and meeting with friends, and at the back were a small bedroom and kitchen. Homes were furnished simply, from mud brick, reeds, and pottery. Life in the village wasn't easy. The men worked in ten-day work shifts, followed by a two-day break. The nearest well was a half-hour's walk away, so water carriers supplied the residents. Many of the women kept small animals for food. When they ordered statuettes of popular household deities like Bes, Isis, or Hathor from the village artisans, they paid one another in trade. Each house contained a small cellar cut into the floor which was used to store the food they received as payment for their work on Ramses' projects. One ostracon describes the mayor's ordering wages to be delivered to the crew working at the tombs, consisting of vegetables, fish, firewood, pottery, small cattle, and milk. Sometimes one of the nobles attached to the royal court might contribute wine as a bonus.

At Pi Ramesse, one of the cities that the Bible records the Hebrew slaves labored to build, an excavation under way has turned up evidence of a very cosmopolitan culture. Workers lived in small ethnic enclaves. There are districts with typical Egyptian houses, but some areas have homes built in Minoan style, complete with bull-jumping scenes painted on the walls, and still others contain row after row of semi-subterranean dwellings like the ones found in Canaan. There are houses that were occupied by Hittites, sections for diplomats and businessmen, and even the headquarters of the Egyptian army. Many of the foreigners who worked in Egypt were prisoners of war and were repatriated to their native lands after working long enough to afford to bribe Egyptian officials. Possibly these foreigners were treated differently than native-born Egyptians living in the same community, but "not like beasts of burden or semihuman beings," says Kent Weeks, an Egyptologist at the American University of Cairo. "Life under the pharaonic system was difficult, but it was difficult for everybody."

More than any other scholar, Weeks is helping change the wider public's image of Ramses. In 1995 he and a team of archaeologists working with him in the Valley of the Kings at Luxor uncovered the opening to a tomb that they dubbed KV5 and that turned out to be the burial chamber of at least several of Ramses' many sons. The Valley of the Kings was the final resting ground of the pharaohs of the

New Kingdom, which according to Egyptian chronology began around 1550 B.C.E. and ended five hundred years later with the demise of Ramses XI, the last pharaoh buried there.

The tomb had last been seen in the early nineteenth century by European travelers exploring the valley, but they had crawled only as far as the opening, made some quick sketches, and turned back. Thousands of years of debris from flash floods had left visible only a small crack in the entrance. Howard Carter, who gained worldwide fame in 1922 when he discovered King Tutankhamen's tomb, began to open KV5 in 1902, but when the workmen dug a little past the doorway and didn't find anything of significance, he stopped working there. Later, in the 1920s, he designated the hillside as a dumpsite for the Tut excavation that was then under way. Tons of limestone chips from that dig were dumped on the tomb, hiding it until only recently. Even after its rediscovery by Weeks, though, it still presented a number of excavation problems to the archaeologists. The waterline from the valley tourist restrooms passed right over the entrance, and a pipe had been leaking into the tomb for decades. Over the previous twenty years, huge buses loaded with tourists had sat with their motors idling right above the tomb, weakening its structure even further. Even so, KV5 still offered the best chance to see a side of Pharaoh that no one knew: the family man.

Throughout Egypt's long history, its rulers liked nothing better than to celebrate their own accomplishments, erecting huge monuments and decorating them with reams of script recounting their military triumphs. In the case of Ramses, that included even voluminous records about a major battle against the Hittites — the Battle of Kadesh — that historians now believe ended in at best a draw. Ramses described it as a great victory for Egypt, thanks to his own bravery in combat. But despite this penchant for bragging, almost nothing is known about the children of New Kingdom pharaohs, what roles they played in the operation of the Egyptian empire, or even their names. The few references that do exist are uninformative. Usually when the eldest child ascended to the throne the names of the younger sons disappeared forever from any official records. And of course, details about the pharaoh's family are of vital importance to readers of Exodus.

The description in Exodus 12 of the killing of the firstborn, the last and most terrible of the ten plagues and the one that finally convinces Pharaoh to relent and let the slaves go, is chilling and spare: "And it came to pass at midnight, that the Lord smote all the firstborn in the Land of Egypt, from the firstborn of Pharaoh that sat on his throne unto the firstborn of the captive that was in the dungeon; and all the firstborn of cattle. And Pharaoh rose up in the night, he, and all his servants, and all the Egyptians, and there was a great cry in Egypt; for there was not a house where there was not one dead." Scripture gives no further details on how Pharaoh felt, but it goes on to record that he summoned Moses and Aaron in the middle of the night and told them to take the Israelite slaves and get out of Egypt. When Weeks began exploring the tomb, one of the first decorations he uncovered was a picture of Ramses' firstborn son, Amun-her-khepeshef, being presented to the gods Hathor and Sokar by his father after his death.

Ramses was in some ways Egypt's greatest patriarchal figure. Perhaps too great, at least from an archaeologist's perspective. He had at least thirty sons by his two official wives, Nefertari and Istnofret, but that number doesn't include those who may have died in infancy or the children of the various minor wives and concubines that he fathered over the years. Apparently his harem eventually included several Hittite princesses, as well as his sister and two of his daughters, although Egyptologists aren't certain whether he consummated the incestuous marriages. According to one Egyptian text that survives, Ramses' father gave him an unusual fifteenth birthday present: two principal wives, six minor wives, two hundred concubines, and the keys to all the harems around the country.

With a birthday gift like this, determining who is Ramses' first son gets a little complicated. "Who is to say he didn't father many children before his first or second principal wives had a child?" asks

Weeks. "What we do know is that Amun-her-khepeshef is his first son by a principal wife."

Fortunately, in contrast to his predecessors, Ramses loved to record not only battles and military strategy but also details about his large family. He listed on temple walls and monumental inscriptions the names of his sons and — even more unusually for a pharaoh — many of his daughters as well. The lists always present the sons' names in the same sequence, probably indicating their birth order. He had images of the processions of the children carved on the wall of at least five different temples. Some scenes show a few of his offspring following Ramses into battle, bringing prisoners of war back to Egypt, or standing in their war chariots. Ramses even put up statues of his wife Nefertari all over Egypt.

The KV5 tomb adds considerably to what is already known about his family. In addition to inscriptions and the names of three of his sons, it is also the source of two inscribed pieces of an alabaster canopic jar bearing the name of Mery-Atum, Ramses' sixteenth son. The tomb itself is very unusual. While most tombs in the valley have on average only eight chambers, more than 150 chambers have already been discovered inside KV5. Archaeologists have rarely found the burial places of sons who didn't succeed their father to the throne, but Weeks speculates that the existence of KV5 may be due to a decision Ramses II made late in his reign: he had himself proclaimed divine while he was still alive, an honor most pharaohs weren't accorded until after they had died. Once he did so, Weeks says, "how can God incarnate still cut ribbons at canals and listen to complaints over real estate? I think he then confined himself to performing the divine aspects of kingly duty and gave his sons the secular responsibilities."

His sons were therefore invested with a status unique to that point in Egyptian history. They weren't true pharaohs, but they weren't traditional crown princes either. They fell somewhere in between, almost in the role of secular semikings. Having been granted this degree of power and respect, they would naturally be given a burial that was more exalted than that due the ordinary son of a king. And Ramses ended up having to bury many of his children. Although he developed a painful periodontal disease in middle age and arthritis that curved his spine and forced him to walk slowly leaning on a cane, Ramses lived a long life, dying in his mid-eighties and outliving twelve of his heirs. His thirteenth son, the Merneptah of the famous stela that provides the first extrabiblical reference to Israel, didn't assume the throne until he was already in his sixties.

In addition to Merneptah, who as pharaoh was eventually buried in his own tomb and not with his other brothers, Egyptologists know quite a bit about Ramses' fourth son, Khaemwese. Khaemwese was admired for his administrative skills, his knowledge of religion, and his expertise in practicing magic. He supervised the construction of many of his father's most famous projects, including Ramses' mortuary temple, the Ramesseum. He also oversaw the restoration of earlier temples, shrines, and pyramids that had fallen into disrepair and were on the verge of collapse after a thousand years in the sun and sand, including those at Giza where Hawass and Radwan had turned up the workmen's cemetery.

But what of Amun-her-khepeshef, son of Ramses and Nefertari? Weeks and his team dug through layers of cement debris in order to retrieve painted plaster and slivers of drawings that were literally lying in puddles on the tomb floor, having fallen off the walls during the flash floods. The effort paid off. According to the drawings the archaeologists had restored, Amun bore several titles. He was Fan-bearer on the King's Right Hand, Heir, and Royal Scribe. His father called him Amun Is on His Right Hand while he was still coregent. When Ramses took over as pharaoh, he changed Amun's name to Amun Is with His Strong Arm, but some of the titles, such as Fan-bearer, were common to most or all of the other sons. Amun had other names, such as Effective Confidant and Beloved of Him, that were exclusively his. Weeks speculates that his many honorifics mean that Amun played an important role in the army. Egyptian records tell of his taking part in battles in Nubia and in western Asia on his father's campaigns there. He even participated in the ill-fated Battle of Kadesh against the Hittites.

The walls of Weeks's downtown Cairo office are decorated with computer-generated maps and charts, and there are books and papers spread across his table. The day I went to see him, Weeks had just returned from a long meeting with the head of the Supreme Council of Antiquities about the following season's work at KV5. His ruddy skin made for an almost violent contrast with his fair hair, and the large-lensed dark glasses he always wears made him seem a little inscrutable. He peppered his conversation with expletives and bursts of humor. When he heard the theory proposed by the guide at the Cairo Museum that Merneptah might be the Pharaoh of Exodus because of the chalky color of his skin, he waved his hands in the air and burst out, "That's dumb!" In fact, Weeks said, until recently he had never given Exodus all that much thought. "I'm an Egyptologist," he explained, "and Exodus isn't an Egyptian story."

Then he wrote a book about his discovery of the tomb, and during his publicity tour readers always wanted to know about Pharaoh's firstborn son and the ten plagues. Weeks didn't have much to tell them at the time, but upon his return to Egypt, he decided to run DNA tests and cranial scans on the remains of three skeletons at labs in Europe and in the United States in order to determine the probability that they belonged to brothers. He planned to compare the results with data scientists have already compiled from Ramses II's mummy. But he was quick to acknowledge that although the amount of information KV5 has revealed about the sons so far is enormous, much work needs to be done. He believes, he said, that scientific tests will eventually be able to determine the cause of Amun's death, and at what age he died. "But how can we prove that he died an unusual death?" asked Weeks. "There won't be a lightning bolt left in his chest where God struck him down."

The Bible had no interest in humanizing Pharaoh, but scenes painted on KV5's walls depict more than just the leader of a mighty empire. Here, beneath the ground, down an endless row of burial chambers, one can still encounter an individualized, empathetic man, his face gentle and pensive, holding his dead son in his arms, and appealing to the gods to ease the child's journey to the next world. In KV5, the nameless Pharaoh of the Bible finally has a name. He is allowed to step outside the category that religious tradition has always assigned him, that of the tyrant, and take on another role, just as universal: a grieving father.

The striking shift in attitudes toward Exodus can most clearly be seen on the movie screen, the perennial barometer of cultural change. In the past Pharaoh was always played as a variation on the theme of the stock villain. It was Moses who kept transforming. In the 1950s, as played by Charlton Heston in *The Ten Commandments,* Moses was characterized as a pillar of moral courage and physical strength. In the 1960s he became the inspiration for modern Jews in *Exodus;* the movie, starring Paul Newman, was based on Leon Uris's bestselling novel, and equated the creation of the modern state of Israel with the biblical escape from slavery. In the most recent version, Steven Spielberg's animated film *The Prince of Egypt,* Moses is a nineties kind of guy, a man of divided loyalties, who remembers the trauma of his days floating down the Nile in a basket via several flashbacks of what psychologists today call repressed memory.

Penney Finkelman Cox, producer of *Prince of Egypt,* traveled to Egypt to research the film. Initially, she says, she approached the trip as an interesting adventure, a chance to add some colorful details and gloss to the biblical tale, which the project's creative team had decided to present as historical fact. The Egyptian government assigned a translator and guide to accompany the group throughout the country. In their two-and-a-half-week stay, Cox and her colleagues visited the Cairo Museum and the pyramids, traveled up and down the Nile, and stopped off at the Valley of the Kings, in Luxor. Along the way, they were treated to the Egyptian point of view about Exodus.

It was a story, Cox felt, that the Egyptians "want to go away." The Egyptologists that they met, and particularly their government-sponsored guide, pointed out that as Muslims, Egyptians venerate Moses too, and that he is the third most important figure in the Koran. But they seemed exasperated that their ancestors were continually portrayed as the villains of the tale.

Cox and her production team listened carefully to the complaints and could see for themselves from the streets and monuments all over the country named for him that Ramses II was a respected leader in Egypt. "The Egyptians argued that all societies have a class system," recounted Cox, whom I spoke to in between her press junkets around the country to promote the film. "If the pharaonic system enslaved and victimized people, then the Egyptians were also victims. The Hebrews weren't the only ones who suffered."

This point of view resonated for the filmmakers when they returned to Hollywood, and in the end the scriptwriters significantly altered the relationship between Moses and Ramses. In the completed film, the two men are portrayed as loving brothers "split apart by history and destiny," said Cox. The movie also features examples of what Cox called "kind Egyptians," particularly the queen, who knows Moses is a Hebrew child when she plucks him from the Nile but is shown as acting out of a sense of humanity and pity for the infant. The ten plagues are shown as causing suffering to Egyptians, innocently caught up in the struggle between Moses and Pharaoh. And the labor force has now become very multicultural. "We gave the slaves different looks and ethnic qualities in order to show that not just the Hebrews are slaves," explained Cox.

On one point, however, the producers refused to make concessions: their version of Exodus is still a story about slaves. "You can't free people who aren't slaves," said Cox. "If you take away that, then you don't have Exodus. There is an Egyptian story to tell here, but that wasn't our story." The Egyptian willingness to reinterpret Exodus had paid off, though. Still, Cox was disappointed to learn that when the movie premiered on the same day around the world, Egypt was one of the few countries where it wasn't shown. The Egyptian censors had stepped in. *The Prince of Egypt* had been banned.

It was probably inevitable that once the image of Pharaoh became subject to revisionism the portrayal of Moses would follow suit. Just as the Bible includes other, more favorable descriptions of life in Egypt than those presented in Exodus, it also contains what the Bible scholar Jonathan Kirsch has called "an anti-Moses tradition," albeit one that has received less attention over the years in sermons and homilies. In one such passage (Numbers 31), Moses is seen sending the Israelites off to war against the Midianites, a desert tribe to which his wife Tziporah belongs and that therefore contains his relatives. Every man among the Midianites is slain, but when the Israelites march back in triumph with their captives, Moses promptly orders the slaughter of all the women and male children and the rape of the virgin girls. In another episode (Numbers 16), when Korah and other rebels question Moses' insistence on being their intermediary with God, arguing that all men should be able to speak to the deity directly, Moses crushes them, calling down divine anger upon them and watching as the earth swallows them up on the spot.

These other attributes of Moses have been neglected over time by institutions and cultural forces that have preferred to see him solely as a powerful symbol of liberation, the embodiment of democratic values. But the complexity of Moses' legacy comes into clearer focus if it is examined in the context of the "Mosaic distinction," a term coined by the German Egyptologist Jan Assmann. This is the idea of monotheism most closely associated with Moses, that all gods but Yahweh are false gods, and that their worship is not only misguided but evil. Despite its success — it has become, after all, the core belief of three major religious faiths, Judaism, Christianity, and Islam — this concept has also spawned a kind of fundamentalism that has often resulted in the eradication of those declared infidels.

For the Bible's authors, Egypt came to symbolize everything that was religiously objectionable, the locus of idolatry. But the hatred and denigration was mutual, Assmann has recounted. The Egyptian priest Manetho, who wrote a history of his country in the first half of the third century B.C.E. (it has survived only in passages quoted by the Jewish historian Josephus), portrayed Moses as a rebellious priest. Having declared himself head of a colony of lepers, Manetho's Moses was expelled from Egypt along with his sickly band. Hecataeus of Abdera, who came to Egypt in 320 B.C.E., included more than a dozen different versions of the biblical story in his own work, all of them strongly anti-Jewish. Many of the most virulent images that would come to dominate European anti-Semitism — those of Jews as aliens and outcasts, lepers and the bearers of plague — turned out to have their roots in Egyptian historical literature dealing with Exodus, Assmann discovered. Assmann saw the long tradition of religious antagonism as beginning in the confrontation between Israel and Egypt and leading directly to the catastrophe of Nazi Germany.

In the hopes of reconciling Israel and Egypt, Assmann began researching Moses' Egyptian roots, believing that it was Moses the Egyptian, rather than Moses the Hebrew of the Bible, who might serve as a bridge between the two sides. But the Moses Assmann had hoped to find proved elusive. The biblical text contains no information at all about what Moses' childhood was like growing up as a member of the court of Pharaoh. We first meet him as one of the many Hebrew male babies whose lives are at risk following Pharaoh's harsh decree calling for their death. Then the tale jumps to the time when he is already a grown man professing a faith whose core idea is that all gods other than the Israelites' Yahweh are false. The ancient biblical interpreters who often rewrote passages and tales in Scripture hadn't been interested in adding more details about Moses' Egyptian background. The Egyptian historians had followed their own, anti-Jewish agenda. In these efforts to counter the biblical portrait, Assmann feared, all hope of finding the historical Moses had been lost.

"Instead," he said during an interview, "we are left to search for what Moses the Egyptian symbolizes."

There is no better place to conduct such a quest than in the Sinai desert, the vast, beautiful, and mysterious expanse of land that has served as the physical bridge between Israel and Egypt for thousands of years. Between 1967, when Israel captured the Sinai during the Arab-Israeli war, and 1982, when it was returned as part of a peace treaty with Egypt, dozens of Israeli expeditions explored and mapped the ancient sites, settlements, and cemeteries that were scattered over the 40,000-square-mile area.

Under international law Israel was not actually permitted to conduct archaeological excavations in Sinai. But archaeologists eager to see if there was evidence of the exodus in the region took advantage of a legal loophole that permitted salvage digs designed to rescue sites that were in danger of being damaged or destroyed by construction projects. All the excavations Israeli archaeologists undertook were therefore labeled salvage digs, although many if not most of them clearly had scientific and cultural goals.

Ethnographic survey work done among Bedouin nomads living in Sinai had already offered tantalizing hints that something might turn up to shed new light on the story. For instance, Israeli archaeologist Ze'ev Meshel noted that some Bedouin customs have precedents in the biblical text, such as a pilgrimage that they make regularly to a spot chosen by the leader of their tribe for several days of worship in the desert. Moses and Aaron initially ask Pharaoh to allow the Israelite slaves three days to go into the desert to worship Yahweh. The archaeologists working in Sinai also turned up scores of nawamis, the Arabic word for mosquitoes. The nawamis are beehive-shaped structures made of limestone, many of them found with their roofs still intact. According to local Bedouin legends, they were built by the Israelites during their trek through the wilderness as protection against mosquito attacks. Upon further investigation, however, it turned out that the nawamis were burial structures.

From the point of view of supporting a traditional rendering of Exodus, the Sinai excavations failed: no proof ever turned up that indicated that the Israelites had wandered in the desert at all, let alone for forty years. But in some respects, what the teams did find was just as powerful and important. Eliezer Oren, an archaeologist at Ben-Gurion University in Beersheba, led an expedition that over the course of ten years probed more than 1,300 sites along the Mediterranean coastal strip of Sinai, the historic route that linked Egypt to Canaan and the lands beyond. They found everything from small ancient campsites, to cities complete with cemeteries, to granaries that the Egyptian army used to supply its troops as they marched toward Canaan.

As they slowly followed the path of the ebb and flow of settlement patterns throughout the northern Sinai, the archaeologists soon realized that the whole cultural reconstruction traditionally proposed for the area didn't make sense. Scholars had always viewed Sinai as an obstacle to interaction between the two cultures, a barrier to interchange. Here the symbolic distance between Israel and Egypt became vividly real, in the form of a vast desert that either separated the two sides or served as the route for military invasions undertaken by either country. And yet, says Oren, the relationship between Egypt and Canaan remained a close one throughout the ages. In most periods the desert was used as a bridge, not a barrier, with the coastal strip in particular heavily settled. Sinai was the main corridor for trade and commerce, through which people moved freely back and forth between the two sides. They met in the middle, on the bridge of Sinai, where the two cultures intermingled and influenced each other. At the temporary encampments that Oren found, the inhabitants left behind pots and jars that originated in both Egypt and Canaan. Inside the burial huts, the nawamis, the delicate shell bracelets, glinting beads, flint tools, and water jugs also reflected the fact that the people who had used them had contacts with both Egypt and Canaan.

The archaeological finds in the Sinai, the whole cultural give-and-take that they represent and that the archaeologists later documented, tell a story. This is the place where Egypt and Israel are finally able to meet, not as adversaries, but as neighbors. It does not appear in Exodus, but there is a hint of this ancient tale in the Book of Deuteronomy, when Moses gathers the Israelites together one last time at the foot of Mount Nebo. On the threshold of a new life in Canaan, Moses urges them to remember Egypt. This is Moses' final speech: he knows that he is about to die and will not be able to enter the Promised Land, and he is filled with bitterness and anger over his lot. At first he urges the Israelites to treat the people of Canaan as God treated the Egyptians, and to smite anyone who stands in their way. But then his fury seems to peak, and in this brief moment, it is possible to imagine Moses recalling his many years living with the tribes of the desert, amid the tools and the bits and pieces of Red Sea shells and inscriptions the archaeologists later found. "Love ye therefore the stranger, for ye were strangers in the land of Egypt," he bids the Israelites, and they set off for the final journey toward Canaan.

Chapter 3

❧

The New Canaanites

Your origin and your birth are from the land of the Canaanite.
(Ezekiel 16:3)

How can you tell an Israelite from a Canaanite?

That is the question that many historians and researchers have been asking as they seek to unravel the origins of Israel. In the Bible, the answer is easy. The Canaanites are the idol worshippers. They hold religious ceremonies involving sex and drink, all part of their broader campaign to entice the Israelites away from the true path of monotheism. They're morally inferior to the Israelites and culturally undistinguished. In the Book of Joshua, entire Canaanite villages, men, women, and children, are eradicated by a victorious Israelite army of tribes that have been freed from slavery in Egypt to march in and conquer the land.

Except that's not how it happened. All the latest evidence indicates that there was no swift invasion around 1250–1225 B.C.E., the time generally attributed to the beginning of the Israelite settlement in

Canaan. Many of the sites mentioned in the biblical account of the conquest — including the most famous of all, the city of Jericho — weren't even occupied during that period, let alone destroyed. Even more significant are finds made in the course of archaeological surveys of the biblical territories of the tribes of Ephraim and Manasseh, located in the central highlands of the West Bank and traditionally thought to be at the heart of the earliest Israelite settlement in Canaan. After studying the remains of scores of villages of that period, the archaeologists concluded that the people living there worshipped traditional Canaanite gods, wrote in Canaanite alphabetic script, and used Canaanite-style pottery. It is difficult to tell an Israelite from a Canaanite because the Israelites and the Canaanites were one and the same people.

In recent years an archaeological reassessment of the Canaanites has been under way, and the new discoveries paint a portrait of Canaan and Canaanite culture entirely different from the one that dominates the Bible. In the Book of Numbers, God instructs Moses to send ten spies to scout out Canaan and bring back a report about the land. When the spies return from their mission, only two, Joshua and Caleb, think the Israelites have any chance of conquering Canaan. The others describe huge cities, prosperous, thriving, and girded for battle. "We came unto the land whither thou sentest us, and surely it floweth with milk and honey," the spies report. "Howbeit the people that dwell in the land are fierce, and the cities are fortified, and very great." In Moses' last speech to the people of Israel before he dies, he reinforces this very same image of Canaan. "Hear O Israel: thou art to pass over the Jordan this day, to go in to dispossess nations greater and mightier than thyself, cities great and fortified up to heaven."

Among the earliest archaeologists working in Palestine, there was great interest in excavating the Canaanite cities listed in biblical itineraries of Joshua's military campaigns. But the archaeologists who uncovered cities like Tel Beit Mirsim, Jericho, and Shechem were surprised to find that they all lacked fortification. Most other cities of the Late Bronze Age, running between the fifteenth and the thirteenth centuries B.C.E., were the same. The reasons for this were never fully explored. In 1997, however, Ze'ev Herzog, an archaeologist working at Tel Aviv University who specializes in this period, published a comprehensive study reviewing the archaeological evidence from excavated Canaanite cities of this period. He found not just a lack of fortifications, but what he described as a "degeneration of every urban parameter" in these cities, including a lack of residential structures, little or no concern for drainage, and no real street network. In fact, most of the settlements consisted primarily of a single large building, which Herzog postulated had served as a palace-fort for the local ruler. Herzog contended that during the time the Israelites would have been fighting their way into Canaan, most of the Canaanite cities had no fortifications and an urban center that probably consisted mainly of the seat of the ruler and a few members of his court. He interpreted this layout as illustrating the overall weakness of political, economic, and social life in the Canaanite cities of the period. The leaders weren't powerful enough to stimulate a thriving urban dynamic. The palace-fort was usually built near the entrance of the city, beside a gate that typically had survived from a previous period. This gave the rulers effective control over the agricultural lands and the farmers who worked them, but was hardly a sign of a flourishing city.

Herzog contended that there must have been a social rift between the elite of Canaanite society and the rest of the population. The city layouts clearly demonstrated that virtually all construction at the sites was done on behalf of the rulers, while nothing was built outside the ruling compound. "The Bible's descriptions of fortified cities were designed to demonstrate how difficult it was to get rid of the mighty Canaanite cities," Herzog argued, "but the archaeological evidence shows a different picture."

There were two major exceptions to this picture of decline. The first was the city of Megiddo, which remained an important urban center throughout this period, although Herzog noted that even here the reality was far removed from vibrant urban power. The other was Hazor, which the Bible calls "the head of all the cities" in Canaan.

Located in northern Israel, closer to Damascus than to Jerusalem, Hazor was one of the key Canaanite city-states. The Bible offers two different stories of the fall of Hazor, which archaeologists estimate took place sometime in the thirteenth century B.C.E. In the Book of Joshua, Jabin, king of Hazor, organizes a coalition of Canaanite kings to oppose the rising power of the Israelites. "And all these kings met together; and they came and pitched together at the waters of Merom to fight with Israel." God tells Joshua not to be afraid, that the vastly outnumbered Israelites will prevail in battle, and the next day they do. No foe is left standing. For good measure, Joshua turns his forces against Hazor, killing the king with his sword. "Every living soul" is put to death and the city is burned to the ground. The Book of Judges remembers Hazor's destruction differently. God has allowed Jabin, king of Hazor, to rule the Israelites for twenty years as punishment for their transgressions. Finally the warrior-prophetess Deborah organizes a group of Israelites, representing the different tribes, to fight the Canaanites. This is no swift battle led by a hard-charging general, but a series of skirmishes that continue until the Israelites triumph. "And the hand of the children of Israel prevailed more and more against Jabin the king of Canaan, until they had destroyed Jabin king of Canaan."

For decades, Bible scholars argued over which of these accounts was older, and hence, they believed, more likely to be a reliable record of what actually took place. Hazor's first excavator, the famous Israeli general-turned-archaeologist Yigael Yadin, wanted to excavate the site in part to determine which version was closer to the truth. He found a destruction layer at the site that he believed matched the time of Joshua's military campaign. But by the late 1990s, Amnon Ben-Tor, who had worked under Yadin and was now conducting a new excavation at the site, wasn't sure, although he was starting to believe the destruction had occurred earlier than Yadin had thought.

Much of Hazor's history is actually known from archives discovered inside Canaanite palaces in Syria and Lebanon. In Mari, on the west bank of the Euphrates River, twenty of the twenty-five thousand tablets discovered there mentioned Hazor. They described it as the center of vast trade, where caravans filled with gold and silver traveled frequently. In Egypt, three letters sent in the fourteenth century B.C.E. by Hazor's king to the pharaoh Akhenaton described the Canaanite's struggle with other local rulers as he acquired new lands. But similar archives had not turned up in Israel. "It's like oil in the Middle East," Ben-Tor would complain. "Everywhere but in Israel." Then Ben-Tor's team uncovered several cuneiform tablets inside the remains of a Canaanite palace on the site. These were the first indication that an archive might be buried in the area, and Ben-Tor had been pursuing it ever since. He was convinced that it lay somewhere inside the Canaanite palace that Yadin had first uncovered, and concentrated the dig's efforts there. It was tiring, tedious work. Some of the volunteers spent an entire summer excavating one small area of the huge complex. The walls of the palace were massive, at one point measuring nine feet thick.

The palace was the best indication of the status Hazor had enjoyed under the Canaanites. The city never recovered its former glory, not even during the days the Bible depicts as its heyday, in the reigns of King David and King Solomon. The city that Ben-Tor believed to have been built by the Israelites under David and Solomon's united monarchy consisted of the city gate and casemate wall, with some rather poor remains within. The Canaanite city beneath it, on the other hand, was truly spectacular. The digging had been done in such a way that the two cities could now be seen side by side. The Canaanites had been master builders, using basalt stone and mud brick to form compact walls. In the vicinity of the palace, there were two pillars still standing that Ben-Tor estimated to weigh five-and-a-half tons each. Beautiful artwork had been recovered, delicate ivory carvings, two basalt lions that had probably guarded the entrance to the palace, statues covered with gold. "The Canaanite architecture is stunning, isn't it?" Ben-Tor asked one day as he showed me around the site. He jumped into the shallow pit where the palace was being uncovered. "It is beautiful, amazing work. The Israelite architecture isn't as good."

The Bible is constantly comparing the Canaanites to the Israelites and finding that they came up short; but the excavations at Hazor show otherwise. For years, evidence has been mounting that the Israelites adopted and built on Canaanite culture, including cultic practices. The Old Testament feasts of Tabernacles, Unleavened Bread, and Weeks — corresponding to the Jewish holidays of Sukkot, Passover, and Shavuot — were basically annual agricultural festivals, and each of them had a Canaanite version. A number of sacrificial terms used in the Bible are similar to those used by the Canaanites, and although Bible scholars can't be completely sure they were appropriated from the Canaanites, it seems likely that this was the case. While the Bible disdains the fertility cult practices that sprang up around the worship of Ba'al, it is perfectly happy to equate El, the chief Canaanite god, known for his wisdom, with the Israelites' god, Yahweh. Much of Genesis describes the patriarchs, Abraham, Isaac, and Jacob, worshipping various manifestations of El. The Bible also adopts certain Canaanite religious themes associated with Ba'al. In the Bible, Ba'al's sacred mountain, Mount Sapan, is transformed into Mount Zion, Yahweh's dwelling place.

At Hazor and elsewhere, the Israelites used Canaanite designs for their own buildings. While I was there, Ben-Tor offered a tour of the site to the volunteers doing the digging. They clambered over the rocks and walked down the narrow winding staircase to the subterranean water tunnel, their voices echoing off the damp walls. The Canaanites' fingerprints were evident throughout the city. Ben-Tor took the volunteers to see the massebah, an open-air place of worship with a slanting basalt pillar located near the city gate. Ben-Tor believed this was a sacred site to the city's Israelite inhabitants, where people might come to make offerings to the gods in gratitude for the birth of a child or a good season's crops, or to request a favor and good fortune. It had been found in the 1950s, during the first excavation led by Yadin. Standing before it, Ben-Tor talked about a small jar that some long-ago worshipper had left at the stone as an offering. Inside the vessel were small bronze objects, including a figurine of a Canaanite deity. When the jar was found, Ben-Tor said, "everyone argued such a find was impossible. People were shocked. They asked, how could it be possible that the Israelites brought a Canaanite deity as an offering to Yahweh?" Ben-Tor paused for effect, standing in the frame of the stone pillar. In his view, that debate was over. "No one would ever make that argument today," he declared.

The most important form of worship in ancient times was sacrifice, the offering of animals to the gods. Praying ran a distant second. People would travel great distances to offer sacrifices at the main cultic centers, usually located in large city-states like Hazor and Megiddo. So many sacrifices were being conducted at those cities that the temples and cultic institutions became veritable butcher shops, slaughtering, cutting, and distributing the sundry parts of the animal throughout the city. The distribution of the animal was often carried out along class lines. The priests got the best cuts as well as the skins. The rich especially prized sheep tails (for their high fat content), animal heads, and the most tender cuts of meat from young animals. The poor got what was left.

Much of what we know about Canaanite sacrifice comes from the Hebrew Bible. At Ugarit, in modern Syria, where a huge archive was uncovered, there are virtually no texts that deal directly with sacrificial practices. There are records of the kinds of animals — mainly sheep, goats, and cattle — that were offered to the gods. One literary text found at Ugarit lists what the god Ba'al sacrificed to other gods, and that probably reflects some of the practices widespread among the general population as well. But even here there are limitations. No one knows exactly how to translate many of the animal names listed as part of the sacrifice ritual, and while scholars believe that some of the words do correspond to better-known terms in Hebrew and Akkadian, there is room for doubt. Canaanite sacrifice is therefore usually reconstructed to contrast with Israelite sacrifice, and is always cast in a very negative light.

During recent excavations at Megiddo, an early cultic complex was unearthed. Inside the many temples uncovered at the complex were tens of thousands of animal bones, one of the largest such troves in the region. This find offered the first opportunity to investigate the Canaanite sacrificial system independently of any textual descriptions, including those in the Bible.

The preliminary analysis demonstrates how closely the much later Israelite sacrifice practices dovetailed with the Canaanite system. The bones were found in a complex that was approximately two thousand years older than any known Israelite entity. And yet, according to Paula Wapnish, who is heading the bones research at Megiddo, "we are hard-pressed to differentiate between ethnic groups when it comes to sacrifice." Throughout the Middle East, the same few species were used for sacrifice, predominantly sheep, cattle, and goats. As discussed in an earlier chapter, researchers until lately were enthusiastic about the potential of identifying Israelite areas by the absence of pig bones. Unfortunately, Wapnish says, "the Canaanites didn't really use pigs for sacrifice either. The fact that later Israelite practices replicated some of this shows that pig taboos are deeply rooted in the area."

That's not to say there were no differences in Canaanite and Israelite attitudes toward God or worship, but Wapnish argues that these are almost impossible to detect from the bones. She cites the Bible's focus on the prohibition of using or touching blood as one such major conceptual difference. Many biblical texts record that the blood of the sacrificed animal had always to be drained and collected by the officiating priest, who spoke the appropriate benedictions as he worked. No comparable rituals regarding the disposal of blood have turned up in the Ugarit texts. Wapnish believes that the Israelite practice has deep roots in tradition since it appears so often in the texts, but even that is difficult to prove on the ground. "If we found a lot of cervical vertebrae, that might indicate that the animals' jugulars had been cut. But you don't find a lot of stuff like that. Vertebrae break up easily because they're spongy. They also have a lot of meat on them. They ended up being used in a lot of stews," she says.

Even so, what has been most remarkable about the finds at Megiddo is that they appear to show that sacrifice was practiced pretty much the same way throughout the Middle East. "If there were differences," says Wapnish, "they're invisible to us now."

It seems clear that the Canaanites and their traditions were an important and key influence on the Israelites. "If they weren't Canaanites themselves," Wapnish said about the Israelites, "then they certainly knew all the Canaanite traditions." And in recent decades the Canaanites have begun coming into focus, outside the overpowering shadow of the Israelites and the Bible. A key piece of the puzzle was found during a 1995 dig in Jerusalem, just south of the Old City, in a small operation beneath a planned tourist center in the City of David sponsored by a group of Jewish settlers calling themselves Elad. As they continued to dig, the archaeologists were startled to discover that the city's ancient water system, long believed to be the work of King David's administration following his conquest of Jerusalem, had actually been built eight centuries earlier by the Canaanites. Investigating Jerusalem in the late 1860s, the British explorer Charles Warren had climbed inside a ten-foot-wide shaft that appeared to be carved into the rock right next to the Gihon Spring, the city's main source of water. A tunnel on the eastern slope of the City of David led to the top of the shaft, which bottomed out not far from the Gihon Spring. Since its discovery, Warren's Shaft had been believed to be the linchpin of the city's water system and the main way that the city's ancient residents took water from the nearby spring.

During the City of David digs in the late 1970s and mid-1980s, archaeologist Yigal Shiloh hired three mountain climbers to climb once again to the top of Warren's Shaft, this time as part of an effort to clean out the area so that tourists might explore the complex. Since then, it had been one of the most popular tourist sites in the city. The archaeologists had found no pottery in the shaft to help them date the site. They speculated that Warren's expedition had removed any shards from the chamber; indeed, they found a rusted bucket that a member of Warren's team had left behind. The excavators working with Shiloh knew, however, that elaborately designed subterranean water systems had been a key part in the planning of important forti-fied cities in Israel. Megiddo had one, as did Hazor, so they dated the system to the time of Israelite rule in Jerusalem. There also seemed to be an underlying assumption that the water system's design was sim-ply too sophisticated to have been a Canaanite creation.

Ronny Reich, the Israeli archaeologist leading the dig under the proposed visitors center, contended that Warren's Shaft was a natural fissure in the rock that had nothing to do with Jerusalem's water sys-tem. Reich's dig had turned up an underground tunnel that circum-vented the shaft altogether and led directly to a pool near the spring. The spring, which until then most had assumed to be outside the city walls and therefore unfortified, was in fact surrounded by a formida-ble system of towers. Soldiers standing guard on one of the towers could easily have picked off anyone trying to infiltrate the city. Arti-facts found in or near the towers indicated they dated from well before King David's time. That would mean that the Canaanites and not the Israelites had built the city's water system.

One morning in August 1998, carrying a huge jerry can of water slung on his shoulder, Reich slowly made his way through the under-ground tunnel that led to the pool of water. He had strung up lights along the way, and they gave off eerie shadows as the damp tunnel snaked toward the pool. As Reich moved carefully through the tunnel, he pointed out to a small group of archaeologists and reporters how clever the Canaanites had been, cutting into the softest layer of the rock, using precise measurements that required a detailed knowledge of geometry to enable them to cut into the rock only as far as they needed. Right next to the pool, sitting virtually on the bottom floor of the planned visitors center, was the spot where Reich had cleared his way through a twenty-five-foot-thick dump consisting of dirt, rocks, and trash that mainly dated to the time of the Second Temple, in the sixth century B.C.E., when people were living on the site.

Eventually Reich and his team had hit the inner corner of what they thought was the remains of a tower built around the spring to protect it. The stones were enormous slabs, some as big as six feet long, three feet high, and three feet deep. They rested in straight layers so that they formed a massive wall. Reich said this kind of masonry hadn't been seen in Jerusalem again until the time of Herod the Great, who ruled in the first century B.C.E. and was renowned as the greatest ancient builder in Palestine.

The area within the tower would have quickly flooded without some sort of exit for the spring water. Reich and the other archaeologists had found a channel cut into the rock that went all the way down the eastern side of the City of David, to a point where the water gushed out into pools. Unlike Warren's Shaft, the Canaanite system enabled the city's residents not only to get their water safely, but to pump it from the spring far more easily than if they had been drawing it through the shaft, as archaeologists had long assumed.

Reich's crediting the Canaanites for building such a system — a conclusion that had appeared a short time before on the front page of the leading Israeli newspaper — hadn't been popular, especially at Elad, which had put up over $2 million to help finance the dig in the hope of illuminating "the links in the chain between the people of Israel and King David," in the words of Yigal Naveh, the manager of Elad's current visitor center. Reich's findings seemed instead a reminder that King David too was a link, in a chain that began long before the Israelites ever arrived here, of conquerors who had left their mark on Jerusalem. Naveh challenged Reich's findings; he handed out the phone numbers of critics to journalists who came seeking comment about the discovery. But despite his benefactors' skepticism, Reich said he felt confident about his dating, because of pieces of pottery that had turned up on the floor of one tower, and within the small crevices between the large stone blocks in another. The pottery dated from the eighteenth and seventeenth centuries B.C.E., a time archaeologists call the Middle Bronze Age.

"People will have to reassess what the Canaanite city looked like," Reich said the morning he took the archaeologists and journalists through the tunnel. Tom Segev, a historian, had come down to the site, drawn by the headlines about the finds. He had sat patiently, his back pressed up against the Canaanite tower, as Reich pulled out maps and explained how the water system had worked. Even as Reich talked, the sounds of workmen building Elad's modern visitor center could be heard in the background. Segev had to raise his voice to be heard over the rising din. "Reassessing what the city looked like isn't what disturbs people about Ronny's finds," he said. "It's the idea of reassessing the Canaanites."

A few weeks after Reich announced his discovery that the Canaanites had built a key part of Jerusalem's water system, Palestinian archaeologists in Nablus called a press conference to announce the discovery of Canaanite homes, dating to around 3000 B.C.E., in a neighborhood in Tel Sofer, in the western part of Nablus, one of the West Bank's largest cities. At the press conference, Jalal Kazzouh, head of the archaeology department at Nablus's An-Najah University, said the discovery's major significance was that it would help the Palestinians write their own version of the region's past. "Israeli research stopped whenever they reached anything dating to the Israelite era in this region," he told a small group of reporters at the site.

For several years now, a group of Palestinian intellectuals, politicians, and scholars has been promoting the idea that the Palestinians are the true descendants of the earliest inhabitants of Canaan. In August 1996 Palestinians from around the West Bank gathered in the town of Sabastiyah to re-create the legend of Ba'al, the Canaanite god of the heavens and fertility, and his struggle for domination over brother Mut, god of the underworld. Teenagers dressed in flowing white robes pulled light wooden chariots through narrow alleyways until they reached a stone stage that had been specially set up in the center of town. There a narrator told the story of Ba'al's tribulations. When he got to the part in the text warning against the Habiru, or Hebrew, tribes who were then on the move in Canaan, his whole face seemed to contort in an effort to radiate the significance of the point to his audience. He recited the tragedies that had befallen the warriors of the various Canaanite peoples, the Amorites, Girgashites, Jebusites, and Perizzites, all smitten by Joshua's rampaging army. As the story reached its climax, with Ba'al dying and then rising to life again, torch-bearing youth formed a knot around the Palestinian minister of culture and danced with him in the center of the square.

The Canaanite festival didn't pay much attention to historical veracity. Sabastiyah, the ancient site of Samaria, was once the capital of the northern kingdom of Israel and boasts mainly Israelite and Herodian remains rather than Canaanite ones. The Canaanite chariots had Philistine birds painted on them, a design belonging to a nonindigenous group that flourished in Canaan, and the festival T-shirts boasted a drawing of a Philistine bowl. But the day's events were in keeping with the long tradition of national pageants, with an emphasis on spectacle and entertainment.

There was a serious message behind it too. After years of everything from disinterest to downright hostility when it came to using the Bible as a historical source, many Palestinians were for the first time embracing biblical historiography, at least in selective parts. There was a growing sense among the Palestinian elite that the Israelis had succeeded in gaining a state not only due to success on the battlefield or political circumstances but from an ability to use the past, especially the biblical past, to help advance a modern agenda. The Palestinians weren't going to be left out anymore. In Sabastiyah, they had effectively declared themselves the new Canaanites, and that was only the beginning. Al-Quds University in Jerusalem now requires all students, no matter what their intended major, to take introductory courses on the history and archaeology of both Palestine and Jerusalem. Canaanites form an important part of the syllabus. "It makes sense to connect Palestinian and Canaanite culture," said Marwan Abu Khalaf, the director of Al-Quds University's archaeology department, during an interview. Abu Khalaf is one of the driving forces behind the change. "Our habits and traditions go back to the Canaanites. Did you know that the Canaanites were actually Arabs? They came from the Arabian peninsula looking for water. Abraham didn't arrive until two thousand years later."

Abu Khalaf's take on the Canaanites' Arab antecedents may have been without much foundation, but his notion of trying to document the Arab contribution to Palestine's cultural past was quite mainstream. The late Albert Glock, the American archaeologist who helped found and head Bir Zeit University's Institute of Archaeology, argued along similar lines. Instead of focusing on the biblical record immediately or exclusively, as he argued Israeli and Western scholars had done, Glock wanted to start with the recent past, during Ottoman Turkish rule before the British mandate period that led to the founding of Israel in 1948. Then, he felt, the Palestinians could keep backing ever further into their past, always searching for and documenting the links between present and past, in the form of cultural continuity in village settlement patterns, domestic and public architecture, and social organization. Glock himself tried to implement that vision by organizing a dig in the village of Ta'annek, in the West Bank. Back in the 1960s, a team of Austrian and American archaeologists had excavated the ruins of the biblical city of Taanach, whose high mound loomed above the Palestinian village. Glock's idea was to excavate the modern village first, to uncover the destroyed walls and mud ovens the villagers had used long ago, to sift through Ottoman tax records, and to interview the elderly villagers in an attempt to trace Ta'annek's more recent history before trying to connect it with Taanach.

But Glock never got a chance to reach Taanach. In January 1992, as he was leaving his office at Bir Zeit University, he was shot at close range by an unidentified gunman. He died instantly, shot twice in the back of the head and neck and once in the heart from the front. The suspects ranged from Israeli secret service agents angry over his provocative archaeological theories at a time of rising Palestinian nationalism, to a Palestinian whose appointment in the department he had supposedly blocked. The murder has never been solved. Many of Glock's students left the country or the field of archaeology. A few articles about the dig at the village appeared, but no final report was issued. Bir Zeit bought Glock's library of nearly six thousand volumes and stored the pottery and other finds from the 1960s dig at biblical Taanach in the basement. Just recently have reports related to the material started to be published.

In 1993, after the Israeli-Palestinian peace accords were signed, Bir Zeit went looking for a new director for the institute. Glock's murder cast a pall over the search. The man they hired, Khaled Nashef, a specialist in cuneiform texts and not archaeology, was impatient with Glock's legacy, his students even more so. Glock's idea of searching for cultural continuity had survived his death, but his theory about starting from the Ottoman period and working backward had not. Most of Nashef's students were ready to jump right back to the Late Bronze Age and the Canaanites. Nail Jelal, one of Nashef's graduate students, had catalogued the more than 250 pieces of Palestinian pottery in the university's collection. Most had been made in the 1970s and 1980s, by aging potters working in small villages in the West Bank and in Gaza, using techniques they had learned from their grandfathers. Jelal carefully recorded the terminology used to describe each piece, the different shapes and forms, the way each had been manufactured, in order to preserve what he considered a dying tradition. As the work progressed, he said in an interview, he realized that handle shapes and certain other forms were very similar to pottery made in the Late Bronze Age by the Canaanites. "Sometimes even the same clay sources were used," Jelal said animatedly.

Another student I talked with had begun working on building a library of animal bones that could be used for comparison with bones found at ancient sites. He had collected thirty skeletons, mainly those of birds, horses, and cattle that he had bought from butcher shops in the West Bank or found lying dead in his village. On traditional Muslim feast days, when sheep and other animals are slaughtered and eaten, he made arrangements with friends and family to save the bones. His goal was to collect bones of all the species native to Palestine. He pointed out that the excavators at Taanach had mentioned finding a lot of animal knuckle bones. Many archaeologists argue that the bones were used in divination rites, but he had another idea. In Palestinian villages, knuckle bones were used in a popular game.

The Palestinian archaeologists had followed the progress of Amnon Ben-Tor's dig at Hazor and the search for the lost Canaanite archives. They had watched enthusiastically as Reich's team uncovered the massive towers guarding the springs inside Jerusalem's walls. The discovery of the Canaanite houses in Nablus — in a dig led by Palestinian archaeologists associated with a West Bank university — was viewed as a chance to shape the emerging new history of the Canaanites in a way that hadn't been possible under the Israeli military occupation. In his office at An-Najah, Kazzouh enthused about building a Canaanite village to draw tourists to the site, along the lines of the pharaonic villages the Egyptians had dug up and reconstructed. The idea seemed unlikely to succeed, considering that the dig had been done on a very modest budget, a few thousand dollars the university had managed to scrounge up. Kazzouh hadn't even been able to finance a fence to prevent the neighborhood residents from throwing trash into the two small pits that contained the Caananite houses.

His office was just as spare. There was one bookshelf with a few books, a piece of old pottery, and a skull. The key to the restroom was kept inside the pottery. "We want the objects to speak for themselves," he said, leading his visitors upstairs to an exhibit he had put together of ancient pottery that the university owned. The pots were jumbled together; there wasn't one sign or explanation of what they were, where they had been found, or to what periods they belonged. Some fancier display cases had been ordered from Europe, but Kazzouh claimed to prefer the current ones, made of a dark brown wood by local Nablus craftsmen. "Those are more traditional," he said. "They reflect Palestinians as the continuation of the ancient Canaanite culture."

Mahogany may or may not have been a cornerstone of Canaanite culture, but Kazzouh's enthusiasm was contagious. He decided to drive out to Tel Sofer to visit the Canaanite houses. Empty cigarette packs, candy bar wrappings, and an old newspaper had been thrown into the pits since his last visit, and he yelled at the village boys who ran out to his car about their lack of respect for Palestine's cultural heritage. "We need to learn as much about the Canaanites as we can," said Kazzouh, staring down into the pits. He still wasn't sure whether the so-called Canaanite homes had been used as houses, as tombs, or as storage, but he was certain that the people who had used them were the "fathers and grandfathers of the Palestinians." He saw the Canaanites as a vehicle for healing the political injustices he felt had been done to the Palestinians. "We need to explain to the whole world who are really the ancient ones in this area," he said. "Where do people think we came from?"

Traditionally there have been three main theories regarding what is referred to as the Israelite settlement in Canaan. At the time, around 1200 B.C.E., huge changes were taking place throughout the Middle East. Egypt, long the dominant power, saw its power begin to slip. A group of pirate types, called the Sea Peoples, were leaving the Aegean and settling in Cyprus and along the coastal cities of Canaan. The Hittite empire, Egypt's main rival, was faring no better, fragmenting into small city-states constantly at war with one another. The great Canaanite city of Ugarit, in the upper part of modern-day Syria, was destroyed. Scholars are still not sure what caused all these problems. Theories have run the gamut from drought to widespread economic collapse, but there's no question that the entire region was in turmoil.

It is to around this time that some archaeologists date the emergence of Israel. Most theories about the Israelites' origins stem from developments in biblical scholarship. Bible scholars had been debating for years the two slightly different accounts in the Bible of how the Israelites took possession of Canaan. The account in Joshua describes a quick military conquest. After a string of Israelite victories, the various tribes divide among themselves the land west of the Jordan. In Judges the tribes first decide who is to get what land, and only then do they go out and try to conquer it; the tribes don't seem to work together as a unified entity as they do in Joshua. Moreover, Judges is fairly open about the fact that the Israelites fail in their attempt to conquer all of Canaan. The book lists twenty cities where the Canaanites remain, including such key centers as Jerusalem, Megiddo, and Taanach.

Much of the relevant archaeology was undertaken with these interpretations in mind. William Albright, who until his death in 1971 was considered the dean of biblical archaeology, defended what came to be called the conquest model. This adhered to the version presented in Joshua, of a group of tribes from outside the country launching a daring and quick military campaign, annihilating most of the local cities, and then settling down on the ruins of their destruction. The peaceful infiltration model, which drew upon the Book of Judges as its source, was championed by Albrecht Alt, a brilliant German biblical scholar. He proposed that the Israelites hadn't conquered Canaan, but had quietly and peacefully moved into the country's central hill region. Only later, when they tried to move into the more fertile areas of the valleys and plains, did conflict with the Canaanites begin. There was some archaeological evidence to support such a movement, but doubts about this idea grew as archaeologists pointed out that there was no way to know whether the people living in this hilly region considered themselves Israelites at such an early date. They pointed out that the people's lifestyle, architecture, and pottery were similar to those found in other areas of Canaan. Then, in the 1960s, a third school of thought emerged. This group, led by a University of Michigan scholar named George Mendenhall and later by a New York Theological Seminary professor named Norman Gottwald, proposed that the Israelites hadn't come from outside the country at all, but had been in Canaan all along. The Israelites were merely discontented Canaanites, peasants in revolt who had launched a Marxist-style revolution to rid Canaan of social inequality. They then headed for the hills, whence they later emerged as the Israelites.

Despite the differences in these various theories, all shared a very important belief. They held that what had occurred was a "singular, epoch-making event in the history of the country," in the words of Israel Finkelstein, the head of the Institute of Archaeology at Tel Aviv University and a leading researcher on the issue of the Israelite settlement. Whether they accepted the biblical account or not, whether they thought Joshua was more reliable than Judges or the other way around, most of these scholars shared the idea that the Israelite phenomenon was unique, heralding the end of an old order and the beginning of something completely new.

At first, archaeology seemed to support that idea. Ben-Tor's dig at Hazor was a typical example. There were the remains of a violent destruction, including the burned brick from a massive fire that had destroyed a rich city. That was followed by the much poorer and smaller remains built on top of it by the next wave of settlers, whom Ben-Tor believed to have been Israelites. Some of the first comprehensive archaeological surveys done in the hill country area had shown a wave of new villages springing up around this time.

Finkelstein had a different take on the phenomenon. He didn't see the Israelites as unique at all. "The Israelite schleppers weren't that much different than the Canaanite shleppers," he told me in 1997 in his office at Tel Aviv University. Outside, a camera crew from Italy was waiting for Finkelstein to finish so they could interview him for a television program in Europe. His controversial views, colorful speaking style, and photogenic looks had helped make him a minor celebrity there. Lately he had been pushing a new idea, that the palace, city gate, and other monumental architecture at Megiddo, where he was overseeing a new excavation, and in places like Hazor and Gezer, hadn't been built by King Solomon after all, but a hundred years later, by King Ahab. If Finkelstein was right, then Israelite architecture in the time the Bible depicts as the golden era of Israelite culture — the united monarchies of David and then his son Solomon — was basically still Canaanite in style. It all came back to the whole question of what had been unique about the Israelites, and the reluctance to acknowledge that at that early stage in their emergence the answer was, not much. The differences between Israelites and Canaanites highlighted in the biblical literature, Finkelstein argued, had only come much, much later.

The evidence for this idea was in a series of comprehensive surveys that had been done in the central highlands of the West Bank in the years following the 1967 war. In those days, Finkelstein, Adam Zertal of the University of Haifa, and the other archaeologists who participated had been young graduate students. Finkelstein had covered the biblical allotment to the tribe of Ephraim, while Zertal had focused on the tribe of Manasseh's portion. Finkelstein had published his results in *The Archaeology of the Israelite Settlement* (1988), a book that made his name in the world of archaeology. These days, only Zertal, formerly head of the archaeology department at Haifa University, is pursuing the survey, having spent every Friday for the past twenty-two years in some other area of Manasseh. In that time he has managed to cover a huge portion of the 800 square miles that the Bible says the tribe received, an area bordered by the Jordan River, the coastal plain highway called the Via Maris, the Jezreel Valley, and the cities of Shechem, now Nablus, in the West Bank, and Jericho.

Archaeological survey work is tedious. One Friday I accompanied Zertal's team as they drove out in jeeps and set to work. Zertal's views have made him controversial. Among archaeologists, his interpretations are considered fundamentalist, since they tend to support the biblical version of events. His colleagues also concede that the enormous record Zertal has compiled of names, places, styles of architecture, types of pottery, type and quality of soil, crops, geology, water sources, proximity to roads — all meticulously entered into a computer for statistical analysis — is the most extensive now available. It paints a fascinating demographic portrait of life in one of the largest and most important areas of the Israelite settlement. Yet Zertal's maverick personality and reluctance to promote his views at conferences have marginalized his work in academic circles.

Among the tightly knit group of friends who have been going out into the field with him every week and the students who participate each season, Zertal enjoys cult figure status. When the Arab countries launched a surprise attack against Israel in 1973, Zertal was a student at the University of Tel Aviv and a father of three children. His unit was sent down to the Sinai desert, one of the bloodiest areas of the war. He was hit by a Russian shell near the Suez Canal, and was one of the few in his unit to make it back alive. He spent over a year in a full body cast; the doctors thought he'd never walk again. As part of his rehabilitation program, he forced himself to learn to walk with metal crutches while doing archaeological survey work in the West Bank. Even today, he'll throw the crutches up on a ridge and then clamber up unassisted. He likes to eat lunch with the group under the shade of an olive tree and drink coffee brewed over a small fire. He'll pull out the Bible to illustrate some connection with what he's found and say with a booming voice, "Archaeology without the Bible is archaeology without a soul."

The results of his survey continue to be published, volume by volume. They demonstrate a change between the Late Bronze Age (about 1200 B.C.E.), when the Israelites are believed to have emerged, and Iron Age I (around 1000 B.C.E.,), the beginning of King David's rule. The number of sites in Manasseh jumped from 39 to more than 220 between these two periods. In contrast to the Late Bronze Age, the settlers of the Iron Age were concentrated in the more difficult to farm mountain region rather than in the valleys and tended to live in small unwalled villages rather than in cities. Zertal argues that this reflects the biblical picture of a new population arriving in the area and being forced into marginal lands because the more fertile valleys were already settled.

Zertal paints a picture of Canaanite-Israelite relations slightly different from the one that appears in Joshua, although elements of it are touched on in the Book of Judges. His examination of the archaeological record sees cooperation and coexistence rather than conflict and battles. The Israelites had no other choice, he posits. Very few water cisterns have turned up during Zertal's survey work, perhaps because carving into the hard rock of the mountains wouldn't have been possible without iron tools. Instead, he contends, the Israelites used collar-rimmed jars, each holding up to fifteen gallons of water, as a storage system. But they had to get the water from somewhere, and Zertal argues it was from their neighbors, the Canaanites. The majority of the 39 sites dating to the earlier period were located near natural water sources, such as springs and rivers. Those would have been the places where the Canaanites continued to live when the Israelites set up shop in the hilly areas. The Israelites would have had to walk several miles through land controlled by other tribes to get to those springs and bring the water back in the large storage jars. They would have needed permission to do it. They weren't fighting the Canaanites, they were probably trading with them.

Zertal's data indicate that something interesting was happening in the hills of Canaan at this time. But how to interpret it? Finkelstein has argued that all the patterns that Zertal describes, such as the sharp increase in settlements, the areas occupied by the settlers, the use of water, had happened before. The waves of settlement following a period of decline in the highlands? The growth and eventual decline of large urban systems? By Finkelstein's count the same pattern occurred at least twice before, during the second and third millennia. The process even followed similar stages — an initial wave of settlement, the emergence of a more advanced administration, and a collapse and crisis.

Zertal's survey has provided the most extensive detail available about what occurred in this one region of Canaan at an important transitional moment, the time when people were starting to build again after the collapse of the Canaanite city-states. Finkelstein has looked at the data for all the surveys and set it into a context of a longer time frame. Their approach to scholarship reflects the differences in their worldviews. The two men don't get along very well. They were friends back in the days when they were both hiking the hills of the West Bank, but over the years they have grown apart. While Zertal's controversial interpretations have left him outside the mainstream of archaeology, Finkelstein's no less controversial ideas have made him a media star. Part of it is personality; Zertal seems to avoid socializing in the tightly knit world of archaeology, while Finkelstein has been a perennial fixture at a wide variety of professional gatherings. Finkelstein has a salesman's personality, charming, outgoing, and quick; Zertal is no less charismatic, but he has the charisma of a cult leader in search of new converts. Neither of them has offered a completely convincing or encompassing vision. There does seem to be evidence that the settlers of the Iron Age period used Canaanite techniques in slightly different combinations, signaling some sort of change for which Finkelstein doesn't always fully account. But it seems to fall short of being a strong ethnic identifying marker that would enable someone to distinguish between Canaanite and Israelite, as Zertal might hope.

Yet taken together, their material and ideas form a compelling demographic picture that hasn't been available until now. One can accept Zertal's argument that the settlers concentrated in the eastern part of the hill country because they were nomads entering Canaan from Transjordan, as the Bible says, or one can agree with Finkelstein that throughout the millennia, settlers always gravitated to the eastern part first because it offered a more moderate climate, better water sources, and land that was easier to cultivate. In either case the conclusion is the same: settlement began in the east. Moreover, Finkelstein's research has shown that despite the passage of a thousand years, during each of the three periods of collapse and subsequent settlement, certain aspects of the inhabitants' lifestyles persisted: the ceramic repertoire was limited, consisting mainly of storage jars and cooking pots, and there was an absence of luxury items such as could be found in other areas, like the coastal plains. The peoples living there were pretty much always an isolated, small, self-sufficient group, struggling to live under environmentally difficult conditions.

Ultimately, the cycles revealed by Finkelstein's and Zertal's work were broken by the emergence of national states, something that took place not just in Canaan but throughout the entire southern Levant. Eventually, huge foreign empires that dominated the region had more impact on the fate of the inhabitants than did the various ecological patterns that Finkelstein detected. Centuries after the fact, the Bible's writers portrayed the Israelite settlement as a unique event in the history of the country, and for them it was, since in their minds it illustrated how God had chosen them and enabled them to survive in the harshest conditions. But what had happened to Israel had actually happened to many other groups of settlers throughout the centuries, both inside and outside Canaan. Israel's fate could never be completely separated from events in the rest of the region.

Adam Zertal was on his way to Mount Ebal, and I was tagging along. At Mount Ebal, the Bible says, Israel first became a nation. The ceremony is described in the Book of Joshua. After slaying the inhabitants of Ai, knocking down the walls of Jericho, and generally wreaking havoc throughout Canaan, Joshua stops to build an altar of stone and make a burned offering to God at Mount Ebal. Before Joshua led the Israelites across the Jordan River, Moses had given him instructions on what to do, telling the Israelites that when they complete this task, "this day thou art become a people unto the Lord thy God."

Joshua fulfills his promise to Moses. As instructed, he divides the twelve tribes into two groups, directing six tribes to stand at Mount Gerizim, a short distance away, and six to stand at Mount Ebal. He then recites the blessings that await the Israelites if they observe God's laws and the curses that will befall them if they do not. He reads out the laws of Moses. Then the nation of Israel packs up and moves on. Another day's battle against the Canaanites awaits them.

The search for Joshua's altar began in the 1860s, when two different expeditions arrived at the mountain. They focused on the southern slope of Ebal, carefully searching on donkey and on foot for signs of an altar. They finally came upon a shallow building, a farm built in the Persian period. They excavated for two days before concluding that they weren't going to find the altar, and filed a report back to their patrons in London. Two other expeditions, by the French, were no more successful.

Adam Zertal arrived at the site in 1980 as part of his archaeological survey work. He only learned later about the four expeditions to the mountain that had searched vainly for an altar. In the course of recording information about the area for the survey, his team came across a large pile of stone that upon investigation turned out to be filled with ash. Attached to the structure were two courtyards, with tens of small compartments cut into the rock. Those too were filled with ash, as well as animal bones and more than one hundred vessels, mainly jugs, small jars, and bowls, part of what Zertal believed had been "presents to the gods." In the middle of the complex leading to the upper part of the building was a huge ramp. The shape of the structure, the ash and the animal bones, its isolation and location on a mountaintop, all led Zertal to conclude that he had stumbled upon a cultic site.

In 1999 Zertal convinced a Norwegian Christian group to contribute money to reconstruct the altar and eventually open it for tourism, and Jewish settlers in the area were raising money to expand and improve the road leading to the site. For some on the Israeli right, Mount Ebal has become a rallying point. The main political body representing the settlers in the West Bank and Gaza Strip, called the Yesha Council, has helped set up meetings between government officials and settler leaders about the future of Mount Ebal. They hope to convince the public that there are historical dangers, as much as security ones, in letting the Palestinians take control of Mount Ebal. "This is our past," says Shuki Levin, who serves as the security head for the Jewish settlements in the region and who regularly arranges jeeps and armed drivers to take Zertal to the site. "And our past should remain in our hands."

In a 1985 article in a popular archaeology magazine, Zertal had gone so far as to claim that the site might be where Joshua's altar was located. These days, Zertal is more circumspect about the Joshua connection. "I'm not saying Joshua built the altar here," he said as we walked around the site. "I don't even know if Joshua was a historical figure. But here is an altar that required organization to build, where the same laws of later Judaism regarding sacrifice are more or less used. Faced with all these facts, how can someone deny that there is a historical nucleus in the traditions described in the Bible about Mount Ebal?"

The day Zertal had chosen for our visit was hot but dry. Viewed from the mountain, the valleys seemed to stretch to the edge of the horizon. A wind picked up, bringing with it the first indications of the approaching fall. The political situation was tense. Mount Ebal sits in a zone contested by Israelis and Palestinians, formally under Palestinian political administration but still within Israeli security control. Our path to Mount Ebal went right around an Israeli military base, and Zertal waved to the young guard on duty.

Zertal had said that at Mount Ebal he saw evidence of the Israelite "will to be different." Certainly there were some signs of this. The pottery at the site was simpler than that found at nearby Shechem, and the area was in a remote location set away from the main city. And yet, in his own preliminary report about the dig's findings that was published in the journal *Tel Aviv*, there seemed to be as much evidence of similarities as of differences. The custom of placing pottery vessels around a ritual structure has deep roots in the Near East. The largest number of animal bones found were from sheep, goats, and cattle, the very same animals that appear at Canaanite sites as well. A simple stone seal was found, together with Canaanite scarabs, pointing to the coexistence of the two cultures.

Nothing was unambiguous; so much seemed to depend on one's point of view. From the top of Mount Ebal, I could see ancient Shechem lying in the valley, shimmering and white. The ancient city of Tel Balata was just to the east. Jordan was over the purple tops of the mountains. To the south was Bethlehem, where David grew up. David's great-grandmother Ruth had been a Moabite; he traced his ancestry even further back to Tamar, a Canaanite. The man the Bible considers Israel's greatest king, the founder of the united monarchy, traced his origins to the crossroads of Canaan, where each side began to see itself as the chosen people living in the Promised Land.

Chapter 4

In Search of David and Solomon

As the Lord has been with my lord the king, even so let him be with Solomon and make his throne greater than the throne of my lord King David. *(1 Kings 1:37)*

The Tower of David is one of the most famous landmarks in Jerusalem. Visitors throng to the museum located inside the fortress at the tower's base. They walk along the citadel's narrow walls through exhibition rooms that chronicle the city's conquest by King David and three thousand subsequent years of history. In the evenings, from the amphitheater in the center of the fortress, they can watch a sound-and-light show, the laser beams bouncing off the walls until they come to focus on the tower itself, the largest of six spread through the site. Silently perched above the Old City walls, the tower seems to guard the city, changing colors from gold to pink to purple depending on the light in Jerusalem. Over the years, it has been transformed into a powerful symbol, a testament to David's continuing hold over the city that he conquered and made the capital of his kingdom.

The tower is in fact an apt symbol, but not of the vision of the past most visitors receive after a tour of the museum. What few people ever realize is that the fortress where the museum is located, called David's Citadel, was actually built in the fourteenth to sixteenth centuries of our era by the Mamluks and the Ottomans, two of the city's many Muslim conquerors. David's Tower wasn't built by David but nearly a thousand years later, by King Herod. The Romans left it standing after destroying Jerusalem and the Second Temple in 70 C.E. as proof of the strength of the city they had succeeded in conquering. Later, the tower served as a mosque for several centuries for Muslim soldiers who were stationed there. The top of the tower is really the minaret to the mosque. King David's name appears more than one thousand times in the Old Testament; there are at least fifty-nine mentions in the New Testament. He continues to dominate the geography of Jewish and Christian traditions and popular imagination. But the historical David is nowhere to be found in the landscape of the city most closely associated with his rule.

Israel and Judah were two of the twelve tribes that became part of what we now call the united monarchy, though no one is sure what the united monarchy was really called. Bible scholars suggest that for the first part of their history in Canaan, these tribes were controlled by a number of autonomous military men who were able to offer them protection. David was probably one such ruler. He was not the first to be given the title of king; according to the Bible, that honor goes to his predecessor, Saul. But the Bible portrays David as the first leader who was able to extend his influence over all of the tribes, controlling territories that would eventually span from Dan to Beersheba. He led the united monarchy for forty years, and his son and successor, King Solomon, is traditionally thought to have ruled for forty more years after that, before the monarchy split into the two rival kingdoms of Israel and Judah.

Most Bible scholars discount the idea that the two kings ruled for forty years each. It's too neat, and forty is also one of those numbers, like seven and seventy, that are a running symbolic motif through many stories in the Bible. In any event, even the Bible says the united monarchy lasted less than a century, a brief moment in the 1,500-year span that has come to be considered the biblical period. Yet the Bible devotes a voluminous amount of space to these two kings, paying more attention to this period than to any other in ancient Israel's history. That should be no surprise. David was considered the best of kings, a man who loved Yahweh above everything, and Solomon was lauded for his wisdom and for his building campaign, especially his construction in Jerusalem of a magnificent temple. The Bible portrays Israel under their rule as a virtual empire, dominating international trade routes, growing rich off tribute and spoils, controlling the area from the Red Sea all the way to the Euphrates River. This was Israel's golden age. Except it didn't happen quite the way the Bible portrays it.

As the Bible tells it, David is the youngest of at least eight sons of Jesse, who lives in Bethlehem, in Judah. He also has at least two sisters. His ancestry is mixed, reflecting the intermingling of the various groups living in Canaan during this time period. He is a shepherd, spending all day in the fields, when he first comes to King Saul's attention in one of the fortuitous events that will mark his subsequent career. His father sends David with bread and cheese to his brothers who are fighting with Saul against the Philistines. At the battlefield, he hears the Philistines' champion fighter, Goliath, taunt the Israelites and their God. "And all the men of Israel, when they saw the man, fled from him, and were sore afraid," the Bible relates. 7- David alone stands his ground. He volunteers to fight Goliath, and moreover, because he is unused to fighting with armor, he meets Goliath in the battlefield with just a sling in his hand and five smooth stones. "Thou comest to me with a sword and with a spear and with a javelin," David tells Goliath when the warrior makes fun of him. "But I come to thee in the name of the Lord of hosts, the God of the armies of Israel, whom thou hast taunted." When the Philistine rushes toward him, David puts a stone in his slingshot and dispatches Goliath with a single shot to the head. It is an auspicious debut to a long military career. David's actions on the field catch the eye of Saul, who puts him in charge of the army and gives him his daughter to wed. Later, Saul comes to regret his decision to promote David, fearing the young warrior's ambition, and even tries to kill David. The attempts are all unsuccessful. David's destiny is clear; God is on his side. Even Jonathan, Saul's son, understands this, and warns David to flee Saul's wrath. After Saul dies, God instructs David to go to Hebron. There he is anointed Israel's second king, and seven years later his rise to power is sealed by his capture of the mountain stronghold of Jerusalem from the Jebusites. Despite the fact the city is well fortified, the Bible reports, David instructs his general to sneak into the city via the "zinnor," which modern scholars translate as a water tower, taking the Jebusites by surprise and giving the Israelites an edge in the battle. Using such stratagems, David eventually conquers Philistia, Aram, Ammon, Moab, and Edom.

The stories about David and Solomon are some of the best-written and best-known in the Bible, but it was Bible scholars and historians, not archaeologists, who raised the first doubts about the biblical portrayal of these rulers. Their examination of the language and style of the text indicated that most of the psalms, poems, and wisdom literature long attributed to Solomon had been written much later. The stories about David, while probably based on some historical events, nonetheless had all been written down hundreds of years after any of the things described by the Bible took place. Nonetheless, despite the growing controversy in the academic world, for most of the past fifty years, archaeologists were sure they at least had hard evidence of the united monarchy.

The lack of archaeological remains that could be attributed to David didn't bother most excavators. They acknowledged that it was troubling that no monumental architecture found in Jerusalem could be dated to this period, and that very few pottery shards from a supposedly flourishing time had turned up despite extensive and continuous excavations at the heart of David's empire. This seemed to indicate Jerusalem wasn't a flourishing major metropolis under David. Nonetheless, it could be explained away. Many archaeologists assumed that pottery from David's time and the remains of Solomon's temple lay under the Temple Mount, inaccessible to any excavation due to the current political tensions between Arabs and Jews over the site. The Bible had never portrayed David as a great builder anyway; Solomon was the one credited with fortifying the walls of Jerusalem, constructing the temple, and embarking on an ambitious and wide-ranging building spree that changed the face of the country.

And if the remains of this didn't show up in Jerusalem, there was always Megiddo. The site in northern Israel now lies off a major highway. There are small restaurants, fruit stands, and fields that line the way. A kibbutz, or cooperatively owned farm, located next to the mound runs a guesthouse that rents rooms by the hour, giving it a reputation among Israelis as a favorite place for illicit trysts. Megiddo itself is a national park, with neatly trimmed lawns, park benches, and an air-conditioned visitor center that sells souvenirs and boasts a model reconstructing the five-thousand-year history of the site.

Megiddo is one of the most excavated sites in modern Israel. At first Solomon seemed to be everywhere. The leader of the first dig, in 1903–1905, uncovered a huge pillar used in cultic worship, an example, he later wrote, of the idolatrous religious practices that the Bible indicated had caused the united monarchy to split apart shortly after Solomon's death. The members of the Chicago Oriental Institute expedition to Megiddo, which began excavating in 1925, uncovered a set of pillared buildings at the site in the late 1930s. The even spacing between the pillars, the spacious rooms, and other details all indicated to the director of the dig, P.L.O. Guy, that the buildings were stables, which fit the biblical stories about Solomon's extensive trade in chariots and horses.

It didn't seem to matter that later excavations and new interpretations led archaeologists to conclude that the pillared buildings, whatever they were, dated to a century after Solomon's rule. Solomon kept popping up at Megiddo. This was in part due to the famous biblical passage 1 Kings 9:15–19, which refers to some of Solomon's building activities: "And this is the account of the levy which king Solomon raised; to build the house of the Lord, and his own house, and Millo, and the wall of Jerusalem, and Hazor, and Megiddo, and Gezer." The Bible goes on to describe how Solomon achieved his amazing building feats using forced labor from among the Amorites, Hittites, Perizzites, Hivites, and Jebusites living in the lands he ruled. Yigael Yadin, who led digs at Masada, Hazor, and also at Megiddo, argued in a number of articles starting in 1958 that the four-entry gate found at Megiddo, and gates found at Hazor and Gezer, confirmed the biblical passage. The building of similarly styled gates, he concluded, indicated that a central administration had directed the construction. The gates became known as the blueprint architecture, the standard style, of the Solomonic era.

The most recent excavators at the site, Israel Finkelstein and David Ussishkin of Tel Aviv University and Baruch Halpern of Pennsylvania State University, began working there in 1994. Megiddo by then had become a type site. The dating of the architecture and the pottery there was used by archaeologists all over Israel for making comparisons and setting dates at other sites. The initial idea of the codirectors had been to clarify some of the dating of destruction layers there. But in the fall of 1996, Finkelstein published the first of what would soon be a series of articles in *Levant,* a British-based archaeology journal, that would change the direction of the dig. The articles challenged the idea that anything at Megiddo had been built by Solomon. One of Finkelstein's codirectors, David Ussishkin, had earlier argued that upon closer examination, the building style used on the gates at Megiddo, Hazor, and Gezer didn't appear to be as similar as Yadin had once thought. Four-entry gates also had subsequently turned up in areas controlled by the Philistines, where Solomon would not have been building, and in other cities during different time periods. Finkelstein's articles went even further. Not only the gates, he wrote, but also the pottery, the palaces, and virtually all the other architecture found at the site had been incorrectly dated to Solomon's days. The true great builder of the biblical period was not Solomon, he argued, but Ahab, who lived a century after him and was reviled in the Bible for being a weakling dominated by his idol-worshipping wife Jezebel. Since the late 1800s, when a group of German excavators led by Dr. Gottlieb Schumacher hired teams of locals and cut an enormous trench through the center of the main mound, there had been five archaeological expeditions to Megiddo. Each had come searching for Solomon. Finkelstein was probably the first one hoping *not* to find him.

From the road I could see huge black tents billowing above the mound at Megiddo. Israel Finkelstein and David Ussishkin had agreed to show me around the site. The tents had been strung up across the areas where volunteers were digging, their only protection from the relentless heat of summer. Dressed in a blue T-shirt, blue shorts, and hiking boots, Finkelstein darted around the site, a camera crew in tow. A key benefactor, an antiquities collector living in London, had gotten wind of the uproar caused by Finkelstein's Solomon articles and decided to withhold funding for the season. In need of cash, Finkelstein had agreed to let a crew from a California-based evangelist television channel shoot a movie at the site and they had been there throughout the summer. Megiddo is mentioned in the New Testament as the site of Armageddon, the future battle between the forces of light and the forces of darkness that will end in fire and brimstone and herald the second coming of Jesus. The film crew's millennial emphasis had made the decision to let them film unpopular among the staff. They found it unprofessional and hypocritical. Finkelstein appeared to be oblivious to his staff's displeasure, but it did seem an odd choice for someone campaigning against the way religious tradition had dominated interpretation at Megiddo.

One afternoon in his Tel Aviv University office, he expanded more on his ideas. He looked tired. Being in the center of public attention had been fun at first; now it felt like one argument after another. "I don't see myself as committed to the Deuteronomist's version of events," said Finkelstein, using the name scholars traditionally use for the scribe or school of scribes that collected and combined Israel's and Judah's histories from Moses through the end of the two kingdoms, in the process giving events a heavy pro-Judah theological and ideological spin. "I'm not ready to buy the negative approach of the Bible's writers to the northern kingdom of Israel," where Megiddo is located, Finkelstein said. "I don't think the cultural openness, the ethnic openness of Israel in the periods before and after David's rule is a negative thing. And I don't see the value of the closed ethnicity, isolation, and xenophobia that characterized Judah" — where David came from — "during this time. I'm ready to take a stand. I'm not for Judah. I'm on the side of Israel."

Despite his professed willingness to take a stand, the dig in 1998 was in some ways a retreat for Finkelstein. In his articles he had also taken some personal jabs at his colleagues, and they were angry at him. He wrote that they adhered to a romantic and sentimental view of the biblical past, that their archaeological interpretations rested primarily on a biblical passage whose historicity and dating were now widely viewed even by conservative Bible scholars as uncertain at best. The articles had been followed by interviews with the general media, some television appearances, and a controversial radio interview that questioned whether King Solomon had built the First Temple. In response, one parliament member had declared Finkelstein and Ussishkin "charlatans." Finkelstein seemed genuinely surprised at the anger his pieces had generated.

The team had been up digging since 5 A.M. They invited me to join them when they broke for their breakfast, provided by the kibbutz. Finkelstein, Ussishkin, and Neil Asher Silberman, an archaeology historian who was helping write a script about Solomon that Finkelstein hoped would be incorporated into a new multimedia presentation at the site in a bid to attract more visitors, sat around one of the picnic tables set up under the trees. "So what if David wasn't as glorious as the Bible says he was," said Ussishkin, as the discussion turned to the criticism the team's work had generated. They had been called anti-Israel, anti-Bible, and anti-Zionist, and that was by their friends. But they didn't think their interpretations were undermining Israel's national history or its connection to the land, as their critics charged. "There's still a connection to the land, there was still a Jewish kingdom here, even if it started later than the Bible says it did," said Ussishkin.

Finkelstein grabbed a hard-boiled egg, spread peanut butter on a sandwich, and cast an eye over Ussishkin's plate to see if he was missing anything good. Waving his sandwich in the air, Finkelstein said, "Why do I have to accept the Bible's version of Israel's history?"

Silberman interjected as the two men bantered back and forth. "Everyone keeps saying that we're deconstructing the Bible," he said quietly. "We're not deconstructing the Bible at all, but reconstructing it."

In a talk Silberman had once given about the history of digging at Megiddo, he had argued that Megiddo, like any important archaeological site, also serves as a mirror, a reflection of who we are at the particular time a dig is taking place. And, in truth, the vociferous tones surrounding the debate over David and Solomon seemed to reflect the mood of the country during the summer of 1998. Israel was celebrating its fiftieth anniversary of statehood, but the new united monarchy was less united than ever before. Israelis didn't seem to share a common culture, especially when it came to the Bible. When the comedian Gil Kopatch gave bawdy interpretations of the week's Torah portion on a Friday night television talk show, the religious parties threatened to leave the governing coalition in the parliament if he wasn't taken off the air. Israeli parliament member Yael Dayan, in proposing gay civil rights legislation, had been heckled by angry parliament colleagues when she cited what she felt were David's homoerotic feelings for Saul's son Jonathan in the Bible.

At Megiddo, Finkelstein had looked in the mirror, and in the uproar that followed, the significance of what he had seen had gotten lost. The crux of his later dating theory rested on complex archaeological arguments, including the dating of a particular kind of Philistine pottery at sites around Israel. When it comes to disputes over pottery in archaeology, there is always room for debate. The dating of pottery is simply too imprecise to result in any hard-and-fast conclusions. In that sense, Finkelstein's theory was as vulnerable to criticism as the one he wanted to puncture. But Finkelstein wasn't just looking at the pottery. Pottery, he said, "was the small details. It's the big picture that convinces me that I'm right." And the big picture that was starting to emerge about settlement patterns, the development of agriculture in the Middle East, and theories about early state formation had convinced even the most ardent supporters of the traditional dating of Megiddo's remains that the Bible's vision of the united monarchy didn't match the facts.

The archaeologists are still debating how much King Solomon really built. There is Finkelstein, who has decided not much, and Amihai Mazar, the head of the Hebrew University archaeology institute in Jerusalem, who basically accepts the Bible's account and believes that Hazor, Megiddo, and Gezer were all built or refortified by Solomon. But Finkelstein and Mazar share an area of common ground that continues to grow larger. No matter where one stands on the debate over dating the supposedly Solomonic palaces of Megiddo or the gates at Megiddo, Hazor, and Gezer, the Bible's broader picture of the united monarchy as the peak of a cultural and architectural flowering, a veritable golden age, has largely been dismissed in recent years. Mazar has written that there is very little justification in even the most traditional interpretation of the archaeological record to merit the Bible's description of David and Solomon's kingdom as a developed state, let alone an empire. Many scholars have pointed out that certain concepts in the Bible's traditional view of the tenth century B.C.E., when David and Solomon are believed to have ruled, no longer make sense, especially in light of excavations around the region. All over the Middle East, in cultures as diverse as Egypt and Mesopotamia, the glory years appeared gradually, evolving slowly from previous developments. If the Bible is right, only in Israel did the years of grandeur emerge suddenly, almost overnight, and then disappear just as suddenly. Another troubling discrepancy has been the idea that monumental architecture began during Solomon's reign but that other signs of advanced public administration — such as monumental inscriptions, administrative records, and inscribed seals — didn't appear in Israel until the ninth century, one hundred years after Solomon died. In every other country of the region, these developments went hand in hand. It also doesn't make sense to many archaeologists that the rulers in neighboring Moab and Damascus didn't consolidate their kingdoms until the ninth century, but that small Israel was supposedly able to develop a flourishing nation-state a century earlier.

After Solomon died, the Bible relates, his son Rehoboam traveled to the leaders of Israel seeking their acclamation as the successor and new king. He was summarily rejected. Truly how united could the united monarchy have been if the northerners displayed such readiness to abandon the Davidic dynasty so soon after Solomon's death? And Rehoboam didn't seem to put up much of a fight either. He went back to Jerusalem without so much as a stirring speech or an emotional plea to try to keep the united monarchy together. Many Bible scholars, using these hints in the biblical text itself and not archaeological finds, have already begun abandoning the traditional view, arguing that the united monarchy was really a "dual monarchy," a time in which the northern and southern tribes shared a king in common, but not much else. When the king died, they all eagerly went their own way, reverting in name as well as in fact to what they had always been at heart, two separate kingdoms with two separate fates. The new archaeological work seems to fit this idea too. Israel and Judah seem farther apart than ever.

If the Bible's picture of a huge and wealthy empire, a united and powerful kingdom, and a period of cultural flowering isn't right, then what were things really like at the time of the creation of the united monarchy? Judah in 1000 B.C.E., when David is believed to have come to power, was only sparsely settled. The tribes living in the northern territories, in what would later be known as the kingdom of Israel, were situated on much more fertile lands. They did not constitute an economic powerhouse, but even at this early stage they were already more established than Judah.

During the Late Bronze Age period, which preceded David's rule, the area to the north of Nablus was heavily populated. Adam Zertal's archaeological survey of this region turned up between twenty and thirty settlements, and most continued to be inhabited as the tenth century B.C.E. began. Finkelstein's Megiddo team did similar work in the western part of the Jezreel Valley, where Megiddo is located, an area that also became part of the kingdom of Israel after the united monarchy split in two. According to their data, there were thirty-seven sites during the Late Bronze Age, and these too continued to flourish into the tenth century.

In contrast, the Judean hill region during the Late Bronze Age had almost no established communities, just six to eight small settlements where it took enormous resources to eke out a meager existence from the rocky, inhospitable terrain. In the Shephelah area, which during the divided monarchy period would form the western edge of the kingdom of Judah, the number of settlements in Judah actually shrank considerably around the time David's rule began, possibly reflecting some kind of environmental crisis. From the outset it seems, tradition, not to mention ecology, geography, and political reality, were working against David's vision of creating a powerful united monarchy.

The gap that exists between the Bible's portrait of rulers of a glorious empire and the picture that is now emerging of rulers of a far more modest entity has caused a group of scholars in Europe to dismiss the Bible altogether. The current controversy can be traced back to the 1992 publication of *In Search of "Ancient Israel"* by Philip R. Davies, a professor at Sheffield University in England and one of the founders of Sheffield Academic Press, which has published many scholarly books that take nontraditional positions on the Bible and archaeology. Unlike most of the works that have followed by scholars making similar points, Davies' book is short, breezy, and fun to read. His basic premise is that the literature in the Hebrew Bible was composed after the fact and therefore yields no real history. There was no ancient or biblical Israel as it is described in the Bible, he contends. It was not before the Hellenistic period, in the second and third centuries B.C.E., that the concept of Israel as an ethnic and religious self-identification even emerged, under the Maccabees.

The book is hardly a manifesto. Nonetheless, Davies and his fellow scholars have been dubbed the Copenhagen School, although only two of them actually live and work in Copenhagen and they don't agree enough even among themselves to fill a classroom, let alone a school. Their critics, and there are many, call them biblical minimalists and revisionists. The group meets twice a year, usually at the general meetings of the Society for Biblical Literature, calling itself the European Seminar for Historical Methodology. That choice of name alone probably helps explain why, despite their protests, the name Copenhagen School has stuck.

In any event, there is something actually appropriate about this name. On the face of it, Copenhagen seems an unlikely place for the seat of a revolution regarding how the Bible is read, understood, and studied. The city is neat and tidy. People ride their bikes around town with flowers and loaves of bread tucked under their arms. There is an expansive public transportation network, very little litter on the streets, a sense of efficiency and orderliness appropriate to a city of commerce and higher learning. And yet there are ghosts everywhere. About twenty minutes outside the main center, there is a huge complex dedicated to the display of five Viking ships, sunk around the year 1000 to block the capital's most important fairway from enemy attack. There are Viking festivals, Viking banquets, Viking plays and theater, and tours of Viking villages. Nordic studies are booming in the academic world. The Vikings are as alive and real in Copenhagen as David and Solomon are in Israel.

Before a group bus tour of the city, Niels Peter Lemche and Thomas Thompson, two members of the so-called Copenhagen School, are trying to figure out why their work angers so many people. They've been called liars, bad scholars, Israel haters, and anti-Semites. Their work has been compared to Holocaust revisionism. These last charges especially disturb them. Lemche's family was in the Danish resistance movement during World War II. His son dug at Megiddo in the summer under Israel Finkelstein. Both men have been invited to speak at major universities in Europe and in Israel. They have written for mainstream publications, including the *Anchor Bible Dictionary*, and even appeared on the cover of *Biblical Archaeology Review*, the popular archaeology magazine. The anti-Semitism charge, they argue, is designed to end the possibility of any sort of debate about the issues. "Once you call someone an anti-Semite, where can any discussion possibly go?" asks Lemche.

Their provocative style is deliberate, though, and in their rush to be noticed they've made some errors. They have suggested that a stela mentioning the "House of David" and found at Tel Dan in 1993 was forged or planted, charges that have made them look foolish and politically motivated. Thompson, with his manic energy and his claims that he fears for his personal safety, sometimes seems a little obsessed. During the bus tour of Copenhagen, he pulls out a photocopied page from the latest article by William Dever, a University of Arizona archaeologist who has written extensively against the Copenhagen School's ideas, calling them nihilist and revisionist. At one point, he described Thompson as "a nasty little man with a nasty little life," a phrase that still makes Thompson livid. Thompson passes around the photocopied page, on which he has written his rebuttals, to demonstrate that Dever has misrepresented his writings, taken things out of context, distorted his theories. But in his anger, Thompson has scribbled his objections in an illegible scrawl that snakes wildly through the paragraphs and crowds the narrow margins of the page.

It's a fine image for how the Copenhagen School works. Its adherents have found the traditional interpretation of David and Solomon and ancient Israel too narrow, too confining. They come up with ideas that spill off the pages, that rankle, provoke, and annoy. They can't seem to stay between the lines. "The Bible should be treated as a narrative, not as a history book," Lemche says. "You can't separate out tiny historical points that might be in it, otherwise you lose the text. The historical Solomon died years and years ago. He's not important. The important thing is the *narrative* Solomon, and what the people who wrote about him had to say about him. That Solomon still exists."

"No one has ever denied the existence of ancient Israel," says Thompson. Lemche was born in Copenhagen, but Thompson moved there after a lackluster academic career in the United States, where, he says, his progress was blocked by his insistence on not taking the Bible at its word. He ended up at the University of Copenhagen, married a Danish woman, and teaches at the university's institute of biblical exegesis, training future seminarians. "Of course ancient Israel existed. But what I am saying is the sense of being a people that you get from the Bible — this ideology of being the people of Israel, the concept of national unity inside Palestine, could not have existed before the Persian period. The Israelites didn't have an ethnic, theological, or historical perception of who they were in David or Solomon's time."

In their effort to show that the Bible should not be read as history, they sometimes go too far. But their detractors fail to give them proper credit for what they have achieved. The bottom line is that when it comes to the big picture, they are often right. Many of their ideas, once considered far-fetched, are now solidly mainstream concepts. For a long time, scholars assumed that the Deuteronomist historian used original documents dating from the time of the two kings when he sat down to write the history of the united monarchy. The image of this historian searching the archives of the palace and the temple for documents, then sitting down to chronicle this glorious era, is largely not accepted anymore. Writing and cultural development all over the Middle East during this period, a time of upheaval and political uncertainty throughout the region, were very limited. So it is simply not surprising that only one extrabiblical reference to David on which there is anything close to scholarly consensus has turned up, in the form of a broken piece of basalt stone mentioning the House of David uncovered at the Dan site in northern Israel in 1993. There is no such reference so far to Solomon. And few archival records, if they existed at all, are likely to have survived in original form for a historian to have consulted when he sat down to work three hundred years after the time of David and Solomon. As a result, anything that was written at such a late date must be read with an eye for the ideological and political viewpoints of its editors and writers. The Bible is not an eyewitness account.

One of the most judicious assessments of the Copenhagen School has come from an unlikely quarter, Bar-Ilan University. Its campus is located in a Tel Aviv suburb, but it has a Jerusalem sensibility. The school is modern Orthodox; courses on Jewish studies are required. Women, even those who are not religious, dress modestly; many of the students are in fact Orthodox. Joshua Schwartz, head of the school's Land of Israel Studies department, was able to hold a conference in

1998 exploring some of the new issues emerging in the study of David and Solomon and the tenth century B.C.E. Most members of the audience were religiously observant, the men wearing skullcaps, most of the women with covered hair and long skirts. Schwartz invited Lemche to speak; he held a luncheon to introduce him to the Bar-Ilan archaeology faculty; he invited Lemche to address a smaller seminar for graduate students. Schwartz conceded it was probably the first time these students had even heard of Lemche's ideas; his textbooks are not standard fare in the Bar-Ilan curriculum. The audience was polite, no one walked out or booed Lemche. Schwartz doubted Lemche had made any converts to his ideas, but he thought it important that the students be exposed to broader intellectual currents outside Israel.

Later, when he spoke to me in his office, Schwartz went even further. He knew that what he was saying was heretical, especially in a place like Bar-Ilan. He even joked about closing the door to his office so he wouldn't be overheard, although he left it open the entire time. He had read the works of Lemche, and Thompson, and many of the others in the Copenhagen School. He disagreed with much that they said and did, but had come to the conclusion that in a fundamental way, they were often on target. "We still don't know much about the tenth century B.C.E.," said Schwartz. The sources used by biblical scribes were written significantly later than the events supposedly happened; religious life in the time of David, and before, was different from the kind of Judaism practiced after the return from exile in Babylon, when the Scriptures were mainly compiled. Schwartz believed it was just too difficult to rely on late sources, as the Bible's writers had to, to reconstruct the distant past and come out with an accurate picture. "Lemche, Thompson, and these others have a point. But they're theologians, not historians. They can't get to small issues. They're not interested in how much a loaf of bread weighed or what the leisure activities described in the biblical text might tell us about the society. I am. They will shout that Genesis and Kings don't tell us anything about the real David and the real Solomon, or even if they really existed. That's probably true. But I don't want to know only that. I want to know about what it can tell us about the kinds of shoes David or Solomon would have worn, what the material culture of Palestine was like, what they did in their leisure time. Once we have these kinds of details, maybe we can look at the entire picture again."

Dever has been the most passionate critic of the Copenhagen School. He never misses an opportunity to bash them. He has stood up at archaeology conferences, at dinners, at lectures, and called the group anti-Semites. In numerous published articles, he has written that the ideology they espouse "poses a threat to biblical studies, to Syro-Palestinian archaeology, to theological and religious studies, to the life of synagogue and church, and even to the political situation in the Middle East." He saves his most impressive invective for Thompson, who dug at Gezer in the 1960s when Dever led the excavations and when the so-called Solomonic gate was discovered. Thompson has said that Dever went looking for a Solomonic gate and therefore found one, and has called him a fundamentalist. The whole fight has gotten so out of hand that Davies, the Sheffield-based academic and publisher, sent out to a few friends an essay he wrote about the debate in which he compared Dever and Thompson to Cain and Abel, and called on both sides to cool down before one of them committed fratricide.

Over breakfast one day in Philadelphia, Dever told me that he objects to the Copenhagen group so vociferously because he thinks their ideas about David, Solomon, and the rise of the Israelite state are dangerous. "They strip away history, but they don't replace it with anything else," he said. "They are nihilists, and nihilism leads to a vacuum, and as we have seen before in Europe, a historical vacuum leads to fascism. And we all know where fascism leads. Jews, of all people, know what can happen. We need to speak up before it goes too far." Dever, who spent his childhood as a boy preacher, traveling the circuit of small southern towns and giving sermons with his father, later converted to Judaism. He now considers himself an agnostic and hates it when Thompson and the others call him a fundamentalist. The label is unfair, but when it comes to the history of ancient Israel, he is a true defender of the faith. Like other defenders of the faith, he thinks that there is one truth, and that he is in possession of it.

On this, the two sides have much in common. Each group has staked out an extreme. The Copenhagen scholars often assume that just because David and Solomon didn't exist as they are described in the Bible, they didn't exist at all. They point out the difficulties of extracting historical information from the Bible, but because it is difficult, they advocate not using the Bible at all. After one session in Copenhagen, nursing a cup of coffee and a bad cold, Lemche had called the middle road "a graveyard for scholars." "This is not some kind of political negotiation," he said. "We are not going to argue, debate, negotiate, and come up with some middle-of-the-road conclusion." But the middle of the road may be the best hope of finding David and Solomon.

One of the European Bible scholars most closely following the new data emerging about the united monarchy period is a German, Hermann Michael Niemann. He has been most struck by the environmental backdrop of the tenth century B.C.E. and how little it seemed to change over time. The landscape against which a David or a Solomon had to manuever and operate hasn't changed much over thousands of years.

Palestine remains a land bridge situated between two far larger powers, Egypt and Mesopotamia, modern-day Iraq. The country's prosperity and development are still dependent on the direction and amount of rainfall, which tends to move across the country from northwest to southeast. This environmental picture allows us to imagine more vividly how things might have been under David and Solomon. In support of his theory, Niemann likes to use an example from a book about eighteenth-century Palestine. At this time, a Muslim leader named Dahir b. Umar took over from his father as high sheikh of Galilee and eventually was able to extend his control from his ancestral seat in Tiberias all the way to the Mediterranean. He became rich by working with foreign traders, and he used his new riches to launch a building program. He fortified his hometown of Tiberias, he enlarged the port of Akko (Acre), eventually making that city his capital. As his powers increased, so did his ambitions. In 1771 he captured Sidon and the next year Ramle, Gaza, and Jaffa and almost took Jerusalem. He ended badly, though. The officials of the Ottoman Empire, which had relied on him and other native forces to try to keep control in Palestine, eventually stepped in to curb his growing powers and he was killed in Akko in 1775.

Reading Dahir's story, one is struck by how closely it seems to follow the Bible's description of the stratagems David and Solomon used to gain and secure power. They too were able to take advantage of the situation in Palestine because the larger imperial powers abroad were too busy with problems at home to exert much control. David, Solomon, and Dahir all arranged marriages for themselves or their family members with other prominent families and local rulers in order to secure power. They positioned sons and relatives at strategically important sites. Just as David had problems with Absalom, so too did Dahir have to deal with rebellions by some of his own sons. At one point, three of them even held Dahir's stronghold at Tiberias, just as Absalom had launched his rebellion from Hebron, the city where David had become king. Most significantly, from David's day to that of Dahir, the north was more important economically and politically than the south. "This is how it could have been in the time of David and Solomon," Niemann concluded in an article published in 1997. "This is perhaps how it often was in Palestine and similar societies under similar conditions."

Niemann depicted David, Solomon, and Dahir as good examples of typical oriental rulers. There are elements of the Bible stories that corroborate this picture as well. Soon after he is named king, David reaches out to the men of Jabesh-Gilead, part of north Transjordan, in the hope of making the people of this tribe his allies. He chooses

Jerusalem as his capital because it is centrally located between Judah and Israel and not strongly identified with any one tribe at the time. Solomon behaves similarly, making scores of political marriages that help secure the borders of his kingdom, embracing elements of the various religious practices of his people. Within the context of theological interpretation, David and Solomon mark the beginning of a messianic dynasty. But even more so, it is clear that they are also men of their region. And seen as part of Palestine's larger history, the Muslim Dahir is as much their spiritual heir as the Maccabees or Jesus Christ.

Niemann's approach appears to allow all the contradictions of David and Solomon to exist together. At the time David and Solomon lived, around 1000–900 B.C.E., Jerusalem was only sparsely populated, as were the areas south of Jerusalem all the way toward Hebron. The cities were remote, hardly at the center of some international trading crossroads as the Bible describes it. The Jerusalem of David and Solomon was most likely a mountain stronghold, not the seat of a huge empire. And yet this new picture doesn't mean that the Bible is completely wrong in suggesting that David ruled there or that Solomon constructed a palace or a temple.

Nadav Na'aman, a historian at Tel Aviv University, has pointed out that David's capture of Jerusalem and renaming it the City of David appear in a wide variety of biblical passages that were written at different times. This would seem to indicate a strong historical memory of David's rule. David's actions, Na'aman writes, were believable in the context of the ancient Middle East, where other regional cities had been named after their founders. It was also common for tribal chiefs to choose to rule from mountain strongholds, and Na'aman argues that the archaeological evidence confirms there were enough settlements inside the Judah region during this period to give David the manpower to create an army. Like many other researchers, Na'aman has painted a picture of Jerusalem as a modest place, and he believes that Solomon's temple and palace, if they existed, were modest too. The search for Solomon in terms of monumental architecture — remains of palaces and temples and walls — has proven use-less, he suggests. Instead, the new data can best be used to create a possible framework in which Solomon or David might have lived. In this sense, the Bible remains relevant, for the actions it describes the two men taking to establish power are actions that Middle Eastern leaders like Dahir were still using during Ottoman times.

In both instances the leaders had tried to expand their preexisting tribal bases and gain support from better-off urban leaders by secur-ing an important central city, Hebron and then Jerusalem in the case of David and Solomon, Tiberias and Akko in the case of Dahir. They had established their leadership credentials through battle, with the enemy who at the time represented the greatest threat to their people. They set up a military corps that was always ready for battle. And most crucially, they recognized the need for a traditional shrine, a shared religious center. They had used religion as a unifying factor against perceived outside enemies. Operating under similar eco-nomic, ecological, and political constraints, these leaders had done similar things.

At Megiddo, Finkelstein and his colleagues are trying to find a new way to promote this message of a shared historical legacy and com-mon ground. Megiddo is like most of the national archaeology parks in Israel: an expanse of beautiful ancient ruins that are virtually impossible to understand in any coherent way. The brochures pro-vided by the national parks authority and the signs scattered through-out the site are dry, conventional, stale.

A new project, begun in 1998, is designed to change all that. There is a "contemplation cove," a small area set up by the archaeologists where people can come to pray, rest, or just look at the sweep of the Jezreel Valley. Tourists can sit in a small area shaded by palm branches, on benches made of huge stones, the remains of one of the palaces built by the Israelite kings. From the top of Megiddo, there is a panoramic view of the purple hills, the rolling valleys with their green and gold and brown flowers and crops, a huge swath of biblical landscape still not ruined by modern development. Undertaken in conjunction with the city of Ename, Belgium, and a group of archaeologists from Belgium, the project will include computer-generated images to allow tourists to see what a palace would have looked like in Solomon's day.

Ann Killebrew, one of the archaeologists digging at the site, and Neil Silberman, the archaeology historian, have been working on a script for this multimedia presentation. One of their key messages is that Megiddo and its heritage belong to everyone. The multimedia show as they have planned it will have various modern narrators superimposed over the archaeological remains, along with reconstructions of the buildings as they might have appeared in ancient times. Among the narrators will be an archaeologist talking about the history of the finds at Megiddo, a Christian couple speaking about the idea of Armageddon taking place at the site, and a member of the Megiddo kibbutz talking about life there now. A Palestinian woman, a resident of the nearby village of el-Lajjun, will also appear. Lajjun, once a thriving small village, has slowly lost ground over the years. Its shepherds used the Megiddo hills as a pasture for their animals until archaeologists started digging there in the 1800s. The founding of the now-prosperous kibbutz at Megiddo on lands once used by the villagers for growing crops has economically marginalized Lajjun even further. Most Israelis have no idea the village still exists. In the program, the Palestinian woman will speak of the rhythm of agricultural life in the village and the way they continue to mark time according to the seasons. Nothing political, but her very presence is a testimony to the broader ideas about David and Solomon and the Bible that are taking shape.

At Tel Aviv University one day, surveying the scholarly ruins of the united monarchy wrought in part by some of his own work, Nadav Na'aman had argued that the latest research has the potential to help forge a new common ground, both within Israel and in the wider region. "What people forget is that David and Solomon didn't unite the monarchy, the Bible's writers did," Na'aman told me. "They united the people, they established the unity, by the act of the writing of the history as they saw it." This was both a reminder of the potential of such an approach and a warning of the dangers of failure, for the very history that had once united the monarchy could not withstand a change in political fortunes and soon ended up driving the people apart.

Chapter 5

⚛

The Divided Monarchy

The Near East Rising

And when all of Israel saw that the king hearkened not unto them, the people answered the king, saying: "What portion have we in David? Neither have we inheritance in the son of Jesse; to your tents, O Israel; now see to thine own house, David." So Israel departed unto their tents. . . . There was none that followed the house of David, but the tribe of Judah only. *(1 Kings 12:16–17, 20)*

Despite King Solomon's gold, his unparalleled riches, magnificent temple, powerful army, far-flung trading network, and reputation for wisdom, the Bible portrays his rule largely as a turn for the worse in the history of Israel. It's not always easy to fathom why, since the Bible also goes to great lengths to demonstrate that under David and Solomon the united kingdoms of Israel and Judah reach the height of their political and cultural power. But by the end of Solomon's rule, it is clear that the Davidic empire is in rapid decline, and the Bible rests the blame squarely on Solomon's willingness to tolerate in his kingdom the worship of gods other than Yahweh. Within just a few years of Solomon's death (thought to be around 931 B.C.E.), the united monarchy totally collapses and the golden age is over. Israel and Judah go their separate ways, the Bible relates, a situation that ends in exile from the land, first for Israel, at the hands of the Assyrians around 722 B.C.E., and later for Judah, driven out by the Babylonians in 587/586.

The time between Solomon's death and the Babylonian conquest is the "divided monarchy," a stretch of 350 years that are largely treated by the Bible as a period of moral decline and religious laxity. The history of Israel is dealt with in a cursory manner. Most of Israel's kings, whether they reign five years or fifty, tend to have their rule summed up with what becomes the standard boilerplate sentence in the Books of Kings: "He walked in the way of his father and did that which was evil in the sight of the Lord." Then the king dies. The only king in Israel who merits more attention is Ahab, and that's largely because his rule coincides with the time of the miracle-performing, muscle-flexing prophet Elijah. In contrast to Elijah, Ahab is portrayed as weak-willed and ineffective, in the thrall of his idolatrous Ba'al-worshipping wife Jezebel, who meets a terrible end, flung from the tower of her palace by order of a usurper king, her blood licked up by dogs. This incident garners more attention than Ahab's military prowess and success in battle. We are left to learn about Ahab's power mainly from the texts of his Assyrian enemies.

The kings of Judah fare only a little better, particularly the righteous Josiah, who institutes a widespread religious reform. Nonetheless, even Josiah's efforts fail to persuade Yahweh to overlook the sins of Josiah's predecessor, and Judah too is eventually consigned to being "carried away captive out of [its] land," as Second Kings relates.

Throughout the telling of this history, there is no question that the Bible clearly considers Israel and Judah sister states, two branches that share the same ethnic, cultural, and religious roots, emerging from some sort of larger Israelite tree. Residents of both kingdoms did worship Yahweh, speak a similar language, and write using the same script. But in other ways, the latest archaeological data don't fit this picture. There are differences in everything from the two kingdoms' pottery traditions to their architectural styles, both of which were influenced in turn by the fact that Israel and Judah had different climates and topographies. Pottery traditions changed much more slowly in Judah, which lay off the beaten track of the main trade routes that brought new styles, techniques, and technology to Israelite industries. Israel's kings built significantly more monumental architecture, in part, some archaeologists now contend, because they did not enjoy the political stability of Judah's rulers. Israel's rulers were looking for ways to impress and intimidate subjects in a kingdom containing numerous foreign groups that had no immediate loyalty to any Israelite dynasty. And even at the height of its power, Judah never commanded the economic resources or the demographics necessary to pursue grandiose architectural projects. In many respects, Israel's sister states could just as easily have been Ammon and Moab, its neighbors across the Jordan River in the central part of what is now modern Jordan. In culture, political development, settlement patterns, and climate, Judah had more in common with Edom, in southern Jordan, than with Israel.

The new questioning that has emerged in recent years among scholars and archaeologists about the Bible's portrayal of the united monarchy has inevitably affected the way people view the divided monarchy as well. The Bible's notion that Solomon's rule is the beginning of the end, and that from there it was all downhill, tells only a narrow aspect of the story. The emerging archaeological picture suggests that Solomon's key achievement was to set in motion the institutional forces that would eventually lead to the appearance of territorial states in Palestine.

This was a critical time in the Middle East, when national boundaries were being decided, and for the first time archaeology is helping to reconstruct the jockeying for power that was taking place throughout the region, not just in Israel and Judah. Among the military powers of the day — under kings like Omri and Ahab in Israel, Hazael in Aram Damascus, and Mesha in Moab — there were frequent territorial disputes, especially along the border areas, which changed hands regularly. The leaders of these kingdoms were beginning to realize that military might was no longer enough, that a powerful army could win a temporary victory but finding long-term security required a different strategy. It was during this time that Israel, in the ninth century B.C.E., and then Judah, in the eighth century, finally developed into flourishing, full-blown states. The demise of the united monarchy, however united it may have been and whatever the extent of its actual boundaries, didn't mark the end of a glorious era after all. It marked the beginning of one.

The research into Israel and Judah in the 1970s focused on the two areas' very different ecosystems. The larger amount of rainfall, the numerous valleys that made the development of agriculture possible, the rich variety of products available to be marketed and sold — all had contributed to Israel's growing prosperity and flourishing trade. These were advantages that Judah lacked, with its drier climate, more mountainous lands, and smaller population base.

Further investigation has led many scholars to conclude that there was a gap of 150 years between Israel's and Judah's becoming states. The mass production of pottery, produced in central workshops and then carried to the peripheries of the kingdom via an extensive distribution network, most likely started in Judah only in the eighth century B.C.E., according to the latest pottery studies. Less work has been done inside the Israelite kingdom, but the preliminary reports from the key site of Megiddo indicate that similar mass production was already up and running in Israel in the mid-ninth century.

There are other clues that Israel became a state much earlier than Judah. Wine and olive oil production, key agricultural industries that formed the backbone of the economies in both Israel and Judah, reached the size of a state industry in Israel by the eighth century and one hundred years later in Judah. Such an industry required insuring that huge quantities of grapes and olives were planted, tended to, and picked, and that wine and olive oil were pressed, bottled, and sent out to market. Running such a system would require a developed political administration to coordinate activities in different areas of the kingdom and to oversee extensive trading networks both inside the kingdom and out. Seals, seal impressions, and other signs of writing, especially administrative and trade records, appear first in Israel, not Judah. Settlement patterns indicate there was a far greater population, living in larger, more organized areas, in the northern kingdom than in the southern one. Even in terms of the two kingdoms' architecture, there were significant differences. Administrative centers that included public buildings and palaces show up first in the north. The size, the quality of construction, the evidence of foreign influence in the building styles, were all more developed in Israel than in Judah. The question is, why?

The explanation seems to lie beyond ecological differences. Israel's richer lands and better climate certainly gave it many advantages that help explain its earlier push toward state formation, but that doesn't seem to be enough reason for such a large time lag. Bible scholars have demonstrated that quite a bit of the information in the Bible describing these time periods is historically accurate. Kings' names and the chronology and years of their reigns have been verified in extrabiblical sources. And yet one of the keys to solving the puzzle of the time lag lies in the history that is missing from the Bible, particularly in events that took place a short distance down the road from Jerusalem in the important Judean center of Lachish.

Readers of the Bible are familiar with the fall of Jerusalem to the Babylonian army in 587/586 B.C.E. But nothing appears in the Bible about the earlier destruction of Lachish, in 701, at the hands of the Assyrian king Sennacherib, despite the fact that, like Jerusalem, it was one of Judah's key monarchical centers. Instead, the account of Sennacherib's campaign in the Second Book of Kings recounts only the confrontation between Sennacherib and Hezekiah, Judah's king. It is a thrilling description. Jerusalem is surrounded, and an Assyrian general, speaking for his king, addresses the people and offers them two options: surrender or die. "Do not let Hezekiah deceive you for he will not be able to deliver you out of my hand. Do not let Hezekiah make you rely on Yahweh," the general says. If the people throw down their arms, he adds, they will be allowed to live, and then deported from Jerusalem "away to a land like your own land," the general promises.

The Assyrian general's arrogance, his mocking of Yahweh's power to save his people, stirs Hezekiah to pray and ask for divine assistance in defending Jerusalem. According to the Book of Kings, an angel of Yahweh is sent out that very night and kills 185,000 Assyrians. When the people of Jerusalem awake the next morning, it is to a city filled with the dead bodies of Assyrian soldiers. Sennacherib, the Bible relates, retreats to his capital, Nineveh, where he is subsequently killed by his sons during prayers.

The story is a reminder of the power of faith. It's not important that the Assyrian account of the campaign, which mentions that Jerusalem was put under siege and avoids destruction only because Hezekiah agrees to become an Assyrian vassal and pay tribute to Sennacherib, doesn't match the Bible's description. Or that the Assyrian records indicate that Sennacherib apparently lived for another twenty years after the war in Judah, and wasn't killed immediately after his return from Jerusalem, as the Bible implies. These points don't matter because this is a theological narrative, concerned with Jerusalem's miraculous deliverance. What is most interesting now, in the effort to piece together Judah's history, is that one of the most important historical events of that period, the devastation at Lachish, is never mentioned in the chronicle.

Sennacherib was downright laconic about his victory in Jerusalem, but he celebrated his triumph in Lachish in style, clearly seeing it as a significant victory. An entire room of his palace in Nineveh is decorated with huge bas-reliefs illustrating the battle scenes and Lachish's burning and destruction. Israeli archaeologists who dug at the site reconstructed the city, and now tourists can see what the Assyrians wrought. It is still a harsh and moving sight, a city in ruins. The city's walls and gateways are burned and broken where the Assyrian army marched in. There is an Assyrian siege ramp thrown up against the wall, and inside the city, a smaller, ineffective ramp that was probably put together at the end of the battle by desperate Judeans trying to protect their city. Some historians now argue that the Assyrian campaign was never directed against Jerusalem, a city unimportant economically to the Assyrians, but rather was an attempt to put down a rebellion in Ekron, about 15 miles west of Jerusalem, and Lachish, about 25 miles southwest. Both were key centers of olive oil production in the region.

Besieged by the Assyrians, Lachish fell. Israel was placed under Assyria's direct control and its olive industry was reorganized. Jerusalem was one of the main beneficiaries of the fall of Israel, eventually expanding into the hills and all the way down to the Negev. The city became the chief market town in Judah and began truly to flourish.

During the time of the united monarchy, the city had been at most a mountain stronghold for a small elite ruling from the hills. But between the eighth and seventh centuries B.C.E., Jerusalem's population grew dramatically, taking in refugees both from Israel and from cities in Judah such as Lachish. Archaeologists have estimated that Judah's population by the late seventh century was roughly sixty-five thousand, with Jerusalem's proportion of the total population of Judah growing from about 6 percent in the previous century to nearly 23 percent. Based at first inside the City of David area, Jerusalem began expanding into the hills beyond. The city's administration started sponsoring huge public works projects, peaking in the eighth century B.C.E., when encircling walls, forts, and water systems were constructed. Evidence of writing has been found from that period, mainly in Jerusalem and sites administratively dependent on Jerusalem. Most important, the surrounding villages and towns showed an increasing economic dependence on the city. None was able to rival Jerusalem, which now came into its own. From that time on, the city served the same role for Judah that Samaria had a century earlier for the Israelite kingdom. It was the engine of growth for an emerging state.

What is a state? Even now, when former empires like the Soviet Union have broken down into small units that are barely self-sufficient economically, or neighbors living in countries like Rwanda or Yugoslavia have turned on each other and tried to eradicate entire ethnic groups, it remains a maddeningly elusive term. Borders keep changing, maps from just a few years ago seem like relics of some forgotten world. Figuring out how to define the entities emerging in the ninth century B.C.E. has reflected a similar kind of confusion.

Over the years, Moab, one of Israel's key rivals at that time, has been described variously as a pastoral community, a tribe, a state, a territory, a simple political state, a monarchy, a kingdom, a tribal kingdom, and a nation. It has also been called a band and a chiefdom, and these lists aren't even complete. Part of the difficulty is that societies are always changing, state development remains in process. Moab wasn't the same throughout its entire history, and so the words used to describe it shouldn't be either, the reasoning has gone.

But the crux of the issue has seemed to be a question that perplexes us even today: how much does a state have to do to be called a state? There are places with barely functioning economies that occupy seats at the United Nations; and there are groups of people, such as the Kurds or the Palestinians, who share a common sense of identity and ethnicity but remain officially stateless. The research being done on ancient societies seems to underscore this paradox. There are numerous examples of nonstates that nonetheless managed to organize large groups of people to complete huge infrastructure projects, construct massive fortifications, or build a water reservoir. Thus it is hard to categorize different societies.

Randall Younker, an archaeologist leading a dig inside the territory of what was once Moab in west-central Jordan, considers himself a student of the Moabites, though his years of work in the field have sometimes left him confused. On the one hand, there are signs such as monumental architecture and fortifications that indicate the Moabites had a state. But his research has demonstrated to him as well that if such a state did exist during the ninth century, it was a state whose social structure remained tribal. Moreover, Younker believes that a similar situation existed in Moab's neighbor Israel. Younker has reached his conclusions by drawing on new research about Moab that has become available in the past few years. One of the most interesting things Younker has found is the striking similarity between Moab's material culture and that of its neighbor to the northwest, Israel.

Younker attributes this to social networks and tribal relationships that spanned the easily crossed Jordan River. At one point, David and Solomon's empire included holdings east of the Jordan, the Bible says, and Moabite texts indicate that in the nineth century B.C.E. the city of Nebo had been in Israelite hands and then was reconquered by Moab's king. Whatever the explanation, the kingdoms of Israel and Moab appear to have buried their dead in similar ways, used similar architectural styles when constructing large public buildings, and served food in similarly styled cooking pots. But various archaeologists have approached the data in different ways. Younker feels uncertain about trying to define the nature of Moab in the ninth century in light of the strong tribal flavor that has come out in the research. Israel Finkelstein, the Israeli archaeologist digging at Megiddo, doesn't hesitate in concluding that Israel and Moab were both full-blown states. "I don't see any contradiction," Finkelstein said one day over coffee at Tel Aviv University. He paused for a moment. The night before, he said, he had been at a dinner party with some friends, all of them Israelis who favored the peace process with the Palestinians and were willing to accept the idea of a Palestinian state alongside that of Israel. Then Finkelstein had asked the guests whether they agreed that the founding of the state of Israel in 1948, however just, had caused the Palestinian people great suffering. "Everyone at the party said yes, and then within thirty seconds had added, yes, but the Arabs started all the wars, they still want to destroy us, their leaders told them to run away from their homes, we're not to blame for their troubles," Finkelstein said. "It was always yes followed by some tribal excuse about how we are not at fault for any part of the dispute." He picked up the coffee cup again and raised his eyebrows over the rim. "So you see why I don't have any problem believing that having a state doesn't necessarily preclude also having a tribal social structure or a tribal mentality."

For years now considerable research has been done on the issue of state formation in the kingdom of Judah. The appeal is obvious. Jerusalem, the City of David, the capital of the dynasty that forms the core of the biblical narrative, was in Judah. The Bible's sensibility represents the perspective of the Judeans. They lasted longer than Israel, which fell just as Judah was starting to emerge as a state. Although excavations of individual sites have been ongoing, until very recently no real systematic investigation of Israel's emergence as a state has been undertaken.

Finkelstein's interest in such a project stems in part from his eagerness to prove his controversial theory that the monumental architecture long attributed to King Solomon, such as the gates in Hazor and Megiddo, and the palaces and public buildings in Megiddo, were actually built a hundred years later, by King Ahab. The results of the archaeological surveys in Judah and around Jerusalem show that, whatever form the united monarchy took, Jerusalem was quite small and sparsely settled during the tenth century B.C.E. Virtually every example of monumental architecture during this time period has been found in the northern kingdom. Hazor and Megiddo lie in ancient Israel. Gezer is the one exception, being based in Judah, although Finkelstein explains away the anomaly by arguing that it may have been considered part of the north during this time period. Why was the major building activity concentrated in the north? And how could a relatively isolated mountaintop capital with few resources have overseen such mammoth construction projects relatively far away from its own economic and political power base?

In Finkelstein's view, considering these questions has seemed to confirm his growing notion that the gateways, palaces, and other monumental architecture must have been built by a northern dynasty, the economically powerful Omrides, with a northern audience and local political considerations in mind. The search for a way to buttress his theory has led Finkelstein to try to determine whether Omri and Ahab introduced a new style of architecture or a new approach to building. Finkelstein believes they did, and has dubbed the style Omride architecture, after the dynasty that created it.

The Omrides are not treated well by the Bible. Omri is virtually absent from the biblical text. First Kings records that Omri came to power after a period of civil war. Omri, described as the captain of the army, overthrew the seven-day rule of the chariot commander Zimri, who had seized power in his own military coup. The fact that Omri established a dynasty that lasted longer than most in assassination-plagued Israel, that during his and his successors' reigns Israel became one of the most powerful and economically prosperous states in the region, is never mentioned in the Bible. Ahab, the son, gets more space than his father, but mainly as a means of emphasizing his ineffectual nature.

The Bible goes to great lengths to make Ahab appear weak and obsequious. In one scene in the First Book of Kings, Ben-hadad, the king of Aram, sends messengers to Ahab, saying to him, "Thy silver and thy gold is mine; thy wives also and thy children, even the goodliest, are mine." These are fighting words in the Middle East, but Ahab meekly responds, "It is according to thy saying, my lord, O king: I am thine, and all that I have." Assyrian inscriptions about Aram and Israel, including one famous inscription by the Assyrian king Shalmaneser, called the Monolith Inscription, provide a vastly different picture. The inscription describes Ahab as an important warrior, able to supply a coalition fighting Assyria with two thousand chariots and ten thousand foot soldiers. Even if these numbers are exaggerated — and historians agree they probably are — the inscription indicates that Ahab was the equal of the leaders of other major kingdoms, not a vassal. He was not the type to meekly tell the king of Damascus that his lands, wives, and palaces were there for the taking.

Finkelstein has not been the first to look at the Omride architecture in the hope of learning more about this dynasty and filling in the large gaps left by the biblical narrative. Nor is he the first to notice some similarities between the architecture employed at Samaria, the hilltop capital built by the Omrides, and Megiddo. The first to do that was Gottlieb Schumacher, who led a 1908–1911 excavation at Samaria for Harvard University. The excavation was conducted poorly. The archaeologists would dig a giant trench and remove dirt and pottery shards haphazardly, making it virtually impossible for later scholars to accurately determine the chronology of the various building layers at the site. Still, Schumacher's advantage was that he also dug at Megiddo, which led him to make the tentative conclusion that some buildings at the two sites had been constructed in a similar style. Some of the excavators at a second dig at Samaria, in the 1950s, conducted by the British School of Archaeology, came up with similar ideas.

Finkelstein's contribution has been to try to articulate the new style, to describe the Omride school of architecture in far greater detail. One of his graduate students, an archaeologist named Norma Franklin, has been focusing on ninth-century architecture and has made a startling discovery: some of the buildings at Megiddo that have been called Solomonic bear remarkable similarity to the Omride buildings at Samaria, down to the marks left by the masons who hewed the rocks for the buildings. Franklin is very cautious about what she is saying, and unlike Finkelstein, she believes that some of the buildings do not need to be redated. But after closely studying the old field reports, the charts and plans, and the buildings themselves, she has noticed a series of mason marks, crossings and hatches that appear on the ashlar blocks used in several structures. She has found fourteen signs on Omride buildings at Samaria, two for which she hasn't found parallels at other sites. But the other twelve signs have all turned up at Megiddo on some of the monumental architecture. It looks as if the same masons, or at least the same school of masons, were working under the direction of the Omrides at both sites.

In his own research, Finkelstein has used this kind of information to argue that the Omrides introduced a new architectural concept to ninth-century Israel. Some of it derived from local Canaanite elements of construction that had been around for centuries. Other features, such as particular kinds of stonework, show up in neighboring

Ammon and Moab, as well as in Judah, albeit at a later date. But the overall design — the layout of the sites and the combination of the features — is distinctively Israelite and Omride, Finkelstein argues.

If we look at sites such as Megiddo, Jezreel, and Samaria, and also Hazor to a lesser degree, we can see they all shared some key similarities. Each of these cities was built on a hill, along an important trade route or routes. Each boasted a massive gate that led directly into a well-paved, large courtyard surrounded by a wall made of ashlar stone with a palace located nearby. The process of constructing these sites was also similar, involving massive operations to level the top of the hill in order to create a flat area for the royal quarters. They contained mainly public buildings, rather than homes or other domestic structures, and were sparsely inhabited, a sign that they served primarily as administrative centers. The palace layout was a foreign import, Finkelstein contends, influenced by Israel's contacts with the north. This layout is unique to Israel. It does not appear even in Jerusalem, Finkelstein argues. Moreover, the key administrative centers in the north and those in the south differed in everything from layout to quality of construction. Looking at the sites in the north, Finkelstein has concluded that the style of building, the scale, even the sheer amount of labor and resources that must have been invested to construct such massively scaled palaces and compounds, had no parallel in Judah at this time.

The hard part has been figuring out why. A number of scholars have sought to understand in detail greater than that provided by the Bible just what sort of society existed in Israel during this formative period. Finkelstein's thinking on this issue originated in part on work that he did studying ramparts and fortifications built at large sites during the Middle Bronze Age period, about 2000–1550 B.C.E. There were real and perceived military threats during this period, but Finkelstein argued that a number of the most impressive structures built then made very little sense from a military perspective. It turned out that many simply served as supports for some of the other architectural features at the sites. Furthermore, he estimated, the amount of labor that must have been needed to construct them was far greater than the small populations living at these sites could possibly have provided. Their construction must have required a centralized, efficient bureaucracy that wielded substantial political and economic muscle. Finkelstein concluded that the very undertaking of these public works projects was a means of propaganda, an important tool with which these emerging regimes tried to establish their legitimacy. He has developed this argument even further in turning his attention to Omride architecture.

The study of the use of propaganda in the biblical world is a burgeoning area of inquiry. It is common even today for states to use bombastic architecture and grotesquely designed palaces as a way of establishing a ruler's or dynasty's right to reign. These palaces are always the first place sacked after an uprising, and it's not only because of the looters' sense that there may be riches there for the taking. They are closely associated with the ruling family's image. Back in biblical times, monumental architecture was virtually the only route available for a king to communicate his wealth and power to a public that was largely illiterate.

Rulers had other ways of demonstrating that they had a divine right to rule. There were victory stelae, inscriptions, coins, and seals. Most rulers used a combination of all of these, but nothing was as powerful as a monumental building, with its sheer size and wide visibility, in communicating a message that would reach all classes of society. The messages were varied, according to the scholarship. The city gate, for instance, was very important, the focal point for life in the city. The huge size of the gates, the attention to detail in the masonry, symbolized both protection from external threats and the promise of security and prosperity within the boundaries of the city itself.

The building activity of the Omrides had as its backdrop Israel's emergence as a state in a time when other peoples too were organizing into nations, most importantly Israel's powerful neighbors Moab and Aram Damascus. Unlike Judah, Israel was not a closed, homogenous community. There was real ethnic and cultural diversity in the kingdom. Omri and then Ahab ruled the highlands area around

Samaria but still needed to consolidate cities like Megiddo in the fertile valleys and lowlands. Controlling this region was a critical part of Ahab's political agenda, since this was where the most lucrative trade routes ran and where most of the manpower for military campaigns came from. Israel's northern border was even more sensitive. The large number of destruction layers at northern sites such as Dan and Hazor indicate that cities on the border changed hands numerous times during this period. Such changes didn't always have to be the result of war. The situation was so fluid, the border so uncertain, that the northern peoples could just as easily have declared their loyalty to one side or the other rather than wait for Hazael, the powerful king of Aram Damascus, or Ahab of Israel to come conquer them in battle.

It was in this world that Omride architecture developed, Finkelstein contends. Omri and Ahab were shrewd. In the valleys, the population remained very stable, according to recent archaeological surveys of the region. As long as the valleys remained politically quiet, it wasn't necessary to introduce some revolutionary change into the political system. Omri and Ahab chose to build, rebuild, and fortify in certain cities for political as much as military reasons. The sites that bear their architectural imprint all dominated important trade or access routes. Hazor controlled rich agricultural land and the trade route to Syria. Megiddo lay atop a valley and the routes to Tyre. The decision to locate the sumptuous, massive, fortified enclosure at Jezreel involved similar calculations. This wasn't about defending the residents of Jezreel from Aram Damascus. Jezreel sat alongside a major highway, and it would have been clearly visible to the many people who traveled along the highway from their homes to the markets and back. The architecture at sites like Jezreel was first and foremost an attempt to find an additional way to shore up Omride power in the heartland without having to use force.

During the ninth century B.C.E., the Omrides' biggest rivals were the Aramaeans of ancient Syria. Of Aram's leaders, Hazael was the most powerful, managing to band the independent Aramaean states into a federation for the first time. For many years, virtually the only source of information about Hazael and the Aramaeans was the Bible. Scholars believe that the earliest likely reference to the "people of Aram" was found in Thebes, on a statue base from the funerary temple of Amenophis III. After that, there are virtually no texts that mention them for close to a thousand years, until the annals of Tiglath-pileser I, the king of Assyria who reigned from 1116 to 1076 B.C.E. In one of his annals, he recounts crossing the Euphrates River twenty-eight times attempting to beat back one threat or another by the Aramaeans. The large number of campaigns alone indicates that they were considered a serious problem. Much of Aram's history has been reconstructed this way, from the writings of people of other states that came into contact with them, including the Bible.

The Bible portrays the Aramaeans as having kinship relations with Israel. One of the genealogies in Genesis lists Aram as a son of Shem, one of Noah's sons. In another genealogy, believed to have been written at a time when the Aramaeans were less powerful, Aram is recorded as the grandson of Abraham's brother Nahor. Additional biblical stories reinforce the idea that there was some sort of tribal connection. In the story about Abraham, his family is portrayed as settled in Aram. The wives of Isaac and Jacob are believed to have been Aramaeans. Despite this history, by the time of King David, the Aramaeans are considered one of Israel's main enemies. David's Syrian wars are described in detail in the Bible, the only source we now have about fighting between the two states.

Still, when it comes to the story of Hazael, the Bible's writers outdid themselves. There is a long scriptural tradition of prophets taking credit for the rise or fall of Israelite kings, but in the Second Book of Kings, Hazael, a foreign king, is portrayed as coming to power largely as the result of a timely visit to Damascus by the Israelite prophet Elisha. Elisha, the Bible relates, goes to Damascus one day, at a time when the king, Ben-hadad, is sick. Hazael is sent to greet the prophet and to find out whether the king will recover. When Elisha and Hazael finally meet, Elisha starts to weep bitterly. Hazael asks him why, and Elisha responds, "Because I know the evil that thou wilt do unto the children of Israel: their strongholds wilt thou set on fire, and their young men wilt thou slay with the sword." Hazael is taken aback by the prediction of his coming power. "But what is thy servant, who is but a dog, that he should do this great thing?" Hazael asks. And Elisha responds, "The Lord hath shown me that thou shalt be king over Aram." Hazael goes back to the sick king and tells him Elisha has foretold that he will recover shortly. The next day the king is dead, smothered by Hazael, some Bible scholars contend, and Hazael ascends to the throne.

Archaeology has moved beyond this story, and a new picture of Hazael has started to emerge. In 1993 and 1994 two fragments of a stela were discovered at Tel Dan, a site in northern Israel near the border with present-day Lebanon. Archaeologists pieced together the fragments into a text of thirteen preserved lines, and based on the scholars' reconstruction, the excavators concluded that Hazael had written it after he conquered parts of northern Israel. There was also a recent dig at Tel Jezreel, Ahab's seat of power and the place where Jezebel was eventually killed. The excavators concluded on the basis of the Bible that the city had been destroyed by Jehu as part of a coup against King Joram, Ahab's son. Not everyone has accepted that conclusion.

Nadav Na'aman, the Tel Aviv University historian, has studied the latest archaeological developments closely, and in a series of scholarly papers that have appeared over the last several years has almost single-handedly rewritten Hazael's history. Na'aman didn't start out looking at Hazael. His major interest was the sources of the Bible. He had embarked on a project to try to determine which sources were more historically reliable, in an effort to learn what the Bible's writers had actually relied on in composing the Scriptures. During a study of the Book of Joshua, in particular the stories about Israel's conquest of Canaan, Na'aman came to the conclusion that in order to enhance the sense of authenticity, the writers had frequently filled gaps in the narrative about long-ago events by dropping in details of military activities that had occurred at later times.

Na'aman believed a similar process had been at work during the writing of the chapters about King David's wars with the Aramaeans. A Judean scribe of the eighth century B.C.E. wouldn't know much about Hadadezer of Aram, David's rival in the biblical stories, Na'aman wrote. Events had happened so long ago, there were virtually no sources or texts that recorded the information. So instead, Na'aman went on to argue, the writer had probably relied on details from the exploits of Hazael and modeled the king in the story, Hadadezer, on him. Na'aman believed that the texts of King David's Syrian wars contained historical information, but not about David or the Syrian wars during David's time. Instead, he thought, historians might be able to glean from these stories details about Hazael's rule and time.

Despite the fact that Na'aman is a historian by training, not an archaeologist, in recent years some of his friends in the world of archaeology have started referring to him as part of the "Tel Aviv University trio," along with the archaeologists David Ussishkin and Israel Finkelstein, who are challenging the nature of David and Solomon's united monarchy. They are all friends, traveling together to conferences, reading one another's papers. But Na'aman is very different, both in temperament and approach. He is soft-spoken, with a birdlike physique and the air of an absent-minded professor about him. His work is the exact opposite of his physical demeanor, though, bold and revolutionary. And although he disagrees with a number of the interpretations of archaeological and biblical material that Ussishkin and Finkelstein have published, in their questioning of traditional biblical and archaeological interpretations, the three could be linked together.

In addition to his theories about Hazael's being the model for Hadadezer in the King David stories, Na'aman has more recently reinterpreted the Aramaean leader's history using the excavation results from Tel Jezreel, where Ussishkin, now Finkelstein's codirector at the Megiddo dig, led excavations. The Jezreel digs have proven crucial for Finkelstein's theories that Megiddo's major architecture should be dated not to Solomon's time but to that of Ahab, in the ninth century B.C.E. The excavators of Jezreel dated the pottery found in the enclosure there to the ninth century, and they have demonstrated that the pottery at Megiddo most similar to the finds at Jezreel fit into Finkelstein's reconstruction of the site's history rather than into the traditional dating scheme. But Jezreel is proving to be a key site for something else as well, the reassessment of Hazael launched by Na'aman. In the Bible, the destruction of Jezreel is described in detail in Second Kings. A message from the prophet Elisha results in Jehu's rebellion against the current king, Joram, son of Ahab and Jezebel. Jehu is given clear instructions: "And thou shalt smite the house of Ahab thy master," so that God may avenge the death of all the Israelite prophets killed by Jezebel when she tried to replace Yahweh's followers with her Ba'al-worshipping loyalists. "For the whole house of Ahab shall perish," Elisha's message continues, "and the dogs shall eat Jezebel in the portion of Jezreel, and there shall be none to bury her."

Jehu sets out to fulfill this prophecy. First he kills Joram with an arrow through the heart. Then he rides on to Jezreel to take care of Jezebel. Jehu enters the gate of Jezreel without a fight, the Bible records, and when Jezebel calls out to him from the tower, he orders the officers to throw her from the window. "So they threw her down," the Bible says, "and some of her blood was sprinkled on the wall, and on the horses, and she was trodden under foot." Jehu then has the heads of Ahab's seventy other sons laid in heaps at the entrance of Jezreel. He moves on to Samaria and becomes king.

This story troubled Na'aman. The excavators argued that Jezreel had been destroyed during Jehu's coup, probably around 842 B.C.E., based on the stories in Second Kings. But the archaeological evidence fit a different picture. During the digging, eight arrowheads had been uncovered, all of them on the southern part of Tel Jezreel, close to the gate and the tower. This seemed to show that, contrary to the description in the Bible of Jehu riding without challenge through the gate into the city, Jezreel had been conquered by force. The city had been destroyed entirely, the archaeological finds revealed. While there had been some sporadic settlement on the site for two centuries afterward, Jezreel had been used intensively by the Omrides for no more than forty years before being abandoned. This too didn't make sense to Na'aman. Why would a king of Israel destroy and abandon a city like Jezreel, with its fortifications and central location? The Omrides had also built the city of Samaria, and that had served as the capital and residence of a number of rulers from subsequent dynasties, who had no qualms about taking over a choice piece of property. There was no reason Jezreel should not have shared the same fate. No reason, that is, unless it had been destroyed by someone other than a fellow Israelite king.

Na'aman looks to Hazael as the most likely conqueror. The Dan Stela provided details of the Aramaic conquest of Israel that hadn't been in the Bible. The text in the Dan Stela indicated that Hazael claimed to have killed both Joram of Israel and Ahaziahu of Judah, and that he ruined the towns and the land in the territories he went on to conquer. Na'aman argues that the archaeological evidence turned up at Jezreel suggests it was Hazael, not Jehu, who destroyed Jezreel and left it in ruins throughout the Aramaic rule in Israel. Based on the excavation reports at a number of other sites in the north, such as Megiddo, Tel Yokneam, and Dan, Na'aman argues that Hazael cut a destructive swath through the Jezreel Valley area as he conquered Israel, destroying at least five major cities. Later, after the Aramaeans were forced to withdraw from Israel under pressure by the Israelite king Joash, most of these towns were rebuilt and fortified. But not Jezreel, which saw most of its functions taken over by its older and larger neighbor Megiddo and apparently never became more than a small village.

Not far from Jezreel, just a few miles from the northern shore of the Sea of Galilee, lies Bethsaida. This was the capital of the Aramaean kingdom of Geshur, which in the ninth century B.C.E. would become part of the powerful Aram Damascus federation led by Hazael. Geshur had a unique connection to Israel. King David had married Maacah, a daughter of Talmai, the king of Geshur. David and Maacah's son was Absalom, who would eventually rebel against David. His death at the hands of David's general prompted David's heartbreaking lament, "O my son Absalom, my son, my son Absalom! Would I had died for thee, O Absalom, my son, my son!" At one point, Geshur also served as a refuge for Absalom. When his half-brother Amnon forces himself on Tamar, Absalom's sister, Absalom murders Amnon in revenge for the insult to her honor. He is forced to flee from David and finds refuge with his grandfather Talmai in Geshur.

Not much is written about Geshur in the Bible, although there is a tantalizing hint that it was a prosperous area. After several years of estrangement following Amnon's murder, David finally allows his general, Joab, to go to Geshur and bring Absalom back to Jerusalem. This is not a full reconciliation. David still refuses to even look at Absalom, and for two years, the Bible records, Absalom manages to live in the small town of Jerusalem and not once see the king's face. Finally in frustration, Absalom forces the issue with Joab, who eventually gets David to relent. "Wherefore am I come from Geshur?" Absalom complains when he makes his case to Joab. "It were better for me to be there still."

Rami Arav, a director of excavations at Bethsaida, thinks Absalom wasn't just being petulant. "Absalom meant what he was saying. Geshur was better off than Jerusalem," says Arav. It started with architecture. Bethsaida was a larger city. Its walls, eighteen to twenty-five feet thick, have no equal in terms of what has previously been excavated in Israel, and the city gate is the largest uncovered inside the current borders of Israel. Even the cult objects were huge. At Dan, in the north, the excavators found small field stones marking outdoor places of worship. At Bethsaida, worship areas were marked by dressed stones four or more feet high. Everything was on a grand scale. "They took their defense much more seriously than the

Israelites did," Arav says. "Everything about their architecture is much more solid and powerful. You see a display of might." But Arav believes that Absalom wasn't just comparing the size of city walls. Unlike Jerusalem, a small stronghold on top of an isolated mountain, Bethsaida was located along the main highway to Damascus, a major trade area. The small finds that have been uncovered during the dig indicate connections all over the Middle East, with Ammon, Egypt, Mesopotamia, Phoenicia, and Israel. The Geshurites prospered from their location along the international trade route, and from the fact that they were the strongest city sitting on the only lake in the area. There was fertile land and water. Through alliances such as the one sealed by the marriage of Talmai's daughter to King David, there was no threat from the west. Geshur continued to maintain good relations with Israel, refusing at one point to join the other Aramaean city-states in a coalition to help Ammon fight a challenge from King David, according to one biblical story.

This changed in the ninth century B.C.E. Arav has found a destruction layer at Geshur dating from around the time Hazael came to power, indicating that Geshur was, in the words of Arav, "annexed, captured, brought in, or whatever definition we take," to a greater Aramaean kingdom, Aram Damascus. Above the destruction is a layer of occupation, representing the city under Aram Damascus's rule. Hazael made some changes, particularly to the ground plan and function of the palace. He added a large partition wall to divide what until then had been used as the throne room into two sections. Two corridors were created above the throne room by the addition of the new wall. A collection of loom weights found inside these corridors has led Arav to speculate that weaving was done here. Arav doesn't have an explanation for all the changes, but there is a sense that under Hazael's rule the palace became a center of activity rather than just a ceremonial place.

The Bethsaida finds have caught Finkelstein's eye as he continues to write about the development of Omride architecture. He agrees with Na'aman that it is plausible to think Hazael was responsible for the destruction of Jezreel, Megiddo, Dan, and other northern sites during his conquest of Israel. He thinks Hazael also destroyed Hazor. "I find it difficult to imagine that Hazael conquered Dan and laid havoc to other cities in northern Israel, east and west of the Jordan, but left Hazor unharmed," Finkelstein says in an unpublished paper. Hazor was the logical place for the Omrides to build some sort of administrative center. It was located right on their northern border, the ideal location for a bulwark against Hazael's expanding powers and imperial ambitions. Finkelstein argues that Hazael also conquered Hazor, then rebuilt the city in a style similar to the one used in Bethsaida. Hazael fortified Hazor with a huge wall, and constructed an edifice on the western end of the city that Hazor's first excavator, Yigael Yadin, contended was a four-room house but that Finkelstein thinks could just as easily be reconstructed as a Syrian-style palace. Finkelstein doesn't think the population changed much when control of Hazor passed from an Israelite to an Aramaean ruler, but he points out that of the four inscriptions found from this time period, three are written in Phoenician or Aramaic (the fourth is not clear enough to decide). Eventually the Israelites conquered Hazor again, and the city changed hands once more. Again Hazor was rebuilt in a very different layout.

The Dan Stela, which provided so many clues for Na'aman's reconstruction of Hazael's rule, was part of a whole new literary genre that came into being, the literature of legitimacy. Back in the ninth century B.C.E., as national identities crystallized for the first time, so did the leaders' need to tell stories about themselves, their gods, and their rise to power. Surviving today mostly on broken pieces of basalt and on stone stelae, such inscriptions were often the first attempts among these new entities to craft national narratives, to tell their version of the people's past and their relationship with a common deity.

Prior to the unearthing of the Dan Stela, the most famous example of the genre was the Mesha Stela, discovered at Dibon in the territory of ancient Moab in 1868 by a Protestant missionary traveling in Transjordan. The thirty-five-line inscription, the longest known royal inscription of this age discovered in greater Palestine, was probably written either just before Ahab's death or within a decade afterward. In it, Mesha, king of Moab, recounts how he was able to deliver Moab from the control of its neighbor Israel, thanks to the support and intervention of Moab's chief deity, Chemosh. The Dan inscription discusses battles with Israel and Judah during this same time period. Here was an early attempt to write a national narrative, one dominated by the uneasy relationships among Israel and its neighbors.

Historians have struggled to understand the political backdrop against which these inscriptions were written. In both instances, the inscriptions recount battles mentioned in the Hebrew Bible, but they differ from the biblical account in key respects, reflecting the fact they were written by the other side. This was a time when Assyria, then the region's superpower, was no longer in control, and so its former vassals, all of whom had long histories with one another as well, were finding their national identities and coming into their own. Moab, controlled once by Israel, had rebelled, and in one of its first acts of newfound sovereignty was taking back its past. At Dan, Hazael, who would continue to fight Israel along its borders for years to come, did the same. Such inscriptions were not appreciated by rival peoples. At Dan, excavators found the stela fragments inside a fortification wall. Apparently after the Israelites recaptured Dan, they broke the stela into pieces and used the basalt blocks for construction material.

For historians of the united and divided monarchies, the discovery of these inscriptions from Israel and Judah's neighbors was a boon. No comparable inscriptions have yet been found in either Israel or Judah dealing with the process of state formation during the divided monarchy period. In the biblical story about Rehoboam, Solomon's son, and the events that lead to the breakup of the united monarchy, Rehoboam is rejected by the Israelites as their king. After his tax official is stoned to death, Rehoboam has to ignominiously flee to Jerusalem in his chariot. The Israelites then proclaim Jeroboam king of

Israel. Jeroboam's first act as monarch of the northern tribes, according to the biblical account, is to strengthen not just one, but two, cities. "Then Jeroboam built Shechem in the hill-country of Ephraim and dwelt therein," the Bible states, "and he went out from thence, and built Penuel." Such public works were a way of assuring the locals that good times were on the way and that they could count on Jeroboam for protection. Jeroboam also set up places of worship to rival the cult based in Jerusalem, and even introduced a new religious calendar of holidays. Here, it seems, was a ruler who understood how to demonstrate the legitimacy of his rule. Perhaps Rehoboam's chief failure was that he never embraced the symbolic power of telling a tale, whether in words or in bricks, that could help unite two sides who now saw themselves as enemies and rivals rather than members of a larger family.

And yet, reading the inscriptions from Dan and Moab is just another reminder of why keeping Israel and Judah united was probably doomed to failure from the beginning. State formation in the Middle East has always been a messy, bloody process. In the Mesha Stela, Mesha describes Moab's oppression by Omri, king of Israel, and Omri's earlier military exploits in Moab, as a way to justify his own territorial ambitions. Hazael in the Tel Dan inscription is no different. He acknowledges that he attacked Israel, but claims his action is justified because the king of Israel had attacked his kingdom first during his father's reign. Based on the hints contained in the biblical text, Israel's and Judah's leaders took a similar approach to determining blame for their own conflicts. There they were, in the ninth century B.C.E., each claiming that the land they conquered historically belonged to their people, using ancient wrongs to justify a political policy that would lead to more fighting. Thousands of years ago, it already seemed impossible to escape the shadow of the past. That shadow would continue to hang over them even as their states came under the control of Assyrians, Egyptians, Babylonians, and Persians.

Chapter 6

❦

Babylonian Exile

The Ones Who Stayed Home

The rest of the people who were left in the city and the deserters who had deserted to the king of Babylon, together with the rest of the multitude, were carried into exile by Nebuzaradan the captain of the guard. But the captain of the guard left some of the poorest of the land to be vinedressers and plowmen. *(2 Kings 25:11–12)*

In 587/586 B.C.E., the Babylonian army marched into Jerusalem and destroyed the temple. Israelite history is replete with setbacks and disasters, but this was by far the greatest calamity yet to befall the people. Surprisingly, the biblical text about this major event is very spare. The coming of the powerful Babylonian army is accorded a brief mention about warriors encamping outside Jerusalem's walls. The siege of the city and the four-month-long famine that ensues receive one sentence. "On the ninth day of the [fourth] month the famine was sore in the city, so that there was no bread for the people of the land," the chronicle reads. "Then a breach was made in the city," the Bible goes on matter-of-factly, and with that Jerusalem falls and the rule of the House of David comes to an ignominious end.

The destruction of the city was the result of a series of fatal miscalculations by Judah's leaders. Nebuchadnezzar, Babylonia's ruler, had taken over Judah in 604/603 B.C.E., the first year of his reign after succeeding his father. Jehoiakim, then the king of Judah, decided not to fight and held on to his throne. But in 602/601, Nebuchadnezzar tried to conquer Egypt, the only remaining power strong enough to threaten Babylonia's hegemony. When the military expedition failed, Jehoiakim saw an opening and rebelled against the Babylonians. It was a serious mistake. He died soon after, so it was his son, Jehoiachin, who had to surrender Jerusalem in 598/597. This time, Nebuchadnezzar took no chances and appointed his own king, a member of the House of David, Judah's traditional ruling dynasty, named Zedekiah.

Eleven years later, Zedekiah aligned himself with Egypt, hoping to push the Babylonians out of the region — and instead brought on the destruction of Jerusalem. The Bible recounts Zedekiah's bitter fate. As Jerusalem burns, Zedekiah manages to escape and make his way toward the desert. But upon orders of Nebuchadnezzar, Zedekiah is hunted down. He is forced to watch his children be killed. It is the last thing he sees, and then he is blinded and carried off to Babylon. The people who survive the massacre are led into captivity and the land lies desolate for fifty years. "Judah was in exile," the Bible laments, adding only that the few inhabitants who were spared deportation were the "poorest of the land," peasants forced by the Babylonians to tend the vines and work the fields. And then the reluctantly related account ends. Judah is no more.

But Judah was not empty after all. Most of the population remained behind, living in the same places they had lived before, except now under Babylonian rule. Just a few miles down the road from Jerusalem, there is virtually no sign of any destruction at all. In fact, archaeologists digging in these areas have discovered that many of those cities actually expanded and flourished under the Babylonians. The people living in them weren't all poor peasants either. Burial caves in use during the Babylonian period have been found to contain gold and silver jewelry, fancy and costly vases and pottery, and other luxury items that reflected the owners' considerable status and wealth, rather than the poverty described by the Bible.

Virtually nothing about all this appears in the Bible. The years of Babylonian rule in Judah are a historical blank, the people's lives and activities in Judah ignored. This situation continues until Cyrus the Great of Persia conquers Babylonia. In 538 B.C.E., he issues an edict allowing the Judeans to return to their ancestral homeland and rebuild Jerusalem's destroyed temple. Some of the exiles begin to return to Judah. It is only then that the story picks up once again.

The biblical image of Judah as completely destroyed, emptied of people except for a few peasants living in misery and eking out a meager existence, has lasted for thousands of years. At the City of David excavations in Jerusalem, it is easy to see why. This area was the original core of Jerusalem, where the Bible says King David began building the capital of his kingdom. Over time, the city spread over the hills, the houses built on the slope that juts out over the valley like the spur of a boot. Today the white and pink stone houses of the Arab village of Silwan cover the hill across from the remains of the City of David. That's how the ancient city must have looked, clinging to the stony terraces cut into the hill.

It's possible to walk along the narrow bridge built for tourists and still get a sense of the Babylonian destruction. In the far corner of the site is the Burnt Room, which got its name from the thick layer of debris that covered the lime-plaster floor when it was discovered. Virtually everything found in that room was charred, including large pieces of wood carbonized from the high temperatures of fire. Next to it stands the Bullae House, where fifty-one clay seal impressions used to affix official signatures to documents were found. The fire that destroyed the building had been so intense that the room turned into a kiln, firing the clay seals and preserving the names of their former owners on them.

The massive destruction of Jerusalem is reflected in these houses, and not just by the thick layer of ashes and debris or the broken pottery that was found scattered all over the floors. One morning during a visit to the site, Jane Cahill, an archaeologist who has supervised digs here, points to the eastern slope of the hill. Heavy, neatly cut blocks that had once been used for construction were found there, a huge accumulation of collapsed building stones that practically covered the entire hill. This had been the result of Babylonian battering rams.

The most poignant find was in what the archaeologists have nicknamed the House of Ahiel because a piece of a broken storage jar bearing the name Ahiel turned up on the floor. There, still embedded in one side of the floor, was a limestone toilet seat. The archaeologists have left it there. The toilet lay on top of a cesspit, and was still in use on the eve of the Babylonian destruction of the city. The seat had two openings, a larger one emptying down into the cesspit, and a smaller one emptying to the side. Cahill speculates that the smaller one was possibly designed for male urination. Right beside the toilet seat was a small clay bowl, probably used for washing hands or for throwing lime into the cesspit.

Cahill and the other archaeologists collected some of the soil in the cesspit and sent it to a laboratory for analysis in the hope of discovering something about conditions in Jerusalem at the time the Babylonians marched in. Before the city fell, the Babylonians had it under siege for eighteen months, and the remains in that toilet vividly illustrated how difficult daily life had been.

The people's diets reflected privation. In the fecal matter, there were the remains of plants, the kind that grow wild in someone's backyard. There were no herbs and spices, few grains of wheat or barley, and no lentils or peas. People had been forced to eat whatever they could find at hand. In addition, there was also a high number of tapeworm and other parasite eggs, indicating overcrowding and unsanitary conditions, and the fact that people were probably eating contaminated, poorly cooked beef and pork.

Standing on that narrow bridge and looking at a two-thousand-year-old toilet seat, it is easy to forget that lately the City of David has been forced into the modern age, becoming the center of a huge political controversy. A group of Jewish settlers eager to see Jews living in Silwan has raised funds and begun purchasing Arab homes on the slopes of the mountain surrounding the ancient biblical capital. Some of the

Arab families living in Silwan claim they were forced out of their houses in the middle of the night or swindled out of their homes illegally. Several cases brought by Arabs have been winding their way through the Israeli court system, although with little success so far. In the meantime, the private organization backing the settlers, Elad (the Hebrew acronym means "To the City of David"), has been building a visitor center on the edge of one family's garden, hoping to attract more tourists to the City of David. Money they have raised is helping fund other digs in the area surrounding the site, including the one led by Ronny Reich, who warmly greets Cahill as we make our way to the ruins. (A few weeks later he will announce that he believes it was the Canaanites and not the Israelites who built Jerusalem's ancient water system.)

Elad members have set up a rest area under the shade of the trees right inside the entrance to the area, with clay water jugs strung up through the branches. The place looks serene, despite the fact that in order to reach the site visitors have to pass under the watchful eyes of two sullen young settlers with machine guns sitting at the entrance. Inside Elad's temporary headquarters, a caravan right next to the rest area, Yigal Naveh is handing out colorful brochures explaining the key sites in the City of David. At twenty-four, he still has a smooth baby face. His shirt is neatly pressed but not tucked in his pants. He wears the knitted skullcap of the religious Zionist movement and talks enthusiastically about David writing his psalms here. He has no time for toilet seats or other finds that might serve as common ground between all the inhabitants of the neighborhood. His head is filled with a loftier vision. On his desk is a proposal by a Jerusalem archaeologist who is convinced David's palace can be found and hopes to launch a dig with Elad's help. "This is the cradle of the Jewish nation," says Naveh.

Back on the bridge outside, Cahill and another archaeologist, Dan Bahat, are talking about the dig Bahat is running here. He eventually wants to get to parts of the hill where Cahill's group didn't have time to excavate further. Behind them, a group of Elad representatives speak loudly among themselves about their own plans for developing the City of David. They talk about the eviction notice sent to the residents of the house in whose garden Bahat has already started digging and wonder when they will move. Signs posted by the Arabs around the site flutter in the wind. Settlers Get Out, they say. Settlements Are an Obstacle to Peace.

In the brochure that Elad distributes to tourists, there are brief highlights of what the group considers the important stops on a tour of the City of David. In Area G, where Cahill's group dug and most of the remains of the Babylonian destruction are centered, only the Bullae House merits a mention. "These are the remains from an archive that went up in smoke with the destruction of the first Temple," the brochure says. The bullae, or seals, are especially popular because many of the individual names on them are found in the Bible. No mention is made in the brochure of the toilet, the most human artifact still visible in what is now just a pile of rocks.

The tour guides who bring groups every day to Area G also make a special point of talking about the clay seal impressions. Dan Bahat looks up at the group now standing above the site and watches as the guide points out the Bullae House. Bahat stops talking about his dig for a moment and presses Cahill's arm. "Everyone loves the idea of the bullae," Bahat says. "But do you know what I like the most? That toilet seat you found, and knowing the remains of the meal the people ate. That moves me more than the bullae." The common humanity of daily life that links the ancient city and modern Silwan hovers unspoken in Bahat's words. But the tour group is already leaving. The guide hurries his charges past the Arab demonstrators. There is no time to talk, either to Bahat or to the Arabs who live in Silwan. The tourists end up missing the real message of Area G and the Babylonian destruction: sometimes the most interesting stories belong to the people who remain behind.

Reconstructing those stories requires an enormous amount of detective work. The Bible's writers hadn't been interested in the people remaining in Judah, even though they and not the exiles composed the overwhelming majority of the greater Israelite nation. In their minds, the exile in Babylon was the great purifying experience in the life of Israel. The Bible records that Jeroboam, upon becoming king of Israel, set up golden idols in Bethel and Dan, probably in an attempt to rival Jerusalem's hold on Israelite religious life. But figurines of a Canaanite goddess have been discovered by archaeologists in Jerusalem, indicating that even in Judah people worshipped more than one god. Monotheism was embraced for the first time in Babylon, and the cultic practices that had angered God and caused all of Israel's problems in the first place were supposedly left behind for good. But the Judeans who remained at home had continued living their lives and practicing their religion much the same as always. This religion could be best described as an ecumenical blending of the various gods. So it was better for everyone, the Bible's writers probably figured, to say that they were only few, and the exiles many. The lives of the people in Judah didn't fit the ideological point of the story they wanted to write.

The text of the Bible does contain some hints that the full story of the exile hasn't yet been told. In the Book of Jeremiah we find the principal remaining record of the first few years following the destruction of Jerusalem. It is clear from the text that quite a few Judeans have not been exiled. There's Gedaliah, a former high-ranking officer under the previous government, who agrees to accept an appointment by the Babylonians to rule what is left of Judah and sets up his administrative center in Mizpah, north of Jerusalem. Joining him are at least five Judean officers as well as their soldiers who, Jeremiah relates, eluded capture by the Babylonians during the battle over Jerusalem and now are in Mizpah ready to swear allegiance to the new regime. Many of the Judeans who had fled across the border to neighboring Ammon, Moab, and Edom come back. And despite the fact that a huge conflagration has supposedly just ended, enough of the economic infrastructure remains intact that these returning farmers are said to have brought in a great harvest after their homecoming, with an abundance of wine, oil, and fruits.

There is even a hint of the tensions that will arise in the future between those who stayed home and the exiles who return from

Babylon. Just as life is beginning to get back to normal, a disaffected member of the House of David named Ishmael, angry that he didn't get Gedaliah's job, slips back into Judah with a group of coconspirators and murders Gedaliah. Ishmael assumes his action will prompt a groundswell of support against the Babylonians and ignite a popular uprising. He miscalculates badly. The people don't want any more trouble and no one comes to his aid. Ishmael is forced to flee, and the Babylonians remain firmly in control.

These small glimpses into life in Judah in the first years following the exile are all we have, and at first Bible scholars ignored them. Like the Bible's writers, they were interested primarily in the people who returned to Jerusalem from Babylon during the Persian era. These were the people, they contended, who oversaw the beginnings of Judaism as it is practiced today. Besides, the destruction of Jerusalem and the temple was hardly a glorious event. The image that most captured people's imagination, inspiring songs, spirituals, and art, was that of an exiled people weeping by the rivers of Babylon as they remembered Zion, suffering in their captivity, and eventually being restored to their ancestral land. The future lay with them, not with the peasants back in Judah.

Some archaeological excavations in cities in Judah found pottery and other material attributed to the years of Babylonian rule. But the changes in the pottery were so slight and incremental that most archaeologists had trouble distinguishing between when the destruction ended and the Babylonian occupation began. The American archaeologist William Frederic Bade, who dug at biblical Mizpah for five seasons between 1926 and 1935, didn't turn up any occupation layer that seemed to belong to the exile period. It was only sixty years later, when a graduate student of archaeology named Jeffrey Zorn was going through Bade's old records and field plans, that it became evident Bade had misidentified several structures, causing him to miss an entire occupation level in his reconstruction of Mizpah's history. The missing layer turned out to be the Babylonian period.

Mizpah, Zorn found, was the key site for understanding what had gone on inside the country during the fifty years after Jerusalem's destruction. In the Bible, Mizpah has a long and disquieting history, beginning well before the Babylonian conquest. The best-known biblical story about the city involves a Levite traveler and his concubine, who is savagely raped and murdered by a gang of men who are members of the tribe of Benjamin. Seeking revenge, the Levite takes a sharp knife and cuts the dead woman's body into twelve pieces, then sends the pieces by messenger to all the tribes of Israel, all the tribes except Benjamin. They all meet at Mizpah, in Benjamin's territory, and from there set out on a grisly civil war that results in the near destruction of the entire tribe of Benjamin. Later, Saul, who is also from the area controlled by Benjamin, becomes the leader of the Israelites and chooses to muster all the tribes at Mizpah for a battle against the Philistines. Eventually Saul will be replaced by David, just as Mizpah is to be superseded by Jerusalem.

But Mizpah had been much more than a biblical crossroads to mayhem and bloodshed. During the period of Babylonian rule, Mizpah had flourished, as had the entire region of Benjamin. This picture, created by Zorn's reconstruction, was in complete contrast to what had previously been known about the so-called exilic period. The clues were all in Bade's site plans. Bade had died a year after his last season of digging at Mizpah, probably due to overexertion brought on by the sheer number of his work commitments. He had been a close friend of the naturalist John Muir, and had worked with him on various conservation efforts in California. After Muir's death, Bade had agreed to be the literary executor and ended up writing a ten-volume biography of Muir and editing his collected works. The money he earned from that mammoth project had gone to fund the Mizpah dig, along with funds from his rich wife and wealthy friends. Before he died, Bade had managed to clear almost two-thirds of the eight-acre Mizpah site. He and a team of more than 150 locals excavated 672 rooms, 387 cisterns, and 71 tombs. More than 23,000 different objects had been catalogued, 15,000 of which were actually drawn. A final report of his findings was never published, but his friends did publish two large volumes of results after Bade died.

One summer, in preparation for a new job as coordinator and tour guide at the Bade Institute of Biblical Archaeology in Berkeley, California, Zorn had been reviewing a large-scale study of the plan of the site. He had gone hunting through the museum's archives and come across a more detailed field plan that Bade had prepared. In comparing the two plans, he started noticing certain irregularities. For one thing, the large-scale plan showed a wall that seemed to run down the center of a house. According to the field plan, the house lay on top of the wall, meaning the house had been built at a later time. In another area, he noticed that directly inside the inner gate to the city was another building. If the two structures had been built at the same time, anyone coming through the gate would have walked straight into the wall of the building. The more Zorn looked at the plans the more buildings he seemed to find that had clearly been built at a later time period.

In the end, he identified in the plans nine large administrative-style buildings and domestic structures that he dated to the Babylonian period. The Babylonians had chosen Mizpah as their center in order to take advantage of the already existing defense systems such as a huge outer wall and the reinforced city gate. They then had launched a major urban renewal, razing most of the small homes and building a larger, fancier city directly on top. According to Zorn's calculations, the largest house of the predestruction period had been no more than 860 square feet. During the Babylonian period, the average house size was almost 1,500 square feet. The walls in the earlier city had been built at a width of only a single stone. The Babylonians rebuilt the city's walls using a mixture of large single stones and double stones for reinforcement. They put down stone-paved floors and preferred using pillars inside their homes. They widened the alleyways so that men on donkeys or horses could easily pass each other in the streets.

In a list Bade and the other excavators had compiled of the objects they found, Zorn found additional information, small finds that no one had known how to date but that additional research over the subsequent years now indicated belonged to the Babylonian period. There were thirty stamp impressions found on jar handles at the site that bore the Hebrew letters Mozah, originating from the estates surrounding the village of Mozah near Mizpah. The Mozah estates probably produced wine for use at Mizpah. Other Mozah stamps had turned up at Gibeon, another nearby wine-producing center during this time period. Fragments of a Mesopotamian-style, bathtub-shaped ceramic coffin were found. Zorn even tracked down at the Rockefeller Museum in Jerusalem a bronze vase that the 1947 report had mentioned as being located in one of the cisterns at the site. He noticed on the base of the vase a small decoration that hadn't been in the published drawing and was impossible to detect in the small, dark photos Zorn had found in the archives. This type of vase is believed to have been a Babylonian-influenced style.

What struck Zorn most about his study was the prosperity Mizpah had enjoyed during the Babylonian exile. A suburblike settlement had even sprung up right outside the city walls as the flourishing city attracted more people to move there. There were very wealthy people living in the area, and not all of them were Babylonian officials.

One June morning, Zorn strides up the hill to the top of Tell en-Nasbeh, the Arabic name for biblical Mizpah. He is tall and built like a football player, and a straw cowboy hat perches incongruously on his head. He is in Israel for his usual summer job, helping run the dig at Tel Dor, on the northern coast of Israel on the edge of the Mediterranean. He flies a pirate flag over the section of the dig he is supervising and goes swimming in the azure waters of the sea after the day's work ends. But Mizpah remains his first love, and today he has agreed to show me around the site.

No one digs here anymore. In the mid-1990s, a group of Palestinian students studying archaeology at Bir Zeit University in Ramallah conducted a small dig at the site, clearing out a small church dated to the Byzantine era that Bade had partially uncovered on the southern edges of the mound. Just down the road, students from Al-Quds University, a Palestinian institution in Jerusalem, have been digging at Khirbet Shuweykeh, a Byzantine site. Chronologically speaking, Khirbet Shuweykeh starts to pick up just as Mizpah is starting to fade. It is as if some of the people in Mizpah for whatever reason packed their belongings and moved next door.

This historical convergence has not been lost on archaeologists in Jerusalem and in the West Bank, and there has even been a suggestion made to Israeli and Palestinian officials to run a new dig concurrently at Mizpah and Khirbet Shuweykeh, an international expedition that would include American, Israeli, and Palestinian archaeologists. The project would offer a new avenue for reconstructing the entire history of the area, and for making connections between what went on at Mizpah and at other sites. It might also contribute further to understanding why, and exactly when, Mizpah ceased to be inhabited.

Zorn has been approached about the idea too, but remains skeptical of the likelihood of its success. There is very little money available for new digs, he tells me, especially when large quantities of material from Bade's original expedition still remain unpublished. There are also logistical difficulties involved with securing the necessary approvals and permits from various Israeli and Palestinian officials. Most critically, with Jerusalem's political fate still contested by the two sides, Zorn doubts the Palestinians will be able to work up any enthusiasm for helping to dig up Mizpah, Israel's other ancient capital.

Each time he visits Israel, Zorn says, he drives past the Israeli and Palestinian checkpoints that mark the border between Israel and the West Bank to see how Tell en-Nasbeh is holding up. The tenth-century wall built by King Asa, Rehoboam's grandson, has seen better days. Tell en-Nasbeh lies on a low plateau that is now used for grazing and farming by the local residents. The farmers have rolled huge boulders up against the wall in order to prevent rainwater from rolling down the hill. That's been great for their crops, but not for the wall, which is breaking up in places. Building contractors cause further damage, regularly coming to pillage the site, taking away the massive hewn limestones for use in their own building sites. From the side of the hill closest to the checkpoints, downtown Ramallah can be seen in the distance.

Walking around the site, Zorn explains how the early excavators could have missed the Babylonian remains. The last year of the dig and the first years of the efforts to publish the reports had taken place during the Depression, when funds for publishing archaeology reports were particularly scarce. Then a few of Bade's key assistants were called away for military service in World War II and had to rush to finish their contributions to the reports. The biggest obstacle was simply the lack of knowledge about archaeology. Many of the architectural forms that had jumped out at Zorn when he studied the plans, such as a four-room house and a double casemate wall, weren't so familiar or well known when Bade was digging. The excavators had thought the four-room house was a temple. The rock-cut installations Zorn immediately recognized as winepresses weren't recognizable at all to Bade's team. Olive presses were misidentified. They had thought the Mesopotamian burial tub was a household storage box.

He stops to scour the ground, hoping to find more Mozah seals that may have turned up when the farmers tilled the soil on the mound in the spring. Zorn has done a special laboratory analysis on the clays of the seals already found here, and it indicates that all the jars came from the same source, in the greater Jerusalem area. The distribution of the seals conforms closely to the area designated in the Bible as belonging to the tribe of Benjamin, from Tell en-Nasbeh in the north down to Ramat Rahel outside Jerusalem in the south. He walks to the edge of the hill and points down toward the valley below. Now everything is fields and weeds. There is a concrete parking lot, and some small houses with tin roofs. Today the area looks bleak and unpromising, but during the Babylonian period, this whole area was part of a thriving suburb, practically reaching the outer walls of the city.

The most recent expedition to Mizpah, Zorn says, found Judean and Babylonian artifacts mixed together, an indication that the two peoples lived side by side at the site. The story of Mizpah was one of conquest followed by occupation. The Babylonians had been like most conquerors, determined to remake the city in their own image. "There's no doubt that a strong cultural echo from Mesopotamia can be found in Mizpah," says Zorn. But even more tellingly, Mizpah's architecture largely continued to resemble the architecture of the pre-exilic period. The locals built the city for the Babylonians, and they built using the same styles they had been using for decades all over Judah. Pottery forms also remained close to what they had been beforehand. Despite the military superiority of the Babylonians, the local people and traditions remained remarkably resilient throughout the occupation of the site.

As we walk around the site, Nebuchadnezzar's strategy seems clear. It would have made sense to set up a new capital at Mizpah once Jerusalem was destroyed. Even now, the walls built by Asa are massive. The town's defense system was basically in place, ready for Nebuchadnezzar's men to move in. "Nebuchadnezzar didn't want to spend money or time on fortifications. He had to get Judah running again quickly," says Zorn. "So he just razed the old buildings inside the city and built nicer ones on top." Zorn paused for a moment, listening to the howls of the dogs roaming around the Bedouin camps on the outskirts of the site. "This was Nebuchadnezzar's strategy all the time," Zorn says, a note of admiration creeping into his voice. "Always very practical."

It was strange at first to hear someone talk about Nebuchadnezzar's leadership style in such terms. The digs at Jerusalem and then in Ashkelon, which was destroyed shortly after Nebuchadnezzar came to power because the king refused to offer tribute, illustrated the extent of his wrath when pushed. The Bible also reinforces this perception of Nebuchadnezzar as a recklessly violent leader, cutting a destructive swath through Judah for no other purpose than to harm the people. Lately the ruler's reputation has been rehabilitated. Oded Lipschits, a young Israeli historian, had begun to see Nebuchadnezzar as misunderstood and unappreciated. In the summer of 1998 he was starting to publish his work. Whenever I visited his small office at Tel Aviv University, with its view of the rolling green campus below, Lipschits could be found studying texts about Nebuchadnezzar's rule. He read the history of the period very differently. Unlike many historians, he incorporated into his own work the reports being published by archaeologists about remains from the Babylonian period. He was convinced that Nebuchadnezzar, while violent, had been precise in his use of violence. The army had spared most of Judah and concentrated its efforts on Jerusalem because Nebuchadnezzar realized that Jerusalem was the source of his problems. "He had no intention of ever destroying Judah," Lipschits said one day in his office. "What would be the economic or military benefit of such a move? He wanted Judah to serve as the source of agricultural products that he needed like olive oil and wine, and as a military base in his ongoing campaigns against Egypt. He destroyed what he had to destroy in order to get the stability he needed to achieve his larger goals."

Lipschits felt that the archaeological information that was emerging buttressed his own ideas about Nebuchadnezzar. Starting in the 1990s, archaeologists had begun exploring the Benjamin region, where the Babylonians had set up their capital, Mizpah, in earnest. The findings by Cahill and other archaeologists working under Yigal Shiloh years before in Jerusalem had been the most important indications that, if anything, the destruction of the city had been worse than even the Bible portrayed it. In some of the cities surrounding Jerusalem, the situation had been bleak too. But it wasn't clear to Lipschits that Nebuchadnezzar's army had been responsible for it all. He speculated that cities like Ein Gedi and Jericho might have collapsed simply because they were too small and dependent on Jerusalem to sustain themselves once Jerusalem's extensive economic and administrative structure was no longer in place. Moreover, as the archaeologists got farther away from Jerusalem, an entirely different picture emerged. There was virtually no evidence of any destruction in cities such as Bethel, Tell el-Ful, and Gibeon. Mizpah had been a flourishing city. Zorn, the archaeologist who had discovered the Babylonian layer at the site, argued that the Babylonians had already begun building the city while they were still fighting in Jerusalem. This too reinforced Lipschits's perception that Nebuchadnezzar had been a shrewd military leader. The Babylonians besieged Jerusalem knowing that they were going to destroy the city. The biblical descriptions demonstrate that the Babylonians were determined to insure that the city would not be built again. The temple was burned, the king's palace torn down. The walls of the city were razed, the residents exiled. Mizpah served as the ideal base for their operations. The city's proximity to Jerusalem assured the Babylonians on the front line of a steady stream of military supplies. The region's agricultural abundance allowed the soldiers to camp outside Jerusalem's walls for eighteen months while those inside the city starved.

Many of the archaeologists whom Lipschits had contacted while doing his doctorate had sent him copies of their unpublished materials about excavations. Some had shown him the pottery and other finds they had collected. The material was troubling, and the archaeologists said they weren't sure how to date it. The pottery was close in style to pottery made before the Babylonian exile, but with enough differences that the archaeologists believed it came later. There were also similarities to the later Persian era of pottery, but not enough that the archaeologists felt comfortable categorizing it as Persian. The pottery, from sites and tombs in and around Jerusalem, seemed to fall in between the traditional pre- and postexilic periods. The idea excited Lipschits because it seemed to provide the first material evidence of what life had been like during the years the Babylonians ruled the region.

In October of 1998, Lipschits organized a conference at Tel Aviv University addressing the question of whether there was now enough material to categorize this Neo-Babylonian pottery that fell in a short time span in the sixth century B.C.E. He urged the archaeologists to bring their strange pieces with them. It was the first chance they all had to compare findings. At the conference, Ephraim Stern, a Hebrew University archaeologist recognized as a longtime expert in the period, gave a speech painting the traditional picture of the Babylonians. "The only thing that remains from the Babylonian period are destruction layers," stated Stern. In his opinion, that was because in 587/586 Nebuchadnezzar had come to destroy. "The Babylonians built nothing," Stern concluded.

Lipschits listened quietly to Stern's lecture, but he saw things much differently. He promoted the idea of a moderate, thoughtful Nebuchadnezzar, championing him at speeches and conferences around Israel. The Babylonians had been clever to appoint Gedaliah as the local ruler of Judah after Jerusalem was destroyed, Lipschits told one group that gathered at Hebrew University to hear him lecture. Gedaliah did not belong to the Davidic line, but he came from a prominent Jerusalem family with a long record of political service. He himself had served as a minister in the government prior to the fall of the city. Lipschits argued that Nebuchadnezzar had hoped to create an alternative to the House of David, choosing a serious leader with extensive administrative experience who could be expected to remain loyal to the empire and rebuild Judah into a thriving enterprise. There weren't more remains that could be attributed to the Babylonians simply because they hadn't been around long enough to launch a major architectural overhaul in Judah. And all signs indicated that the nature of their rule tended to favor keeping things the same whenever possible.

This conservative approach wasn't turning up just in pottery, although Lipschits felt that the pottery displayed at the Tel Aviv conference, odds and ends that couldn't be easily categorized because they were so similar to what people had been doing for decades, confirmed his notion. There were also clues in the biblical text itself. When the Babylonians first took over Judah, Lipschits pointed out to me one day, they allowed the king, Jehoiakim, to remain on his throne, despite the fact that he had been appointed to his job by the Egyptians. "I think they figured that anyone willing to accept Egyptian rule for so many years would be willing to accept Babylonian rule too," said Lipschits. He pushed the books about Nebuchadnezzar to one side of his desk for a moment and pulled out a Bible. Quickly, his voice picking up speed as his finger moved along, he summarized the history of Babylonian rule as recorded in the Second Book of

Kings. Nebuchadnezzar had been incredibly patient, Lipschits argued. When Jehoiakim rebelled, his son was allowed to succeed him. The son cut a deal with the Egyptians, so Nebuchadnezzar marched in and removed him from office. But even then, the House of David was allowed to continue in power. Those who were pro-Egyptian were deported to Babylon. The rest were allowed to stay, and Nebuchadnezzar appointed Zedekiah, another king in the Davidic line, to reign. He even left the heads of the previous rebellious administration in place to help out Zedekiah and signal Nebuchadnezzar's willingness to let the people run their own lives. "He hoped that the various measures would keep Judah loyal to him while he fended off the Egyptians," Lipschits argued. "It was a calculated risk."

Judah was small and militarily inferior to Babylonia, but its stability was critical to Nebuchadnezzar because the kingdom shared a border with Egypt, the only power in the region able to challenge Babylonia's hegemony. When Zedekiah and his ministers renewed their contacts with Egypt, Nebuchadnezzar realized that his gamble had failed and he had to act. Jerusalem agitated against Babylonia with the leaders of the neighboring provinces. At Lachish, one of the major cities in Judah, archaeologists had found a text written in ink on a piece of broken pottery describing the arrival of "the commander of the host, Coniah son of Elnathan," who stopped at Lachish on his way to Egypt. Lipschits ascribed great importance to the estimated dating of the letter to the ninth year of Zedekiah's rule, the same year Judah's rebellion against Babylonia began. It provided further confirmation that Zedekiah's government had been in some sort of alliance with the Egyptians. Jerusalem's destruction had not been the result of wanton violence or the impulsive nature of an all-powerful ruler. Babylon wanted to remove the House of David from power because it had proven disloyal time and time again. Jerusalem was targeted for destruction because the city was the only major center of resistance to the Babylonians' continuing rule. "The Bible's writers have a theological explanation for Jerusalem's destruction, but there is a political one as well," said Lipschits. "The city was razed because Judah's leaders made a huge mistake. They were blinded by their messianism. Jerusalem was destroyed because they read the political map incorrectly."

As Nebuchadnezzar has begun to look different, so has the Babylonian Exile. Founded in 1973, the Babylonian Jewry Heritage Center has helped launch a quiet revolution in the way the exile is viewed. Most major research centers tend to open in major cities like Jerusalem and Tel Aviv, but the Babylonian Jewry Heritage Center consciously chose downtown Or Yehuda, a working-class suburb on the outskirts of Tel Aviv. The center is a short drive from an upscale mall that has opened, part of the city's plan to revitalize and attract more affluent residents. Despite its efforts to gentrify, Or Yehuda still sports the drab look of a city built in the 1950s. The apartment buildings take up entire blocks, square, squat, gray buildings whose only splash of color comes from the shirts, towels, and underwear hanging out of the windows to dry in the hot afternoon sun. Israelis flock to Or Yehuda on weekends, filling up the small, family-run restaurants that have sprung up one next to the other. They serve Oriental food, huge chunks of meat and vegetables cooked on skewers, fried balls of chickpeas tucked into pockets of freshly baked flatbread and spread with hot spices, colorful chopped salads that arrive in small white china dishes, all at low prices. Many of the city's residents are immigrants who arrived in Israel from Iraq in the 1950s.

Many Jews from Middle Eastern countries found themselves cast adrift when they arrived in Israel, urged to leave behind their traditional mores and transform themselves into Israelis. The Iraqis were ridiculed for their heavy, Arabic-inflected accents and their "Iraqi pajamas," the long, Arab-style traditional dress still worn in Iraq. Here was a twist on biblical history: this time around, the generation of exiles returning from Babylonia to Palestine weren't treated as the elite. The peasants in Judah were finally having their revenge. The museum's purpose was to instill pride in Iraqi Jewish culture, in the flourishing Jewish community that had sprung up during the exile in Babylonia and continued a thousand years after King Cyrus had given the Judeans the option of returning to Palestine.

At first glance, it seems that despite that mandate, the museum prefers to focus mainly on the Jews' longing for Zion. There are photographs of Zionist youth groups in Baghdad, grainy black-and-white images of youths on nature outings or at the gymnasium. There are pictures and archival material related to the secret Mossad operation, code-named Operation Ezra and Nehemiah, that brought 124,000 Iraqi Jews to Israel over the years 1950–1952. It is as if the curators felt they had to illustrate the famous verses in the Book of Psalms about life for the Jews in Babylon: "By the rivers of Babylon, there we sat down and wept, when we remembered Zion." It is one of the most beautiful poems in the Bible, moody and evocative and filled with longing. Over the years, it has come to form a central part not just of Jewish tradition, but of Western cultural images of exile. Certainly the feelings evoked in that poem express part of what life must have been like in Babylonia for the new arrivals, and yet it was hardly the whole picture, as the rest of the museum bears out.

Even as they emphasize the longing for Zion, the curators couldn't help re-creating an amazing picture of a rich and vital Jewish cultural life that seems to contradict this posture of suffering. Over the 2,600 years that Jews lived in Babylonia, now modern-day Iraq, Baghdad became famous for its centers of Jewish learning, the Nehardea, Sura, and Pumbedita, and for its development of a kind of Jewish government-in-exile that helped sustain a sense of community and ethnic identity. As the darkened corridors of the museum hall, lit only by flickering slides, lead deeper inside the building, a transformation takes place. Grainy black-and-white photos give way to a colorful re-creation of Baghdad street life in the Jewish quarter. The scene bursts with life and vitality. There are goldsmiths and tailors, small craft shops, a butchery, stores selling knickknacks. As visitors wind their way through the scene, it ends in a large airy hall dominated by a re-creation of the Great Synagogue of Baghdad, ornate and grandiose, the synagogue that tradition says was built with ashes taken from the ruins of the destroyed temple in Jerusalem.

The museum's isn't the only new picture of the exilic period now coming to light. Historians have been examining cuneiform records found during digs at former city centers in Babylon and reexamining what exile was like for the Jews there. Some of the new research was presented in the fall of 1998 at a conference sponsored by the Babylonian Heritage Center in honor of Israel's fiftieth anniversary. The Book of Chronicles states that the deportees from Judah were servants in Babylon, but in fact that wasn't the case for most of the exiles. Instead, they obtained land from the state and were considered the king's tenants. Fathers were able to bequeath the land to their sons. Most positions in the empire were open to Jews. Some were engaged in crafts and commerce, others absorbed into huge state projects that paid salaries from the state treasury. Former Judeans even got posts in the imperial administration and rose to senior positions. A huge bureaucracy was needed to run such a far-flung empire. Educated, literate exiles like the ones from Judah were quickly integrated into the civil service.

One of the speakers at the museum conference was Oded Bustenay, a historian at Haifa University who has done considerable scholarly work on Jewish life in Babylon during these time periods. Bustenay carefully studied cuneiform documents that had come to light during excavations at Nippur. These tablets, called the Murashu texts, contained the records of a large Babylonian family banking firm. Although they dated to a later period, about a century after Jews first settled in Babylon, it was clear from the texts that over the years Jews had prospered in agriculture, trade, and finance. Bustenay argued that although too many years had passed ever to determine precisely the status of the exiles, the Murashu texts showed that there was no formal discrimination against the Jews. They made the same kinds of contracts and were charged the same interest rates as any other group. They were not sold as slaves, as the Bible had indicated, but treated as freemen, subject to taxation and draft into the imperial army like everyone else. They were even allowed to keep slaves themselves. Contrary to the impression left by the Bible, Bustenay concluded, the Jews in exile were hardly marginal elements, living on the fringes of Babylonian society. They hadn't needed King Cyrus's edict to empower them. They were already free.

Jerusalem must have looked strange to the first Judeans who returned to the city following Cyrus's edict. Virtually all of those who had been exiled from Judah had died by then, but their children had been nurtured on stories of Jerusalem's beauty. The Babylonians had never rebuilt the city during their rule. Nehemiah, the man who eventually became the governor of the reconstituted province under the Persians, records that he sat down and wept, as if in mourning, when he first heard about the condition of the city from Judeans who had returned there. When the Persians took over, Jerusalem was still a shell of its former glory. And yet, as the archaeologists have continued to explore the city, it seems that even in Jerusalem, amidst the worst of the wreckage of Babylonia's destruction, life went on.

Gabriel Barkay was running a salvage dig at a site named Ketef Hinnom in Hebrew, on the shoulder of the Hinnom Valley below. Near the St. Andrew's Scottish Church, which sits on a knoll that looks toward the Old City, Barkay discovered a series of caves cut into the rocky ridge running right below the church. It turned out that the church's apse was sitting directly over a cave used for several centuries as a burial chamber for wealthy Jerusalem families. Digging out the caves was no easy task. People had buried their dead on top of whatever remains already existed inside, making more room by pushing the bones closest to the door farther in.

From each cave's opening, one had to descend down several steps into the heart of the chamber. On each side of the cave were rock-cut benches that looked like shelves, on which the corpses were laid out after burial. In one cave, raised pillows had been carved out of the rock benches, with headrests and openings for the neck cut into the stone. The bodies had been laid head-to-toe in pairs, fitting neatly inside the rock grooves.

Over the years, tomb robbers had managed to clean out most of the caves of any goods that were buried there, but in what came to be marked as Cave 25, Barkay stumbled upon a treasure. The rock from the cave's ceiling had collapsed, hiding the entrance. A repository located under one of the benches had been blocked from view. Inside that repository was one of the richest finds ever made in a burial tomb in Palestine, over one thousand different objects that had belonged to the more than ninety-five people buried there over two centuries.

The tomb's artifacts showed that the burial cave, probably belonging to several generations of one family, dated from the seventh to the fifth centuries B.C.E. Included among the finds was pottery that excavators soon determined to be typical of the Babylonian period found at other sites around Jerusalem: carrot-shaped bottles, flasks, oil lamps with flat bases, decanters whose bottoms widened out into a sack shape. There were even fragments of a bathtub-shaped clay coffin like the one found at Mizpah, and arrowheads of the type used by the Judeans during the battle against the Babylonians, some of them bent from battle.

To Barkay, it was important enough just to have found evidence that the burial tombs were in use even after Jerusalem had been destroyed. But the relics also showed incredible wealth. There were bone and ivory objects, and small cream-colored glass vases, expensive luxury items that were crafted by hand before the invention of glass-blowing techniques had made glass more widely available. There were more than 250 kinds of pots, gold and silver jewelry, and a pendant decorated with the huge head of a bearded man. Some of the jewelry contained precious rare stones.

The church above the tombs had been erected in 1927 to commemorate the men from the Scottish regiments who had died during General Allenby's campaign to capture Palestine from the Turks during the last days of the crumbling Ottoman Empire. After Allenby captured Jerusalem, a shipowner and church elder from Edinburgh had proposed that a church be built there to serve as a war memorial. Allenby himself laid the foundation stone, which can still be seen outside the church at the corner of the steps that lead inside to the main foyer.

The whole building seemed to be a memorial to the dead. Barkay, just before giving me a tour of the site, sat down in one of the wicker chairs in the foyer. He had deliberately chosen a spot above the tombs of servicemen buried in the church. He gave a wry smile and pointed to the four orange-colored squares beneath his feet, noticeable in an entire floor covered with mud-brown tiles. "Back in the 1930s, one of the wives of the ministers here complained about bad dreams caused by the tombs," Barkay said. "So they resealed everything and marked the tombs with the orange tiles."

There are other ghosts too. Bullet holes from fighting between the Israeli and Jordanian armies in Jerusalem during the 1967 war pit the walls in the building. At the entrance of the church are four flags designating the regiments of the servicemen who fell in battle in World War I. At the rear are memorial plaques listing the names of the dead. On the floor in front of the communion table is a brass plaque that recalls the story of Robert the Bruce of Scotland, who wanted to have his heart buried in Jerusalem. After his death, a knight on one of the Crusades had carried the king's heart in a casket, intending to bury it once he arrived. Instead, the knight was killed en route, in a battle in Spain, and the king's heart had to be returned to Scotland.

The entire site was a reminder of centuries of conflict. Outside, the bells of St. Andrew's began to peal, calling people to prayer. A slight breeze stirred as worshippers made their way slowly up the hill, passing the burial caves on their way to the church. During the days of the Second Temple, Pompey used this area for his encampment opposite the walls of Jerusalem and from here attacked the city. The siege wall with which Titus sealed off the approaches to the city to suppress the First Jewish Revolt in 70 C.E. ran by this hill. One ancient burial cave had been reused as an arms dump and ammunition store by Turks stationed here during World War I, their rifles laid out on the rock-cut burial benches that dead Jerusalemites had once occupied more than two thousand years before. Other caves had been damaged when some of the stones were used to build the road to Bethlehem during the Ottoman period. Each group in turn, it seemed, had scavenged off the dead, reusing stones to build their churches and buildings.

More than any other place in Judah, this resting place of the dead illustrated how life had continued after every calamity and destruction. "I'm not saying that Jerusalem was a flourishing city after the Babylonian destruction. It wasn't," said Barkay. "These are the remains of people living on the fringes of what had once been an important city. But they continued to live here." Jerusalem's size and importance had ebbed and flowed, its fortunes fluctuated, and yet the remains of the dead continued to accumulate. Here on the summit, atop burial caves, surrounded by war memorials to lost soldiers, amid architecture built by people using bits and pieces of the past, the view was very clear. The Bible's writers had acted as if Jerusalem ceased to exist when they were no longer there. But people continued to live under the Babylonians not just in Judah but in villages in neighboring Ammon as well.

Chapter 7

❧

Lot's Children

What Really Happened to the Ammonites

Thus were both the daughters of Lot with child by their father. . . .
And the younger, she also bore a son, and called his name Ben-
Ammi — the same is the father of the children of Ammon unto
this day. *(Genesis 19:36–38)*

In the Bible, Israel has no shortage of enemies. There are the
Amalekites, who try to kill them as they make their way out of
Egypt; the Edomites, who refuse them free passage during their long
trek in the desert; not to mention the Canaanites, the Philistines, the
Perizzites, and the Egyptians, all of whom vex the Israelites in various
ways. The Bible's writers don't like any of them, but they single out the
Ammonites, next-door neighbors and rivals, for special contempt.
According to the Bible, the patriarchs of Ammon and Moab are the
two sons who result from a drunken incestuous union between Lot
and his daughters that occurs in the aftermath of the destruction of
Sodom and Gomorrah. And that's only the beginning. Throughout the
Bible, the prophets continually rebuke the Ammonites for their supposed treachery against the Israelites in the field of battle, predicting
doom and a bitter end if they keep it up. The Ammonites' national

god, Milcom, is described in the Bible as especially bloodthirsty and cruel, possible to appease only through throwing children into a fire. And in a final flourish, readers learn that although the child of inter-marriage between an Israelite and a foreigner can be considered part of the people of Israel by the third generation, the offspring of marriages between Israelites and Ammonites are to be permanently excluded.

Then, suddenly, the Ammonites are gone from the biblical text. After the stories about the Babylonian destruction of Judah, very lit-tle is heard of the Ammonites. There are a few scattered references, then silence as to their fate. For many early biblical scholars, it was puzzling that after looming so large in the minds and imaginations of the Bible's writers, the Ammonites would disappear from the biblical record. But for a variety of reasons, most assumed that Ammon prob-ably shared Judah's fate as described in the Bible, with the Babyloni-ans also destroying Ammon's cities and exiling its people. In the 1930s, the American rabbi and scholar Nelson Glueck traveled to Jor-dan, conducting one of the most extensive explorations of the area around the Dead Sea since the days when nineteenth-century adven-turers tried to penetrate the area dressed in disguise to avoid detec-tion by Bedouin tribes living there. Based mainly on the results of a surface survey of remains rather than in-depth excavation of any of the ruins, Glueck concluded that the Ammonites did in fact cease to exist around the time of the Babylonian destruction of Jerusalem. His conclusions became so widely accepted among scholars that no one raised the prospect that Ammon's history should be considered as being separate from that of Judah. But even before archaeologists and scholars began in the 1990s to reexamine Judah's fate under the Baby-lonians, a group of American scholars were already starting to argue that east of the Jordan River, the story of the Ammonites might turn out to be different after all.

The first clue to the unknown history of the Ammonites turned up in a water reservoir at Tell Hisban. Hisban, known as Heshbon in ancient times, is only a half-hour's drive south of Jordan's capital, Amman, but far off the beaten track for tourists. During their first season of digging, in 1968, the archaeologists uncovered a huge fill near the top of the mound that marked the fifty-acre city. But it wasn't until 1973 that they hit the bottom and realized it was a reservoir. Covered in plaster and able to hold up to two million gallons of water, it was probably built between 1000 and 900 B.C.E., when the town was expanding and the villagers needed more water. Soon afterward, Hisban was largely abandoned, with the reservoir being put back into use only two hundred years later. No one knows why the city was abandoned, or from where the villagers got the water to fill such a large pool in the first place. When the archaeologists discovered it, the reservoir was filled with layer after layer of pottery, dirt, and bricks, the remains of the succession of cities that had existed at the site, been destroyed, and then rebuilt by the next inhabitants over the course of thousands of years. Most interesting to the archaeologists were the hundreds of pieces of broken pottery found among the debris over several seasons from 1968 to 1978. Six of them turned out to be ostraca, pieces of pottery with text written on them.

At first, the specialists examining the writing weren't sure of the language. Until then, very few Ammonite texts had been found. There was an inscription containing eight lines of Ammonite writing discovered on a small bronze bottle on the campus of the University of Jordan. There was also a dedication written on a piece of limestone at the top of the Amman Citadel that dated to the ninth century B.C.E. On that one, the name of the Ammonite god Milcom could be made out, but overall the inscription preserved only ninety-three letters of the Ammonite style of writing, not much to go on for deciphering other texts.

After close examination of the Hisban ostraca, which included photographing the pottery underwater to make the ink stand out more clearly and arduously replacing word breaks between the letters, they could make out the text. Several of the Hisban pieces turned out to be lists of commodities to be used as trade items. The texts had been written in the Ammonite language, but using Aramaic script. This was an important clue for dating the pottery. Like most of the languages of neighboring people, Ammonite script gave way to Aramaic when scribes adopted that language as the common way of communication throughout the empire under the Assyrians. But the shape of these particular letters became common even later, when the Persians ruled the Levant area. That meant that the ostraca at Hisban had been written in the late sixth century — well after the period of Babylonian rule that scholars had assumed ended Ammon's existence.

The notion that the Babylonians conquered the Ammonites is suggested in a history of the period written in the first century C.E. by the Jewish historian Josephus. It also rests in part on a story recounted in the Book of Jeremiah about King Baalis, who ruled Ammon during the early years of the Babylonian Exile of the Judeans. A renegade Judean prince named Ishmael came up with a plan to avenge the House of David and the destroyed temple by killing Gedaliah, the scion of another prominent Judean family who had been installed by the Babylonians as governor of Judah. King Baalis supposedly supported the plan, even giving the rebels refuge in his city after the murder. Josephus wrote that after Gedaliah was murdered, the Babylonians took revenge on the Ammonites for their complicity in the plot and destroyed them.

In the mid-1980s, a dig at Tell Umayri, near Hisban, suggested otherwise. The site had been discovered by a group of archaeologists working with Andrews University, a religious institution associated with the Seventh-Day Adventists, a Protestant evangelical group founded in North America in the mid-nineteenth century. They had arrived first at Hisban in the 1960s, hoping to find signs of the Israelite destruction of ancient Heshbon that was recorded in the biblical story recounting Moses' successful battle against King Sihon, who refused the Israelites safe passage through his territory after their escape from Egypt. When the archaeologists encountered no remains of a major destruction, they launched a regional sweep of the Madaba Plains area, the land east of the Dead Sea running from Amman in the north to Madaba and Tell Jalul in the south. The search turned up four additional candidates all within a six-mile radius of Hisban. The Hisban group renamed itself the Madaba Plains Project in 1982 and over the years undertook digs at all four sites.

Umayri had been one of them. It was located close to Hisban, but much about the site remained a mystery. In the twelfth century B.C.E., there had been a violent destruction at Umayri. The evidence of ruin was everywhere: several feet of debris, burned wooden beams, piles of seeds spilling from broken jars, bricks discolored from fire, even the scattered bones of what turned out to be at least two human beings. No one was sure who had originally built Umayri or who had destroyed it.

At the western edge of the city, three large buildings dominated the area. There were basements in the first two, a rarity for that time period. The basements, the buildings' large size, the thick walls, all indicated that they had been used for administrative purposes rather than as private homes. Adding to that idea was a small seal found in the pit just below the building complex. The seal contained several typical Ammonite names, and was written in Ammonite with the same sixth-century Aramaic script found at Hisban. The archaeologists concluded that based on the location of the seal, the buildings had probably been erected after the Babylonian destruction of Jerusalem.

There was also another important find, a small lump of clay that one of the volunteers had plucked out of the soil that was being sifted near the top of the mound. This was an Ammonite seal showing a winged scarab beetle with sun discs, crescent moons, and Ammonite letters surrounding it, all well-known royal symbols. In the first line of the seal, the name of its owner could be made out: Milcom'ur, a form of the name of the national deity of the Ammonites. Other lines on the seal indicated that its owner was a high official of a king named Baalyasha, believed to be a slight linguistic variation on the Baalis mentioned in Jeremiah. This too seemed to confirm the idea that the buildings were remnants of an Ammonite bureaucracy, one that had continued to function even after the Babylonians destroyed parts of Judah.

Oystein LaBianca, the head of the Hisban dig, thinks he knows how the Ammonites found a way to survive. Back in 1968, after graduating from college, he headed to the Middle East. He hiked through Jordan, even spending a night in a cave at Petra, the fabled city of the Nabateans cut from the red rock of southern Jordan. He ended up joining the first expedition at Hisban, headed then by Siegfried Horn, a professor of theology at Andrews. LaBianca had immigrated to the United States from Norway when he was thirteen. He liked to tell people that he was descended from the Vikings.

At the time, he hadn't thought much about the night he spent in the cave in Petra, but later it came to form a key part of his ideas about the Ammonites and the ancient history of Jordan. In a group where most of the men have short, tidy hair and neatly trimmed beards, LaBianca is the closest thing to an Adventist hippie. His blond hair is unruly. He is always late to meetings. Not long ago, on the night before a major celebration that he was running to commemorate thirty years of digging at Hisban, he suddenly realized he had no more clean shirts to wear. He got up at 3 A.M. and handwashed them in the moonlight. Later, he kept the president of Andrews, where he works as an anthropology professor, waiting an hour in the car for a luncheon while he got dressed.

Over the years, LaBianca has developed a theory about what he calls "indigenous hardiness structures," or in simpler terms, survival strategies that he contends enabled the local population to adapt to any number of uncertainties and changes. The Ammonites survived, he says, because of a strong sense of tribalism, organizing themselves by clans and powerful families. The political situation in the ancient world changed quickly, so people were always ready to move on, switching easily between living in caves, tents, and houses depending on the circumstances, not to mention the weather. They relied on small-scale water collection for farming rather than risk the construction of an elaborate water system, and they ate home-grown foods instead of those brought in from foreign markets. Kings came and went, so they had learned to rely on themselves and not to expect too much from a central government. They developed a culture of hospitality that created a network of sharing favors and information, and an emphasis on personal honor in order to assure that individuals and families didn't shirk their responsibilities to each other.

LaBianca's night in the cave in Petra has come to symbolize for him how the locals really lived, as well as their ingenuity and ability to adapt to whatever change came their way. At Hisban, for instance, the archaeologists were surprised that there were a number of time periods for which they found no pottery or architecture on the mound and during which it appeared no one had been living at the site. But additional work eventually turned up an entire underground network of caves honeycombed under and around the main site, and they had been in use throughout the city's history. In fact, elaborate cave villages had sprung up around Jordan during different periods. Amman began as one, eventually expanding into a metropolis. And during the Ottoman period, when taxes were high, there were only three towns in all of Jordan listed in the official tax collection records: Husn, Salt, and Kerak. Unrecorded and unmentioned were the hundreds of cave villages throughout the country during the same period, including one at Hisban, whose residents spent most of the years of Ottoman rule living underground in order to avoid tax collectors.

For the Madaba Plains archaeologists, one of the biggest appeals of searching for the Ammonites has been the realization that the culture and lifestyle described in the Bible can actually be seen much more clearly in Jordan than in Israel. Over the years, Israel has shifted away from an agriculture-based economy. Huge swaths of biblical landscape have been taken over by new housing projects and even bigger highways. The Israelis have established biblical parks (one is called Genesis Land) in an effort to re-create for tourists as well as Israelis what ancient life was actually like. There, actors dressed in traditional garb bake flatbread over a fire, press olives in a stone olive press, make pottery on an ancient wheel. In Jordan, there is no need to go to a park to see these things. The continuity between the traditional lifestyle still followed in many villages and the one emerging in the study of the Ammonite sites is remarkable.

In a 1997 book produced for a popular audience, the Madaba archaeologists purposefully keep switching between the lives of the ancient Ammonites and those of modern Jordanians. They show how many aspects of life in modern Jordan — from concerns about agriculture to the way homes are built, the daily diet, even the emphasis on hospitality — have their roots in life four thousand years ago. "The ancient Ammonites," the authors write, "are the ancestors not only of modern Jordanians but in many ways of all of us."

This is a nice notion, but even so until recently most Arab countries did not encourage the study of their countries' histories prior to the Islamic period, which began in Jordan in 636 C.E. with the Muslim victory in the Battle of Yarmuk. There was a trend, especially among the Arab elite, to discount the creation of the modern Arab states, which had mainly emerged as the European colonial powers, primarily Britain and France, divided up the region, sometimes arbitrarily setting borders. By the 1980s, this attitude had slowly started to change. The new borders, not to mention the Arab leaders in charge of them, proved more resilient than most people had originally suspected. Arab governments, seeking to shore up national secular identity against a rising tide of Islamic fundamentalism, began emphasizing the connections between the ancient and present occupants of the land.

The Maronite Christians started promoting the notion that the modern Lebanese were the descendants of the seafaring Phoenicians. Turkey invested huge funds in preserving monuments built by the Hittites. The Shah of Iran held a grandiose fiftieth birthday party for himself in the city that had served as the ancient capital of the Persian empire under King Cyrus. Saddam Hussein sank millions into a project to rebuild the ancient city of Babylon. He even had special bricks made stamped with a likeness of himself and a proclamation declaring himself the new Nebuchadnezzar. There were some signs of change in Jordan too. The Jordanian government began making an effort to promote its ancient archaeological sites both at home and abroad, launching a series of public service announcements on television urging people to protect and visit the country's antiquities. Al Kutba Publishers, run by a Jordanian journalist named Rami Khouri, published six small guidebooks and two children's books in Arabic about Jordan's past and even more titles in English. By 1998 Khouri was working on a book that would list every site in the Hebrew Bible, the New Testament, and the Koran that had a link to Jordan.

Still, many Jordanians haven't exactly embraced the Ammonites, as became evident at a conference devoted to the history and archaeology of Jordan held in Copenhagen in June 1998. Dr. Osamah Abu-Qorah, curator of the archaeological and heritage museum at the University of Jordan, chairman of the school's archaeology department, and a professor of biblical archaeology, stood up to give a speech about the Jordanian perspective on the Bible. It was a moving moment. Here was a Jordanian scholar addressing a forum of Americans, Europeans, Jordanians, and Palestinians, all archaeologists and scholars interested in reconstructing the ancient history of Jordan. He had a chance to articulate for the first time the emerging Jordanian vision of this history.

Dressed in a conservative business suit, his face sweating a little, he gave a broad outline of the controversies surrounding the history of the Israelites, recounting some of the theories involving the Israelites' entry into Canaan from Jordan. But the theories were all well known in the literature of fifteen years ago. He didn't incorporate any of the new finds regarding the Ammonites, Moabites, or Edomites being done right in his own backyard. In fact, he seemed to ignore them.

"The Hebrews and the Israelites constituted part of Jordan's population in ancient time," he concluded. "Their social, ethnic, linguistic, and religious history is one of the most important highlights in the region, and concerns us in Jordan."

Later, some of the others attending the conference tried to figure out the motivations for the speech. Was it due to a lack of access to the latest data and information? A fear of saying anything too political or controversial at a time when things seemed so uncertain in the region? Whatever the reason, among the archaeologists who had been working so hard to bring the Ammonites and their history to the attention of Jordanians, there was a sense of disappointment. Abu-Qorah had had a unique chance to claim the Ammonites as Jordan's own. Instead he seemed to prefer the Israelites.

In his column in the English-language *Jordan Times,* Rami Khouri often writes about the link between Jordan's modern identity and its past. In the archaeological record of the architecture of Petra, the art of Umayyad castles, the deities of the Ammonite, Edomite, and Moabite kingdoms, Khouri sees, he has said, "evidence . . . of long traditions of religious faith, cultural pluralism, trading contacts with other economies, and, most dramatically, a willingess to interact in peace with other cultures and absorb from those cultures some of their most positive dimensions."

Leen Fakhoury, a professor of architecture at the University of Jordan and the president of the Friends of Archaeology Society, which lobbies for the preservation of antiquities, has worked hard to bring Jordan's past to the public. Her office is covered with posters, maps, bulletin boards announcing field trips to various sites, and pictures of past events. Young and attractive, with hair down to her shoulders and wearing a hip black trouser suit and expensive jewelry, she seems far removed from the Ammonites but still sees a connection between herself and them. "The Ammonites aren't a living entity in my mind," she said one afternoon. "But the partnership I feel with them is [one of] sharing the same place. I look at how they used it, and how I am using it. When the Ammonites were here, they had a specific economic, political, and social situation. We are still relics of this."

Yet even those who show interest are hard-pressed to find a way to see Ammonite culture. The main center is at the Amman Citadel Museum, located on the hill that most archaeologists agree was the capital of ancient Ammon. Behind the building is the domed entrance hall of the Umayyad Palace Complex, dating to the eighth century C.E. There is a public area, reservoir, and plaza, and a square with steps leading to a large mosque. Outside the museum entrance stand impressive Roman columns, the remains of the Roman occupation of the city. Visitors can walk through the columns and see downtown Amman, watching the roll and sweep of the small hills that now mark various Amman neighborhoods and serve as points of reference for the locals when they are giving directions.

While it's true that the Citadel Museum is probably Jordan's premier archaeological museum, that isn't saying much. The Jordanians had housed their most important archaeological find, the Dead Sea Scrolls, in the Palestine Archaeological Museum, more popularly known today as the Rockefeller Museum, in the eastern half of Jerusalem. When the 1967 Arab-Israeli war broke out, the Jordanians hastily made plans to move the scrolls to Amman for safekeeping. They weren't fast enough. The Israelis captured east Jerusalem in the last days of the fighting, and along with it the scrolls and the museum.

Despite the beautiful view from outside the Citadel Museum, things are disheartening inside. There are few visitors, and the ones who make their way around the small hall are primarily foreigners. An elderly woman can often be seen moving up and down the aisles with a mop and bucket, her shoes making a clicking sound as she washes the brown tiles. The display cases are poorly marked. Most of the important Ammonite finds aren't even on display but stored in boxes downstairs or at the Department of Antiquities office in Amman. But more than thirty statues found over the years in the vicinity of Amman are in the Citadel Museum. They are remarkable works, double-faced limestone heads, gnomelike creatures, some of the eyes inlaid with beads. A few are inscribed with Aramaic letters. During the 1998 season, the archaeologists at Umayri found fragments of several more statues. None of the pieces seemed to fit with any of the others, but even taken separately they revealed how spectacular the artwork had been. There was a large eye, a chin and mouth with a painted beard or tattoo, and other parts of the body, including a shoulder, a heel, arms, and legs. Taken together, the statues and fragments are probably the most important evidence of just how advanced Ammonite culture actually was; there is no comparable artwork known among the Israelites during the same period. But those who aren't familiar with Ammonite history find it difficult to understand the significance of the work in front of them. The signs are cursory and stilted. There is a musty, old-fashioned air to the entire museum.

The museum is a reflection of the tentative approach many Jordanians have to their own history. In the fall of 1998 the first National Cultural Heritage Week was launched by the Friends of Archaeology. On the opening day, the mayor led a walk through downtown Amman that started from the Citadel Museum, wound its way through the city streets, and ended up at a special exhibition of Jordan's antiquities in the gleaming white Amman Municipal Hall. The idea was to show the continuity between the past and the present, the site of ancient Amman and what it has become.

It was an uphill battle. Only 150 people showed up for the walk. The exhibition, which included pictures of various excavations, a display of children's artwork, and live demonstrations on how to make mosaics, attracted mainly schoolchildren and representatives from foreign organizations. Toward the end of the week, a play was held downtown called *Al-Da'ira* (The Circle). It used the legend of the two Canaanite forces of fertility, Ba'al and Asherah, to illustrate how drawing upon the resources of cultural heritage can offer a solution to modern-day problems. It too was poorly attended.

That week, sitting in her comfortable home in a fashionable Amman neighborhood, Kathy Sullivan, the head of the education committee of the Friends of Archaeology and one of the prime movers behind the festival, was trying to figure out how to get the message across. She had persuaded the hostess of a popular television program called *Whaqt Al Farah* (Times of Happiness) to publicize the children's art exhibition. One of Sullivan's ideas had been to dress up one of the children as a Roman soldier and have him talk about life in Amman during this period. She planned to give the child an artifact to display on the show, the head of Tyche, who was the goddess of Amman during the Roman occupation. Sullivan recalled that the television hostess had been reluctant to show the head, saying, "I don't want anybody to call up and complain about portraying the kids like gods, and I don't want to confuse the children that there were several gods." She had received a similar reaction from people who saw the poster that she had prepared to mark the heritage week. She had used a picture of a Roman head on the poster. "Some people said it was nice, but asked me why I didn't use something Jordanian," Sullivan recalled. "I said it is Jordanian. Jordan was influenced by so many peoples and cultures that were here throughout the years. But they said, 'This is not our heritage.'"

To Sullivan, this was part of the problem. Jordanians knew about Arab history and Islam, but virtually nothing about the Ammonites, the Nabateans, or the Romans. They were all viewed as foreigners, not integral parts of Jordan's history. The same arguments had been raised about the influx of fast food chains and even the Internet. Yet the latest archaeological discoveries were showing that the Ammonites had survived for so long because they had been open to outside cultural influences and trade with their neighbors, always finding a way to adapt these things to their own circumstances.

Sullivan, chatty and friendly, grew even more animated as she drew the connection. "The lesson is that you can use these things that came from outside your area or your native culture without losing who you are," she said. "I think they should feel proud of the people who came before them and how resourceful they were. They should feel that this strength is something inherited."

How did the Ammonites do it? How did they manage to survive the upheaval in neighboring Judah, and their own leader's role in the ensuing political chaos? Even as digging at Umayri proceeds, other members of the team are combing the hillsides in the hope of understanding what role Umayri played in the wider area. Dotting the surrounding countryside are more than seventy ancient farmsteads, all built in the monumental architectural style that seems to reflect government patronage. Each of the farmsteads contains one or more winepresses, a water cistern or two, and one or more caves around the main building that could have been used for storage. Virtually all of them were built in the same time period, the mid-sixth century B.C.E., when the Babylonians ruled in Judah.

In his summary of the finds published in the 1990s in the Jordanian Antiquities Department's annual survey, Larry Herr, director of the Umayri dig, suggests that these farms may provide a possible explanation for how the Ammonites managed to escape Babylon's wrath. The Ammonite monarchy sponsored the construction of these grape plantations, complete with winepresses and all the equipment necessary to produce wine, in order to pay tribute to Babylon, Herr writes. Umayri served as the nerve center, where the production, collection, and shipping of the wine took place. Royal administrative seals have been unearthed at the site, and many record the sale, storage, and shipment of wine to Babylon and other destinations.

The Babylonians destroyed where they couldn't compromise, but they preferred compromise. Jerusalem's constant rebellions, the unending machinations by a group of conspirators bent on restoring the House of David to power, left Babylon no option. Ammon's willingness to pay taxes and supply wine and other goods that were necessary to an expanding empire, provided a different route. The Babylonians, Herr contends, were willing to make a deal. The Ammonites, ever practical and resourceful, were too.

The archaeologists digging in Ammon still aren't sure what ultimately did the Ammonites in, but they now agree that Ammon reached the apex of its cultural achievements under the Assyrians and then the Babylonians. Apparently the Ammonites continued to survive even under the Persians, who became the region's superpower after Babylon weakened. Dealing with empires, trading with outsiders, was good for Ammon.

Ammon's continuing contact with the outside world is illustrated mainly by two additional seal impressions found in one of Umayri's administrative buildings. They are stamped onto the handles of jars. There are no intricate royal symbols or pictures of scarab beetles like the ones embellishing the earlier seals turned up at the site. The letters are large and crudely shaped, the script dating to the time of the Persians.

The seals are difficult to read, but Herr is convinced that the first three letters are part of a typical Ammonite nickname, Shuba, short for Shub'el. The next word consists of three consonants of the national name Ammon. Herr recently spent a year working at the William F. Albright Institute for Archaeology in Jerusalem, and he was struck by the similarity between the Umayri seals and the so-called Yehud seals, which got their title from the Persian name for the province of Judah. The Yehud seals, used on Judean jars as a marker in the Persian provincial tax system, are written in the same Aramaic script as the Shuba seals. Herr theorizes that the Shuba seals are the Ammonite version of Yehud seals.

Here was LaBianca's hardiness principle in action thousands of years ago, as the Ammonites made an almost seamless transition from running their own show to living under the mercurial Babylonians and then the Persians. The Shuba seals were found in the same administrative complex at Umayri that had housed the Ammonite monarchy that produced the Milcom'ur seal. These buildings had undergone only minor architectural additions between the time of the Ammonite kings and the time Shuba was collecting taxes for the Persian empire almost a hundred years later. And the jars on which the Shuba seals were stamped contained goods that the Persians collected as taxes. One of those goods had probably been wine, the same thing the Ammonite kings geared up to produce in the farmsteads around Umayri in order to keep the Babylonians at bay. The Ammonites had found a way to survive. Life went on, pretty much as it always had.

At Hisban, it hasn't been easy trying to find a way to make the entire sweep of this unusual history relevant to the villagers. At one point,

LaBianca had signs prepared and installed throughout the site, explaining to tourists and villagers what they were seeing. But the next summer when he came back to dig, all the signs had been destroyed. "I learned my lesson after that," he told me recently.

He approached the mayor and asked if there was someone in the village who spoke English well and might be willing to work as a liaison between the village and the dig. The mayor appointed the local schoolteacher, Mafouz Abdul Hafez, a Palestinian refugee from the West Bank who had moved to Hisban after the 1967 Arab-Israeli war.

The two men hit it off. Abdul Hafez explained that the signs had been made of plastic and that the village teenagers liked to come down to the site and pick them apart for fun. So their first project was to put up new signs. This time, Abdul Hafez organized a group of villagers to cut huge pieces of wood and paint them brown. They constructed a time line in Arabic and in English to greet visitors to the village and explain the whole history of Hisban, from its beginning as a "traditional Amorite stronghold," where the Bible says Moses and the Israelites fought the powerful King Sihon, through the Ammonites, right up to its present-day incarnation as the home of the Ajarmeh tribe. Other signs explained basic archaeology terms. A huge pile of broken jars and handles was left there for the teenagers to pick up. Someone even drew a map of the entire site on one sign showing the various periods and what had been uncovered from each one.

The next step was to try to turn Hisban into an open-air classroom. A twelve-week lesson plan was proposed, each lesson designed to teach the students about archaeology — what tools archaeologists use, and the various techniques they apply to try to figure out a site's history — as well as to convey information about the many different groups that have lived in the city over time.

The curriculum LaBianca, Abdul Hafez, and a few others produced, which is still being reviewed by the various Jordanian ministries, reflects some of the dilemmas that arise whenever the Ammonites, and hence the Bible, come up. Despite the site's importance in helping unravel the history of the Ammonites, the curriculum touches on them only briefly. The notion that Hisban is a former Amorite stronghold, while prominently displayed on the signs for tourists, isn't mentioned at all, in part because LaBianca himself says he's not so sure that the biblical confrontation between Moses and King Sihon even took place at Heshbon. Instead, the curriculum emphasizes the site's Islamic history, and the relationship of its modern inhabitants to the ancient ones, no surprise given the fact that the Ajarmeh tribe is Muslim. But part of LaBianca's personal journey from focusing on biblical Heshbon to looking at the sweep of history that resulted in modern Hisban has meant letting Hisban determine how to remember Heshbon, and that isn't always such a simple matter.

While I am there, Hisban's mayor, Yousef Msalam al Awalda, comes to check on preparations for the thirtieth-anniversary party for excavations at the site. A mercurial man, he has been boycotting the dig for nearly a week, angry over LaBianca's insistence on choosing the people who will be responsible for various aspects of the celebration rather than leaving it to the mayor. Stopping briefly to talk, the mayor doesn't seem all that interested in Ammonites. "I'm not aware that there are any biblical connections to Hisban," he demurs. Instead, he launches into a convoluted history of the linguistic variations in the name Hisban over the years. Does he feel any connection with the ancient Ammonites who once lived here? "Of course I do," he answers. "They are the first ones here and we are the second ones. We're part of history. As the Koran says, 'We have found our fathers, and we will follow in their footsteps.'"

The mayor would probably be stunned to learn the history of those fathers that the archaeologists have been uncovering. In a report about the 1998 season in Jordan, Herr, LaBianca, and two other archaeologists note the strong similarities of the material culture at Umayri and Hisban with finds in the highlands of Cisjordan, north of Jerusalem. The same type of pottery has been found at a number of sites associated with Israelites in Canaan, including Shechem, Itzbet Sartah, and Taanach. The architecture is similar too. A seal and a potter's mark found at Mount Ebal, outside Nablus, are identical to two found at Umayri, all on the upper handles of collared jars. "Every early Iron I site in the northern hills has a pottery assemblage very similar to ours," Herr says. This has not been the case with sites in Transjordan. "So far the parallels with sites in Transjordan, most of which seem to be [established] later . . . are not strong," the report states. Herr believes that the people who eventually became the Ammonites may originally have been members of the biblical tribe of Reuben, the firstborn son of Jacob and Leah. The Bible scholar Frank Moore Cross pointed out that, despite the changes over the years in many of the stories, the tribe of Reuben is always listed in the Bible as the firstborn of Jacob in Israelite genealogies. Since these genealogies tended to represent the development of tribes, Cross argued, the tribe of Reuben must have been the first of the groups later composing Israel to achieve a measure of success. Herr concurs. For Herr, the idea that Umayri began as a Reubenite settlement fits nicely with his religious conviction that the Bible's account of tribes moving into Canaan from east of the Jordan River has a historical basis. If true, it also provides a richer history of the Ammonites than the one the Bible imparts.

Reuben's history is complex. The biblical text conveys an inconsistent view of Reuben. After Rachel, Jacob's preferred wife, dies, Reuben has sexual relations with her slave, his father's concubine. This is seen as an attempt by Reuben to challenge his father's authority, an act upon which the Bible's writers frown. But in the Joseph story, Reuben is portrayed in a better light. He is the one who attempts to save Joseph when his other brothers want to kill him out of jealousy for his favored status with their father. Later, after the Israelites enter Canaan, Reuben's tribe asks to be allowed to remain in Transjordan. The tribe is assigned territory there. Then Reuben, like the Ammonites, seems to disappear from the historical record. In the Mesha inscription, written in the ninth century by the king of Moab, the tribe of Gad is described as having dwelt in the area, but there is no mention of Reuben.

Hisban's mayor will never read the excavation report, which appeared in an Andrews University journal, but it is probably just as well. Just after the digging at Hisban began, the archaeologists convinced the Ministry of Public Works to put up road signs to the site in the hope of attracting more tourists, who generally bypassed the village in favor of trips to Petra or the Roman-era Jerash. There was much back-and-forth between the two sides over the wording for the signs, but finally everyone agreed: Hisban, Ancient Biblical and Islamic Heritage Site. The signs went up and in between them sprang up the lively side-of-the-road commerce that is so ubiquitous in Jordan. There were small stands selling freshly brewed Arabic coffee, the owners resting in the shade of the trees with only the huge brass spouts of the coffeepots visible on the side of the road; and Egyptian potters in traditional Arab dress, waiting patiently in the breakdown lane for customers, their distinctive white-and-pinkish pottery in hundreds of shapes and sizes winking at the cars driving by.

In the village, there were complaints, first to the mayor, who then brought them to the attention of the ministry. It was about a year after the June 1996 election of Benjamin Netanyahu as Israel's prime minister. The peace process had stalled and the signs became a strange focal point for the growing frustration. The problem was that there had been no good way to translate the word "biblical" into Arabic. The Arabic word for the Bible is "the book," but that wasn't quite right. So the ministry chose to invent a word instead, "Torahonic," from the Torah, or Hebrew Bible. Hisban, Ancient Torahonic and Islamic Heritage Site, is what the signs actually read.

To the locals, "Torahonic" could mean only one thing: Israelis. If Hisban is an Israeli site, people asked in complaints that began flooding the ministry, then what's to stop the Israelis from trying to take the site back? "There was talk about Israel invading Jordan to conquer Hisban," says LaBianca. "There was concern that somehow those signs affirmed the presence of Israelites in the region."

LaBianca argued that Western tourists would be particularly interested in Hisban's biblical connection. The ministry wouldn't budge. "Torahonic" had to go. Then the archaeologists came up with a compromise. Why not call Hisban an ancient Ammonite site? "Not many

Jordanians know who the Ammonites are," says LaBianca. "But they know they weren't Israelites."

So the old signs came down and new ones went up: Hisban, Ancient Ammonite and Islamic Heritage Site. Tensions eased, the controversy passed. Even the archaeologists were pleased. The Ammonites may have disappeared from the Bible, they thought, but at least they had a place on Jordan's highway signs. Except even here, the Ammonites didn't quite get what was due them. The villagers in the area love to use the sign to hang handmade posters announcing weddings or giving directions to family celebrations. In just a short time, the lettering in the word "Ammonite" was scratched and faded, making it hard to read.

Today at least, though, the Ammonites are back on center stage. Hundreds of people have gathered at Hisban for the celebration. There are two large white tents placed on the edge of the site for refreshments. Later in the day, there will be a tour of the dig. The visitors will walk in small groups and look at the reservoir. They will see the remains of the military fort built by the Greeks on the mound's summit, and hear how armor scales, stones for slingshots, and arrowheads were all found inside it. They will be shown the small Roman temple on the summit. Under the Byzantines, Hisban had two churches with beautiful mosaic floors and its own bishop. Later, the Muslims who conquered the site built a small inn within the Roman and Byzantine remains. The city's governor during that time even added a bath with running hot and cold water, with a view of all that was happening in the city and surrounding countryside, not to mention the coolest, most refreshing breezes. On a clear day, the governor would have been able to make out Mount Nebo's peak in the distance.

For now, the sun is unrelenting and people sit in white plastic chairs that have been set up inside the ancient amphitheater, the site of a temple during the Roman period, a church under the Byzantines, a mosque under the Muslims. The choice of locations is intentional, a further illustration of how each succeeding group built on the remains of the ones who came before.

A member of the royal family, Prince Raad, has arrived, sporting a jaunty black cap and a white short-sleeved shirt. The speeches begin, with everyone eager to say a few words. The prince, the tourism minister, the head of the Department of Antiquities, the Hisban parliamentary representative, the mayor — all take turns at the microphone. The audience sits patiently in the intense heat as boys from the village dart in and out of the rows of chairs, passing out cold glass bottles of Pepsi. When it is LaBianca's turn, he takes the audience step by step through Hisban's long history, pointing to the water reservoir constructed by the Ammonites and other sites in chronological order, right up through the Roman temple on top of the mound. "Hisban is a classroom in which we meet the people who made the history of the world," he tells the audience.

The Bible is another history of that world. It is well known that the Bible castigates the Ammonites mercilessly for the battles they fought against the Israelites. It is even written that they may never be accepted as converts into the congregation of Israel, supposedly because they stood idly by while the Babylonians destroyed Jerusalem. But there is a small story in the Bible that is usually overlooked. When Jerusalem was destroyed, when the Babylonians ran rampant through Judah, the Bible says, many Judeans crossed the Jordan River and found sanctuary among the Ammonites. So despite the way they are described in the Bible, there was once a sense of kinship, however distant, and a recognition of a common fate. The Ammonites had been willing to take a chance and open their borders to the outside world, despite the dangers involved. It turns out that Ammon was not always Israel's enemy; it was also a place of refuge during a time of upheaval. Our view of ancient Israel's relationship with Edom is undergoing a similar transformation.

Chapter 8

❧

Esau's Birthright

A New Look at the Edomites

And Jacob sod pottage and Esau came in from the field, and he was
faint. And Esau said to Jacob: "Let me swallow, I pray thee, some of
this red, red pottage; for I am faint." Therefore was his name called
Edom [red]. And Jacob said, "Sell me first thy birthright." *(Genesis
25: 29–31)*

While the Scriptures treat the Ammonites with unremitting
contempt, the feelings they express about the Edomites,
the Israelites' neighbors in southern Jordan, are much
more complex. Like all the tribes in the region, the Israelites and the
Edomites share a long history. Over the course of hundreds of years,
they try to conquer each other and often find themselves competing
for the best access to important trade routes. Despite the ongoing tensions, the Bible admonishes the Israelites, "You shall not abhor an
Edomite, for he is your brother." Curiously, most of the prophets
ignore this prohibition, calling down some of their harshest predic-
tions of hail and brimstone on the heads of the hapless Edomites. For
years, Bible scholars have debated the source of the prophets' anger.
Many speculated that it reflected a sharp sense of betrayal resulting from some unnamed Edomite perfidy. Edom's actions stung all

the more, this theory suggests, because Esau, the patriarch of the Edomites, was Jacob's twin brother.

What exactly the Edomites might have done, though, is never made clear in the biblical text. Take the story about Jacob and Esau, twin sons of Isaac and his wife Rebecca. They are portrayed as always fighting. They fight in the womb over who is going to be born first, and Esau emerges with Jacob's hand wrapped around his ankle. They fight over the all-important birthright of the firstborn son, which Jacob eventually wins through deceit, his mother's timely assistance, and the fact that the dying Isaac is too blind to see which son stands before him demanding a blessing. All this certainly explains why Esau, and his descendants, might harbor ill will toward Jacob and Jacob's descendants, and yet the story doesn't permit such an interpretation. Jacob and Esau, after years of not seeing each other, eventually meet up again. Jacob expects war, and comes offering gifts, hoping to placate Esau. Instead, Esau greets him warmly, says he's prospered since they last met, and the two part on friendly, if not brotherly, terms.

Even the books of the prophets are vague about what exactly Edom's transgression is. Some scholars, using various prophecies that appear in Jeremiah and elsewhere, have speculated that Edom may have been militarily active against Judah in the Negev, the desert area bordering Judah and Edom in the south, when Nebuchadnezzar attacked Jerusalem in 587/586 B.C.E. after Judah's king Zedekiah openly rebelled. The prophets don't explicitly state this, focusing more on Edom's inaction in the face of Jerusalem's plight under the Babylonians, and the Edomites' gloating and rejoicing when Jerusalem finally fell. Still, the military domination theory has persisted. In addition to the biblical texts, supporters of this theory point to some letters found written on pottery shards at an archaeological site in Arad, in southern Israel. Some historians contend that these letters, alluding to an Edomite threat, support the idea that the Edomites, taking advantage of Judah's weakness at the time of the Babylonian military campaigns, invaded and possibly conquered at least part of the Negev.

Indeed, the archaeological work done in the Negev in the past few years has turned up a wealth of pottery and religious objects traditionally associated with the Edomites, who at the very least cast a long cultural shadow there in the seventh and sixth centuries B.C.E. This is also the period during which, Bible scholars believe, the Jacob and Esau traditions were either written or revised to show some sort of kinship between Judah and Edom.

But what kind of relationship was it? At Qitmit and Tel Malhata, two sites in the Negev, excavations by a Tel Aviv University archaeologist, Itzhaq Beit-Arieh, produced beautiful painted pottery that closely resembles finds in Edom, cooking pots in the so-called Edomite style, and inscriptions bearing the name of the deity Qos. Qos is usually considered the national deity of the Edomites, although other groups possibly worshipped this god as well. Beit-Arieh himself believes that these finds fit a picture of military domination. "The Judean kingdom would not have permitted the Edomites to live and worship in the Negev or to build shrines to their god," says Beit-Arieh. The finds, combined with the indications of hostility in both the Bible and the Arad texts, complement the traditional picture of Edomite military invasion in the area, he argues.

But recently a new interpretation has been offered by a group of archaeologists and historians who have examined the Qitmit and Malhata materials as well as work being done in Jordan. Such reevaluation is common in archaeology, in part because the dating of pottery, which often provides the foundation for interpretations of material remains, is an inexact science. In the case of the Edomites, though, this situation is intensified by the fact that so much about their history remains hazy and incomplete, even by the standards of ancient history. Edom lay on the agricultural and political margins of Transjordan. Archaeological surveys of the remains of settlements indicate that Edom was probably settled later than Ammon and Moab, and never as densely. Even at the height of Edom's power, in the seventh and sixth centuries B.C.E., the only full-blown city that existed was Buseirah, which probably served as the capital. The rest of the sites are small encampments and villages.

There is no artwork that parallels that of the masterful Ammonite statues, or literature that has been found comparable to the Hebrew Bible. This was not an urban society so much as a collection of tribes who for a time were held together under a loose administrative umbrella.

And yet the Edomites did have some material advantages, which Assyria was able to exploit, starting in 734 B.C.E. after Tiglath-pileser III turned Edom into a vassal state, and intensifying in the seventh century. Edom held some of the region's richest copper deposits, far more extensive and significant than those supporting the Timna mines in Israel during the same period. Recent archaeological surveys indicate that Feinan, 25 miles south of the Dead Sea, was the most important mining center of its day, the heart of a vast trading network that extended throughout the Mediterranean basin. Edom also sat on the all-important Arabian trade route that ran through the Beersheba Valley and connected Arabia and Transjordan with the Mediterranean at Gaza. This route zigzagged its way through the Negev desert and the ever-changing swath of no-man's-land where Bedouins, Egyptians, Judeans, Edomites, and Assyrians all met to trade, deal, and exchange information. Desert shrines were set up where traders of various religions and nationalities could pray and make offerings to their deities as they traveled back and forth through the harsh desert. The Edomites did have a strong influence in the Negev at this time, but it was commercial and cultural more than military, the new interpretation contends.

This idea casts a new light on the Bible as well. Against the political backdrop of the seventh century, the prophets' harsh words reflected the intense jealousy that Judah must have harbored of Edom's prosperity during this period. This was a time of competition and jockeying for power. The Judeans feared economic domination by Edom, which continued to benefit and expand with the backing of its superpower patron Assyria. Even the tale of Esau and Jacob reads somewhat differently when viewed in this light. Business motifs run through the story. Jacob is described as the quieter of the two brothers. He prefers strategizing in his tent, the precursor to today's lawyer or investment banker, while his brother Esau is a workingman, out in the fields hunting and producing food. The most famous scene in their relationship involves quite literally a buyout, when Jacob uses Esau's momentary hunger and weakness after a day's hard work to pressure him into selling his birthright for a bowl of pottage and some bread. After his final deception, convincing his blind father to give him the blessing that should rightfully go to Esau, Jacob runs away. Jacob escapes to an area of Canaan where relatives are living, but his business machinations continue. He cuts a deal with Laban, his father-in-law, whereby Jacob ends up with the best of Laban's flock. When Jacob returns to his native land, two wives, concubines, servants, and eleven children in tow, his first instinct is to try to buy Esau off again. He sets up a meeting with his brother and makes him a generous offer: 200 female goats, 200 male goats, 200 ewes, 20 rams, 30 camels and their colts, 40 kine, 10 bulls, and 20 donkeys and their foals. Bible scholars have noted the ten-to-one ratio of female to male goats and sheep, indication that Jacob's gift, already huge, promises to increase further over time. This is payment with interest for the unfair business practices. Esau does the unexpected. Instead of attacking Jacob, he embraces him, tells him that Esau Inc. has prospered in the intervening years, and that he doesn't need Jacob's riches. Then Esau proves how much better he is at business this time around. With only the slightest additional prodding from Jacob, Esau decides to take the gift after all. The two men soon pack up their belongings and part company with a handshake, the birthright deal finally sealed. In that moment, something else about their complex relationship becomes clear. Jacob and Esau aren't just brothers. They are also business rivals.

If Esau did manage to prosper in Edom, it was probably from copper, not from hunting or working the fields. Edom was an agricultural backwater. It got far less rain than its northern neighbors Ammon and Moab. In the south, conditions were rarely good enough for any farming or agriculture to take hold. In the north, where enough rain did fall in good years to sustain some crops, the water supply was so unstable, the mountains and hills so forbidding, that Edom was more often than not cut off completely from the rest of Palestine and even central Jordan. It was copper that turned tiny, isolated Edom into one of the key centers of overland and sea trade routes that extended beyond the Middle East, possibly as far east as Central Asia.

One of the earliest records we have of the term "Edom" is in Egyptian documents dating from the reign of the pharaoh Merneptah, who ruled 1236–1223 B.C.E. It appears in a group of letters that served as models for schoolboys learning how to write. There are also references from the time of Ramses II (reigned 1304–1237) and Ramses III (reigned 1198–1166). In one inscription, among accounts of conflicts with various other groups, the pharaoh also brags about his victories against Edom. "I razed their tents: their people, their property, and their cattle as well, without number, pinioned and carried away in captivity, as the tribute of Egypt." Few archaeological remains had been found in Edom over the years. Many archaeologists and historians wondered why Egypt would have bothered with such a deserted place. The answer again was probably copper. Egypt had mining interests during both Merneptah's and Ramses III's reigns in Timna, located on the western side of the Arabah Valley. They must have conducted their raids with an eye to securing their own mines and competitive interests.

Archaeologists had conducted extensive surveys of Edom in the late 1960s, early 1970s, and mid-1980s but had been unable to find any pottery or other remains that dated earlier than the eighth century B.C.E. Then in 1997, three archaeologists excavating near Feinan in southern Jordan stumbled onto an ancient graveyard. Feinan had been the place in Edom where copper mining activities were concentrated. In Wadi Fidan, located near the mines, the archaeologists excavated sixty-two graves, which contained eighty-seven human skeletons. Their survey of the site led them to believe there were at least 3,500 more graves in the cemetery. None of the burials they uncovered contained any pottery, but there were many beads, probably the remains of pendants, necklaces, or bracelets, as well as textile and leather shrouds, copper and iron rings and bracelets, wood bowls, and pomegranates. It was the seeds from one of the pomegranates found in a sealed grave that gave the archaeologists a tentative date for the finds. Radiocarbon testing indicated the burials had taken place within the tenth or ninth centuries B.C.E., dating earlier than any of the previously excavated Edomite settlements, and around the time of the Egyptian inscriptions and Egypt's mining activities at Timna. Although there was no specific evidence linking the graves to copper mining, the proximity of the cemetery to Feinan led the archaeologists to conclude that some of Edom's first settlers were apparently miners. Other archaeologists working in Ammon were also discovering extensive remains of metalworking. The earliest evidence of steel in the Near East was jewelery found in burial sites in the Baq'ah Valley, north of Amman. At Tell el-Hammeh in the central Jordan Valley, archaeologists in 1996 and 1997 unearthed at least three furnaces and found heavy ash and slag remains around the walls of a building, all signs of a large-scale iron industry there, perhaps even the center of the region's iron industry. These discoveries have led some archaeologists to conclude that the development of an iron and steel industry around this time may have contributed to the rise of the Ammonite state. Feinan's copper probably played a similar role in Edom.

The approach to Feinan winds through valleys, low hills, and past a spring. The remains of walls and towers lie haphazardly across the site. Clusters of stones arranged in small circles dot the hillsides; archaeologists speculate that they served as either burial places or hearths. From a distance, the tops of the hills look dark and forbidding. They are covered with heaps of copper slag, the refuse of an extensive smelting and mining operation that apparently spanned thousands of years.

According to the German Mining Museum, in Bochum, Germany, which has reconstructed the history of copper production at the site, the earliest copper mining at Feinan was in the Chalcolithic era, around 4500–3300 B.C.E. This is the period now referred to as the Copper Age. Previously most of what was known about the era when the copper trade first flourished in the Middle East had come through discoveries in Israel. One of the earliest and most important finds had been an entire Copper Age village in Shiqmim, a village located in the Negev desert. Shiqmim had first been discovered in 1950, not long after the founding of the state of Israel, during early survey work done in the Beersheba region. A later survey, from 1977 to 1980, revealed that Shiqmim had been a large settlement center surrounded by six smaller sites. There was a network of underground rooms. Apparently the first settlers had built their homes into the hillsides and used the rooms to store grain. Then as mud and sediment filled the stream nearby, they moved further inward, erecting mud-brick houses atop stone foundations and constructing large buildings where communal activities took place. Many of the most important finds at Shiqmim were related to copper. There were the remains of copper ore, slags, and even three pits where the ore was smelted and cast. An analysis of the small traces of copper found in the slags showed that the copper tools in the village, such as axes and chisels, had been made of the same material. It wasn't easy work to make copper tools, requiring a temperature over 1,981 degrees Fahrenheit to melt down the ore, and for every copper axe at Shiqmim, the archaeologists turned up more than two hundred made of stone. Earlier researchers at the site had speculated that the origin of such metalwork had been in Anatolia or even Armenia. At the time, no one thought to look closer to home. In 1962, there had also been the amazing find in a cave (later known as the Cave of the Treasure) located near the top of a canyon called Nahal Mishmar, on the west side of the Dead Sea. Archaeologists exploring the cave there had discovered 429 copper objects wrapped in a reed mat. The horde was spectacular, including everything from ivory pieces to scepters, copper vessels, and mace heads. Casting such objects would have required copper ore rich in arsenic or antimony, two elements not found in the mines based in Israel. The initial assumption there too was to look far beyond the region's borders for the source of such ore. The German Mining Museum's work in Jordan was critical in determining that the source of the copper ore both at

Shiqmim and Nahal Mishmar, along with other copper sites in and around Beersheba in the Negev, had been Feinan.

At Feinan during this period, the copper production was on a large scale but unsophisticated. The miners dug out ore that was closest to the surface. They worked quickly using grooved basalt stone picks, not bothering to smooth out the low entrances and narrow galleries of the mines. Still, even if the mining process was rudimentary, the trading network that spun out from Feinan was far-flung and intricate. There was extensive exchange between Feinan and Beersheba in raw copper ore. Feinan supplied the ore, which was then smelted in small furnaces and crucibles set up in village workshops throughout the Beersheba Valley. That was only the beginning. From there, it went around the world.

Andreas Hauptmann, who heads the Feinan project for the German Mining Museum, has done chemical analyses of the ore remains at Feinan in Edom. Over the years, he has managed to retrace sizable stretches of the ancient trading network in the region. To do so, he says, he often found himself following the path of a new network as it emerged in the wake of various Arab-Israeli peace agreements. At first, things seemed promising. The trail from Feinan had led to Israel, so Hauptmann crossed the newly opened border between Israel and Jordan in the south and went to analyze the famous copper finds from Nahal Mishmar. That's when he discovered that many of the objects had been made from copper mined in Feinan. He next flew to Turkey. Turkey was openly expanding its military ties with Israel, and trade between the two countries was close to reaching the $1 billion mark. Copper objects made from Feinan ores were being excavated there at a site in Anatolia.

And yet, each time Hauptmann returned to the Middle East to do more research, he noticed that things had gotten more difficult. Travel between the countries remained possible, borders were still open, but relations grew tenser, the waits at the checkpoints longer, and the questions about his frequent trips into and out of Israel more intense.

Hauptmann found frustrating the contrast between the flourishing and open trade network that existed in the region as early as 3000 B.C.E. and the much narrower opportunities in the present day. "You are angry every time it is so difficult to cross a border, and you know that in ancient times people traded and material was exchanged," he says. "Maybe it was difficult then too, but economics was the major point."

The copper trail that Hauptmann kept following was Esau's most valuable inheritance, and in the seventh century B.C.E., mining activity at Feinan, which had ebbed and flowed depending on political circumstance for more than three thousand years already, now reached its peak. Archaeologists had long debated why. Hauptmann believed it was due to the Assyrians and he wasn't alone in that idea. He speculated that Assyria had made Edom its vassal in part because it wanted to control the mines and the copper trade in Feinan. There was another, even larger mining site located within the Assyrian empire, in Cyprus. But copper production there was controlled by the Phoenician port cities, whose relations with Assyria often were strained at best. It was far easier for the Assyrians to take charge of isolated Edom. He believed that they had invested an enormous amount of financial resources and technology in the project. The miners working at Feinan during this period didn't have the benefit of rich ores located near the surface. These had already been tapped out by previous generations. They had to sink deep shafts, some as far down as seventy meters. Once they reached the ore, they extracted only the highest-grade material, which was embedded in rocks deep inside the mountains.

It was an amazing operation. Hauptmann likes to quote a passage from the Book of Job that he says "describes what mining must have been like at Feinan in the seventh century," the time when most scholars believe Job was written: "For there is a mine for silver, And a place for gold which they refine. Iron is taken out of the dust, And brass is molten out of the stone," the passage begins. It then goes on to describe in further detail the difficult life of the miner. "He breaketh open a shaft away from where men sojourn; They are forgotten of the foot that passeth by; They hang afar from men, they swing to and fro. As for the earth, out of it cometh bread, And underneath it is turned up as it were by fire."

The miners literally worked in the debris and the ruins of their predecessors. They didn't bother clearing the hills of old slag that had accumulated over thousands of years of smelting at the site. Instead, they recycled it. Using anvils and hammers, they first crushed the old slag. They collected droplets of copper ore that remained in it and then resmelted them to extract the tiny amounts of copper that earlier miners hadn't been able to reach. The crushed slag had other uses as well. It was one of the materials used in the manufacture of domestic pottery and lined the insides of the furnaces at the mines. Sometimes the workers in charge of the furnaces threw some back into the fire in order to aid the smelting process. The mines themselves also showed evidence of the introduction of more advanced techniques. There were entire underground networks of shafts and galleries. The miners dug two shafts next to each other, one for mining out the ore and transporting it up to the furnaces, the other to allow the miners to descend even further underground. Nothing like this had been done before at Feinan.

"This kind of operation required a huge organization," says Hauptmann. "You need many people to run the mine, they have to be fed, their houses have to be built, they need to be transported to and from the mines to their villages near the site. You have a large number of furnaces and they all need fuel. There has to be a system for the fuel to reach the furnaces, and up to five people have to constantly man the furnaces. This was industrial-scale production of copper."

Hauptmann has traced the extensive trading network that existed throughout the region during the Copper Age by using geochemical studies and other scientific techniques to create a kind of "fingerprint" for Feinan's ores, slag, and finished metals. With this in hand he can analyze a copper tool in Anatolia, ore found in a site in Beersheba, or a slag heap halfway around the world from Feinan and determine if any of the copper originally came from Edom. Coming up with a geochemical fingerprint for the seventh century has been more difficult because technology by then had advanced to the point that tin and lead were being added to the copper, making it much harder to determine the original source and composition of the metal. Still, the extensive remains at Feinan, the enormous and complex operation that was established there, can mean only one thing, Hauptmann contends. Call it the Assyrian fingerprint on Edom.

Assyria's rule in the Middle East, in the eighth and seventh centuries B.C.E., changed the face of the region. Some states were incorporated as provinces into the empire, complete with Assyrian officials and administrative structure. Others paid tribute to Assyria but remained nominally free to run their daily lives, although an Assyrian official was usually posted at the court in order to keep tabs on what was happening in all corners of the expanding empire. Inscriptions report that delegations from these states visited the court of the Assyrian king Sargon II, who ruled from 722 until 705 B.C.E., and were treated very well, receiving costly gifts. The visiting kings were hardly poor themselves, thanks to the new economic opportunities. One inscription relates that Sargon received gold, ivory, stones, willow seeds, perfumes, horses, and camels from a delegation that consisted of the "kings of the seashore and the desert." Scholars believe that this wasn't tribute so much as gifts given by heads of state who were eager to expand the increasingly profitable trade between themselves and Sargon's political and economic representatives in the outer reaches of the empire.

No one is sure if Assyrian officials actually ruled from Edom or whether the state paid tribute but was left largely to its own devices. During two excavation seasons in 1994 and 1996, a joint Dutch-Jordanian team of archaeologists uncovered what the excavators considered to be a distinct new cultural phase in the early seventh century B.C.E. at Tell Deir Alla, located in Ammon in the central Jordan Valley. The remains were found inside and around large walls and some mud-brick buildings atop stone foundations dated to that period. Among the finds were iron daggers and the first appearance of sand core glass bottles, indications of strong Assyrian influence. The archaeologists also found a bronze ring, two carbonized wooden spindles, loom weights, and a large basalt grinding bowl that showed signs of the Assyrians. Despite their excitement, they were still unsure whether a whole new group of people had moved in and lived there, or whether the finds indicated how powerful the cultural influence from the north had been in Transjordan.

The same situation existed in Edom as well. Piotr Bienkowski, an archaeologist who has excavated Edomite sites in Jordan, questions whether the German Mining Museum's Hauptmann is giving enough credit to the Edomites themselves for developing the copper technology found at Feinan. There is no evidence of the physical presence of Assyrian officials living in Edom, he contends. Nonetheless, Bienkowski concurs that Edomite officials made the standard pilgrimages to the Assyrian royal court in Nineveh (in northern present-day Iraq) in order to pay tribute, and that these visits to the heart of Assyrian power must have left a deep impression on them. The wealth was staggering, and when they returned home, they copied many of the fashions they had seen. In Edom, potters adopted the Assyrian style of decorations on their wares. The so-called palace architecture, which got its name because it followed the layout of the Assyrian palace, flourished at this time in Edom, Palestine, and north Syria. More advanced technology was introduced, including a faster wheel for making pottery, which led to similarities in pottery between all the Levantine countries that were in contact with Assyria. "Pax Assyriaca" is how Nadav Na'aman, the Tel Aviv University historian, describes this time of cultural interconnection and expanding trade networks, as well as of jockeying for economic power and market share.

There haven't been many excavations in the Edomite homeland, east of the Arabah Valley, which extends from the southern end of the Dead Sea to the Gulf of Aqaba. But the picture that has emerged is that Edom reached the height of its prosperity in the seventh century. One of the most important sites is Tell el-Kheleifeh, which lies a few miles north of the Gulf of Aqaba, and over which Judah and Edom fought because it controlled the gateway to Africa and the Arabian peninsula. There is also Buseirah, the capital city, which like Tell el-Kheleifeh reached the peak of its development in the seventh century. Tawilan and Umm el-Biyara may have been established a little earlier but flourished at the same time. Archaeological surveys of the settlement patterns during this time period indicate a sharp surge in population and in the number of settlements. Edom wasn't alone in experiencing a demographic boom. Archaeologists in Israel also have demonstrated that southern Judah, particularly in the Beersheba Valley, had a dramatic increase in population during the period of Assyrian hegemony. Borders were not always clear, and the people of Judah and Edom, not to mention Assyrian and Egyptian traders, Bedouin tribes, and others, moved back and forth. Digs all over the Negev have turned up pottery similar to that found in the Edomite sites, as well as seals and inscriptions mentioning the name of the deity Qos.

But nothing has matched the finds at Horvat Qitmit, an ancient shrine in the Negev desert. Among the discoveries were more than eight hundred figurines, some in the shape of three-horned goddesses and sphinxes; reliefs; seals; cooking pots using forms that have turned up at sites inside Edom; and bowls that rest on feet molded in the shape of an animal's ankle bones. Itzhaq Beit-Arieh, the Tel Aviv University archaeologist, discovered Qitmit during a survey of the surrounding area. He is now excavating Tel Malhata, a settlement located just a few miles away. His interest in Malhata was sparked by tests that he ran on the Qitmit pottery indicating that the material he had identified as Edomite ware had actually been made locally, inside Judah's Negev. Qitmit had been a shrine, but there were no residential quarters. Beit-Arieh felt that the pottery must have been made at nearby Malhata.

Qitmit and Tel Malhata are in the middle of the desert, isolated amid the rolling sand dunes. But they tell a story about the fate of trade networks in the Middle East. Beit-Arieh calls both Edomite sites, even though they lie in the part of the Negev controlled by Judah. Malhata is now part of an Israeli air force base, and the whole area demonstrates how, since antiquity, this has been the crossroads of many different cultures. Beit-Arieh has to meet visitors at the gate, and obtain special security permission for them to enter the site. On the day I went to Malhata he was driving a jeep and had on a funny hat that made him look like he was wearing the cap of a mushroom. He has spent most of his career digging in the desert, first in Sinai during the years before Israel returned that piece of land as part of the Egyptian-Israeli peace treaty, then at various sites around the Negev.

The drive to the mound where Beit-Arieh was digging was littered with the remains of all the various peoples who had been there in the last forty-odd years. It was hard to talk, since Israeli fighter planes kept taking off and landing from nearby airstrips. There would be an incredible quiet when the desert itself seemed to be breathing, broken suddenly by a huge roar that seemed to shake the clouds. As he drove through the flat lands, Beit-Arieh pointed out a former camel rider station that the British had used when they controlled the Negev before the founding of the state of Israel. The jeep picked up speed, passing by a British military fort and a watchtower. There were also the remains of a school for the Bedouin tribes that had been shut down when Israel turned the area into an army base and moved everyone out. But Bedouins still came to the site because right next to the mound was a cemetery. The local sheikhs made special arrangements with the Israelis when they wanted to visit their dead.

The presence of the cemetery had stalled Beit-Arieh's efforts to dig there. The local Islamic movement had gotten wind of the ongoing excavations and complained to the head of the base, saying it was a violation of the sanctity of the dead to dig at the cemetery. The air force commander asked Beit-Arieh to stop. He complied for a while, then did what has always been done in the desert. He went to pay his respects to the head of the Bedouin tribe and the leader of the Islamic movement. Over small cups of bitter coffee, Beit-Arieh suggested that the leaders appoint someone to join the dig. He would receive a small salary, and his job would be to insure that the archaeologists didn't disturb any of the graves. "They agreed, and the young man they sent came to the dig one day and never came back," said Beit-Arieh. But Beit-Arieh had continued to pay him a full salary at the end of each dig's season, as they had agreed. And in deference to the Bedouins' wishes, he wasn't digging on the cemetery site, even though he suspected that he would probably turn up important buildings from Malhata there. The laws of the desert and the tribes still ruled, just as they had in the seventh century B.C.E.

Standing on the top of Malhata's mound, he pointed to Qitmit, which could be seen clearly in the distance. Over a quarter of the pottery at Malhata had been identified as Edomite in style, Beit-Arieh said. He hadn't found the kilns yet, but he had also uncovered figurines, such as one of a flute player with a double-stemmed flute, that were so close in form and technique to the work at Qitmit, that he was convinced the artists probably lived and worked at Malhata.

Everything was mixed together at these sites, making them the perfect place to observe the interaction of two ancient cultures that shared a common regional tradition but were beginning to develop their own particular national identities. One of Beit-Arieh's colleagues had analyzed the cult objects found at Qitmit and demonstrated that the artwork there, often quirky and humorous and displaying a mixture of various shapes, had drawn from a variety of Levantine sources, not just one. The styles, the themes, the shapes of the bowls and jars, reflected Judean, Syrian, Phoenician, Edomite, and Moabite traditions. This wasn't the only instance either. At sites in Edom proper, the pottery showed both Judean and Edomite elements, and so did quite a bit of architecture, including fortresses. And Qitmit hadn't been the only site in Judah where Edomite cultic objects were discovered. Excavators working at 'En Haseva, about 20 miles southwest of the Dead Sea in the Negev, had found an ancient religious center that they dated to the same period. They had found seventy-five cultic objects there, including limestone altar stands similar to others found at contemporary Israelite sites and three cult stands that were human-shaped and were similar to artifacts at Qitmit. Other finds seemed to mix the two traditions, such as bowls decorated with projecting triangles that were found at both Edomite and Judean sites, and clay pomegranates that were common in both Edom and Judah.

In his office in Jerusalem, the excavator of 'En Haseva, Rudolph Cohen, said the presence of Edomites inside Judean territory perplexed him. Like Beit-Arieh, he had initially assumed that this indicated the Edomites had pushed their way in militarily. "Why would Judah let the Edomites set up their own shrine?" he had asked.

Lately, though, he had reconsidered. Religion in Judah during this time was eclectic. It was possible that some of those worshipping Qos had been Judeans. 'En Haseva also sat on a commercial route that had been very important during the Roman period, and perhaps during this earlier time as well. "I don't think the Edomites invaded the Judean Negev," Cohen said. "I think what we are seeing there is more of the commercial and cultural shadow of Edom on Judah, rather than a military one."

Beit-Arieh didn't rule out the commercial explanation, but largely he had evaluated the site and the finds in the context of the Bible and therefore come up with a more militant interpretation. "The Bible reflects a historical reality," he pointed out during a conversation in his cluttered office at Tel Aviv University. "Judah's unremitting hate for Edom, the hostilities between the two sides, runs through the Bible. Why let them trade inside Judah?"

The explanation for this lies outside the Bible, goes the new scenario, in the wider history of the region during this period. Qitmit and Malhata both sat along the great trade route that connected Arabia and Transjordan via the Beersheba Valley with Mediterranean ports. There were alternative routes from north Arabia to the ports of Philistia that didn't run through Edom or Judah, but Assyria's economic strategy in the region changed at this time. Controlling the Arabian trade was always a primary goal of the empire. At first, Assyrian leaders were content to depend on various agreements with the leaders of Arab and nomadic tribes to control border crossings and trade routes. But after Assyria was forced to intervene militarily in Philistia to insure control there, Assyrian officials decided to direct trade through the territory of far weaker Judah and Edom. Qitmit lay at the gates of this crossing point for Assyrians, Phoenicians, Philistines, Judeans, and Edomites. It was the first site those coming from the south would see; it was the last resting point for those heading south into the vast deserts of Arabia. Qitmit was a temporary oasis for those who hoped to make money out of the desert.

While the Assyrians were directly involved in the area, things went smoothly. The Assyrians weren't altruists. They took the largest share of revenues from the growing Arabian trade that resulted from the network they set up. But everyone else prospered too. Qitmit wasn't the only site to flourish during this time. There was greater settlement activity throughout the entire southern area of Judah and Edom, more developed agriculture, new wealth. But Assyria was soon forced to withdraw from the scene. There were problems at home, intrigues to be dealt with at various corners of the empire. The successful rebellion of Egypt in the second half of the seventh century began a period of steady decline, culminating in the capture of Nineveh by a coalition of Medes and Babylonians in 612 B.C.E.

Once the Assyrians loosened their grip, the southern trade didn't end overnight. Relations continued, caravans still moved across the desert. But all the disputes, the rising nationalistic ideologies, the suspicion and mistrust that the Assyrian presence had kept in check now came out in full force. Faced with growing instability, traders soon found alternate routes outside the Negev for moving their goods into and out of Arabia. Qitmit was abandoned. The Judeans and Edomites learned the same lesson of the market that would still prevail a couple thousand years later: in times of political strife, the money moves elsewhere.

Piotr Bienkowski is musing aloud about the Edomites one rainy evening in Copenhagen in June 1998. The bar where we are sitting is on a pretty cobbled side street that has been turned into an enclosed marketplace, closed to traffic. Families stroll up and down the lanes, ignoring the rain. Inside, the tables are packed, umbrellas strewn everywhere, the din of constant conversation rising. The waitress brings beer, coffee, and nachos. The annual conference on the history and archaeology of Jordan is meeting in Copenhagen. Bienkowski has just come from a session he had organized for the various archaeologists working in the areas of Ammon, Moab, and Edom to compare pottery finds and ceramic traditions, and he is due to give a speech about the Edomites the next day. The question that most perplexes him, he says, is "What is an Edomite?"

The root of the problem, he explains, is the use and meaning of the word "Edom." The name is believed to derive from a Semitic root meaning red or ruddy, and most scholars have assumed it was given to the area because of the red-colored sandstone there. The Bible's writers, perhaps seeking to tie Esau to Edom, pointed out that Esau was very red at birth. Throughout antiquity, "Edom" was used to mean many things, first a geographical area, then a political state, and also an ethnic group. Some of the pottery types found at Buseirah that are now considered "Edomite" also showed up at sites in the Judean Negev but were not present at all the sites in Edom, such as the mountaintop sites around the city of Petra.

Trying to recover the histories of the peoples mentioned in the Bible is always difficult, Bienkowski goes on, but with the Edomites the task is further complicated by the fact that everything scholars do know points to their remaining at heart a group of nomads, elusive and largely unseen. "We really know nothing about the Edomites for certain," Bienkowski says. "We don't know when the kingdom was formed, or why it was formed. We don't know how the material culture changed, and what it was in different parts of Edom. We don't know when Edom stopped existing, or why — if their sites were destroyed, or if they simply went out of existence. We don't know what happened to Edom afterward. That's why I find them so fascinating. It's this giant scholarly puzzle."

The excavations inside Jordan are too limited to answer Bienkowski's questions. Crystal Bennett, the British archaeologist, excavated the Edomite city of Buseirah from 1971 to 1974 and again in 1980. Bienkowski worked on the dig. But Bennett died before starting to write a final report, and Bienkowski is now trying to publish it. It is a frustrating task. He is working with material that relied on methodologies now out of date, that might answer some questions, but not necessarily the ones that are relevant to current debates.

That's why Beit-Arieh's work at Qitmit and Malhata, and Cohen's finds at 'En Haseva, are so important for Bienkowski. The data and finds are more recent, and they offer a chance to make comparisons with the finds at Buseirah. Bienkowski and a colleague have studied the figurines and some of the decorated pottery in Judah and in Buseirah hoping to better understand the relationship between the two entities. Despite the remaining uncertainties, their conclusion is fascinating. To date, the finds from Qitmit and 'En Haseva provide the closest parallels yet for aspects of Buseirah's material culture. Bienkowski hasn't relied on the biblical story about Jacob and Esau for much help in unraveling the puzzle of the relationship between Edom and Judah. "The Bible's writers wrote about Edom, but with their own biases. Besides, it's clear from their descriptions that they never visited there," he argues. Still, Bienkowski's interpretation shares something with that of the Bible's writers: it leaves future possibilities open.

Outside the bar, the rain has started to taper off, leaving tracks down the large panes of the windows that offer a view of the busy street. It is warm inside, the voices at the bar hum pleasantly. It is easy to accept the notion that the ending remains unwritten, at least for the time being. Jacob and Esau are still locked in their embrace, the Judeans and Edomites are sitting down to pray together at Qitmit. They haven't yet parted ways. There is still a chance for Judah and Edom to become part of something larger, before the region goes back to being nothing more than a collection of warring, petty tribes. Yet there's no escaping the realization that in Jerusalem, Judah's capital city, the newly returned exiles from Babylonia squandered a similar opportunity.

Chapter 9

꼭

Return to the Promised Land

Thus saith Cyrus king of Persia: All the kingdoms of the earth hath the Lord, the God of heaven, given me, and he hath charged me to build Him a house in Jerusalem, which is in Judah. Whosoever there is among you of all His people — his God be with him — let him go up to Jerusalem, which is in Judah, and build the house of the Lord, the God of Israel, He is the God who is in Jerusalem. *(Ezra 1:2–4)*

The two hundred years when the Persians ruled the Middle East marked a watershed in biblical history. About the fifty-year period following destruction of the First Temple the Bible's writers remained largely silent. They wrote little of the exiles' life in Babylon, they ignored what was happening back in Judah. Then suddenly, King Cyrus and the Persians conquered Babylon and took over its vast empire, virtually without a fight. A declaration was issued that ethnic groups living in exile were free to return to their ancestral homelands. Over time the Judeans, led by a scribe and religious figure named Ezra and by a Persian-appointed Jewish governor, Nehemiah, moved back to Judah, rebuilt the temple, fortified Jerusalem's walls, and instituted a religious reform. For the Bible's writers, the return to the Promised Land marked a new beginning, the rise of the new Israel. So it is surprising that for years, despite the momentous events taking place during the period, the Persian era simply didn't interest modern scholars.

Part of the problem was that the Books of Ezra and Nehemiah, the major biblical sources on this subject, are actually very spare, compressing the rule of several Persian leaders and a couple of hundred years into a very short text. That made it harder for historians to sort things out chronologically; even today no one is sure who arrived in Jerusalem first, Ezra or Nehemiah, or when. Most scholars simply accepted the brief record of events in Ezra and Nehemiah and left it at that, preferring to focus their critical attention on later periods when Palestine was under Greek and Roman rule, the time when Judaism and Christianity as they are practiced today first began to take form. Archaeologists too skipped over this time. They rarely published pottery from this period. Sometimes they didn't even bother saving their finds, instead digging down to earlier periods that dealt either with the emergence of Israel in Canaan or with the so-called golden era of David and Solomon.

Then very recently, there was a sudden burst of interest in what really happened in Jerusalem after Ezra and Nehemiah showed up. Study groups devoted to what came to be called the Second Temple period, spanning the time from the arrival of the Persians in the mid-sixth century B.C.E. to the Roman destruction of the Second Temple in 70 C.E., were organized by the Society of Biblical Literature, based in Atlanta, Georgia, and serving as the main umbrella organization for Bible scholars and historians. The prestigious Cambridge History of Judaism series brought out a volume on the Persian period, and other scholarly texts began appearing as well. The main reasons for the increased activity actually had little to do with the Persians. For centuries, biblical scholars had assumed that the descriptions of many events in the Bible were written down shortly after the events occurred. But starting in the 1970s and 1980s, new doubts were raised, first regarding the historicity of Abraham and the patriarchs, but then extending as far as King David and King Solomon. Soon, more scholars began to argue that when it came to the composition

of the texts making up the Hebrew Bible — the Old Testament —
the Persian period had probably seen the most significant literary
activity.

This idea was given additional driving force by the burgeoning
scholarship concerning the Dead Sea Scrolls, the oldest surviving
copies of the biblical texts and long considered the most significant
archaeological find of the twentieth century. The first of the scrolls
had been discovered in 1947 by a Bedouin shepherd chasing after a
lost goat in the hills near Khirbet Qumran, on the northwest shore of
the Dead Sea. He threw a stone into a cave, heard some pottery shat-
ter, and clambered through the narrow opening to see what he had
hit. Inside, he found jars filled with ancient parchments. Scientific
analysis showed them to have been written over a three-century span
starting around 200 B.C.E. During the next several years, ten more
caves with scrolls and manuscript fragments were discovered in the
Qumran area. The manuscripts, which eventually numbered some
eight hundred, postdate Ezra's completion of the Law of Moses (or
Pentateuch) by several centuries, but lately they have had an enormous impact on how scholars view the writing of the Bible. The
Books of Ezra and Nehemiah describe Ezra's returning from Babylon
carrying with him a kind of proto-Bible. In the Book of Nehemiah,
Ezra assembles the children of Israel in Jerusalem for what is called
the first public reading of the Pentateuch, perhaps around 445 B.C.E.
Men and women make the trip in inclement weather to Jerusalem,
and Ezra, standing on a pulpit made of wood and surrounded by the
leaders of the community, reads the Law from early morning until
midday for seven days. Then the people feast and celebrate an event
that is clearly supposed to represent an updated version of the handing down of the Torah at Mount Sinai.

Tradition ascribes to Ezra the editing of the Pentateuch — the first
five books of the Old Testament — in its present form. Scholarship on
the Dead Sea Scrolls has called this idea into question, although it
took a while to happen. Only eight of thirty-eight planned volumes of
scroll material were published in the first forty years after their discov-

ery. Until very recently, most of the texts had remained in the control of the scholars charged with reconstructing, translating, and publishing them; debate was virtually impossible, since few outside this small group had ever seen the actual manuscripts. But in 1991 a new editor of the scrolls was appointed by the Israeli government; under his aegis twelve more volumes of scrolls were published, four in 1997 alone. In terms of wordage, more than 90 percent of the scroll finds are now in print. This material, finally available to a wider group of scholars, sparked a new look at both the makeup of the Hebrew canon and the revising of individual volumes. What now became evident was that, among the scrolls and other documents found in the Qumran caves were many versions of the biblical texts, in fact all the books of the Hebrew Bible except Esther. These manuscripts didn't contain merely minor textual variations that could be attributed to the mistake of a copyist. They clearly showed that over the course of centuries many of the best-known stories in the Bible, from Abraham and Sarah's sojourn in Egypt described in Genesis to parts of Exodus and the Book of Samuel, had been intentionally reworked — updated, many scholars speculated, to reflect current concerns. Also found among the caves were many texts of works not included in the traditional Hebrew canon. Hundreds of years after Ezra supposedly brought back the version of the Pentateuch that we use today, many books not now contained in the Hebrew Bible were clearly still considered part of the mainstream Jewish library. The conclusion was quite staggering: the writing and editing of the biblical texts and the establishment of the final canon had obviously involved a much more fluid and complicated process than previously thought.

This notion invariably led back to the Persian period. Among Bible scholars, Ezra had long been considered the final editor of the Pentateuch. In fact, Ezra is still remembered in Jewish tradition as second in importance only to Moses when it came to the shaping of the laws. He may very well have brought back with him from exile in Babylon some sort of early draft of the Hebrew Bible, completed his editing in Jerusalem, and had the laws read to the public as part of the revival of religious life that occurred during this period, as the Bible records. But the Dead Sea Scrolls scholarship indicated that the rewriting and revising hadn't stopped with Ezra.

The archaeology emerging about the period seemed to fit this idea too. In light of the new biblical scholarship, some archaeologists were going back and studying the records of old excavations with Persian-level layers to see what they could learn about the Persian period. Some of their finds were quite dramatic. Around 450 B.C.E. a series of fortresses located on strategic trade and military routes had been built throughout Judah. There were signs that, just as Nehemiah indicated in his memoir, the walls of Jerusalem had indeed been fortified around this time too, even though Yehud, as the Persians renamed the province of Judah, was small in comparison to other places in the Persian empire that had remained without extensive fortifications. As the archaeologists sought reasons that could explain Yehud's relative importance, they began to see the fortification of Jerusalem as well as Ezra's religious reform not just in theological terms, as the Bible's writers had, but as a window into a larger Persian imperial policy. A clearer picture of Palestine in the sixth through the fourth centuries started to come into focus.

In the Bible, Ezra comes across as a harsh man in many ways. He has no sympathy for the people who have remained behind in Judah and managed to keep things going after the Babylonians destroyed Jerusalem. In fact, the Bible portrays him as ripping his garments in anguish soon after his return when confronted with the news that the Israelites have intermarried with the Canaanites and other groups living in the area, and adopted some of their religious customs. He is continually praying to God not to exile everyone again as penalty for such transgressions. He then declares a stringent ban on intermarriage, something not done before in Israelite history, and even oversees a mass forced divorce of Israelite men and their foreign-born wives, destroying entire families without a second thought. Under Ezra and Nehemiah, it is no longer enough to live on the land or even to worship Yahweh in order to be considered part of Yehud. They attempt to end the plurality of religious belief that had existed up until that time, arguing that membership in the new Israel requires observing the sabbath and the holidays the way Ezra instructs and marrying exclusively within the Israelite community. The Bible and later Jewish tradition portray all of this as a religious reformation, treating Ezra as one of the founders of Judaism.

But archaeologists and historians were discovering that there were other, more political considerations at stake too. It was part of Persian imperial policy at this time to allocate territories to particular ethnic groups throughout the empire and to allow them relative autonomy to run their own affairs. The Judeans received Yehud, but they were dependent on the goodwill of the Persians to remain in the land of Israel, and that meant following Persian requirements to restrict and maintain tight rein on who belonged to the Israelite community and had land rights. Intermarriage, these scholars argued, constituted a threat to the Judeans' continuing control of the land and so had to be forcefully suppressed. Ezra brought to bear his political instincts as much as his religious inclinations when he read the Torah aloud to the people that week in Jerusalem. Ezra wanted to establish a religious status quo, but in truth a centralized religious authority never really took hold. This was a community seeking to define itself, and as they would continue to do in the coming centuries, the Israelites sought this definition above all through their literature. As the Dead Sea Scrolls indicated, hundreds of years after Ezra's time, the only orthodoxy Israelites shared was a love of the Torah. They certainly didn't agree on what the stories meant. Ezra's program succeeded at the time because he was able to make the Pentateuch relevant to his community based on an artful and ruthless understanding of the particular historical circumstances in which his audience lived. In this sense, Ezra should probably be considered not so much the Pentateuch's final editor as its first interpreter, part of a long tradition that continues to this day. Ezra pushed for viewing the Torah narrowly, as a set of rules to be strictly followed. But the Bible's lasting power has come from the fact that it is not dogma, as Ezra wanted people to believe, but a living document whose meaning changes depending on who is doing the reading.

If one goes by lists in the Ezra-Nehemiah books of families who move back to Judah from Babylon, there were approximately fifty thousand people who returned to Jerusalem from exile. The new archaeological data suggest otherwise. In Palestine during the past century twenty-two sites have been excavated that are attributed to the time when Judah was Yehud, and more than one hundred others have been identified on the basis of archaeological surveys that rely on collecting pottery that lies on the ground. Charles Carter, an associate professor of religious studies at Seton Hall University, analyzed the various archaeology reports as part of a broader study about Yehud that he published in 1999. He came to the conclusion that the population of the province grew from around 13,450 toward the end of the sixth century B.C.E. to 20,825 by the second half of the fourth century. That's a 55 percent increase, an impressive jump, but still Yehud was about a third smaller in size than scholars had previously thought. Most of the settlements in Yehud were small, with perhaps 125 people at most living in them. Jerusalem was the only major city in the province, probably two to three times bigger than the next largest town. But even Jerusalem never reached its former glory. The Babylonian army that marched into town in 587/586 B.C.E., burning the temple and exiling the elite, pretty much destroyed Jerusalem. Archaeologists excavating the city and the surrounding areas had determined that people continued to live in Jerusalem even after its destruction, but the city didn't extend much beyond the City of David, the small, traditional center of the city. Under the Persians, Jerusalem reached probably only 20 percent of its former size.

Still, Jerusalem became a capital again during this period, and that's really the most important point in terms of understanding the significance of Yehud to the Persian empire. The Persians were always struggling to maintain their empire, and at first they didn't pay much attention to Jerusalem or to Yehud. Cyrus the Great had been the one who supposedly gave the order allowing the Judeans, among other ethnic groups, to return to their ancestral homeland, but he died suddenly in 529. His successor, Cambyses II, spent most of his reign trying to conquer Egypt, the only power left in the region capable of opposing the Persians. He didn't last long on the throne. While off in Egypt, he learned of a revolt against his rule and had to rush back to Persia, where he died under mysterious circumstances. The next few rulers were kept busy trying to shore up the empire, which continued to be plagued by revolts in various holdings. The constant turmoil at the Persian royal court had dire consequences in Jerusalem. The rebuilding of the temple in Jerusalem came to a halt shortly after it began, and the number of people returning to live in Yehud slowed to a trickle. Only in the mid-fifth century B.C.E., when Artaxerxes I took the throne, did things begin to change. He brought with him a new strategy for keeping his western front quiet. Yehud's day had finally arrived.

One of the first problems that Artaxerxes I had to deal with was a revolt in Egypt. The Greeks, who were gaining power in the region (under Alexander the Great they would eventually push the Persians out of Palestine), were giving the Egyptians support. There are even indications of defections within the Persian empire to the Athenian side: Dor, a province in northern Palestine, is listed as a member of one of the Greek military leagues for the period 460–450 B.C.E., during the height of the Egyptian uprising. Suddenly, small poor Yehud, with roads that led directly to Egypt and its central location for garrisoning the Persian troops needed to quash the Egyptian uprising, took on new importance.

There are some hints of Yehud's changing fortunes in the Bible, but overall it is difficult to detect the extent of the transformation. The Ezra-Nehemiah books contain few references to any historical events. But the emerging archaeological record has helped fill in the picture. Throughout the Persian kingdom, fortresses were built at this time along the major and minor routes linking the various provinces together. In Yehud alone, more than ten fortresses, dated to this period through pottery remains found inside the structures, were built. Excavations at some of the fortresses show they featured similar design and were built using standardized plans. They were almost always located overlooking an important roadway rather than close to a population center, demonstrating that their principal function was to protect key routes from attack and help solidify administrative control rather than to defend cities. The fortresses appear to have been abandoned just a few decades after they were established, indicating they had been built in response to a specific strategic condition, and that once the threat to the empire posed by the revolt in Egypt no longer existed, the soldiers occupying them moved out. Another sign of the increased militarization of this time, archaeologists determined, was the presence of a particular kind of jug at these sites. Studies of the clays used to manufacture the jugs indicated they had been made in southern Palestine in the mid-fifth century B.C.E. What was most interesting was that they had been found not just in Palestine but as far north as a military cemetery in Anatolia, Turkey. The archaeologists who studied the distribution patterns of the jugs speculated that imperial troops had used the pottery while stationed in southern Palestine, and had then taken it with them upon being redeployed to Anatolia after the Egyptian revolt was quashed.

While the Books of Ezra and Nehemiah do not mention the Egyptian revolt, there are clues in the Bible about Yehud's newly expanded role. Ezra writes that shortly after the former exiles begin rebuilding the temple, some of "the people of the land," described as enemies of Judah, approach Zerubbabel, the governor of Judah under Darius I, offering to help. Zerubbabel and the Jewish leaders turn them down. In a fit of pique, they send letters back to the imperial court arguing that Zerubbabel, who is a descendant of King David, and the group surrounding him are not to be trusted. "They are building the rebellious and the bad city," they write in one missive. "Be it known now unto the king that, if this city be builded and the walls finished, they will not pay tribute, impost, or toll. . . . This city is a rebellious city and hurtful unto kings and provinces, and they have moved sedition within the same of old time, for which cause was this city laid waste." The letters, the Bible reports, apparently hit home and the king orders them to stop working. This attitude apparently changes under Artaxerxes' rule, at least according to the Book of Nehemiah.

Nehemiah approaches the issue differently. Unlike Ezra, he makes sure he gets imperial approval for rebuilding Jerusalem's walls before setting out for the city. Even so, it is clear that he is operating under different political circumstances. The new archaeological work has demonstrated how unusual it was for the Persian rulers to agree to the fortification of a city; excavations of other former Persian provinces have indicated that very few urban centers at this time had walls. The fact that Jerusalem was allowed to build one, the archaeologists argue, indicates that the central authorities understood Jerusalem's importance in the fight against the growing Greek influence in the eastern Mediterranean. And indeed, when the familiar protests arise at the news that Jerusalem is once again being rebuilt — this time from the leaders of neighboring provinces Samaria and Ammon — the response from the royal court is different. This time, the building proceeds, and the walls of Jerusalem are refortified.

Jerusalem's walls were part of a broader transformation that was taking place in the city's status, one best illustrated by a number of archaeological excavations done around the city in recent decades. As part of an ongoing survey of the Jerusalem area, the Israeli Antiquities Authority turned up signs that the city had been rebuilt during the Persian rule. There were the remains of winepresses, storage rooms, and olive presses at a number of farmsteads surrounding Jerusalem. In one section of the city, a storage room and sixteen winepresses were discovered, indicating that the site may have served as some sort of industrial complex for manufacturing wine for the city's elite. Carter, the historian who had closely studied the Persian era, argued that the many settlements inside and surrounding Jerusalem could be interpreted as satellite villages whose function was to produce all sorts of goods that the inhabitants of Jerusalem consumed, bought, traded, or used to pay taxes. Farther south, in Ein Gedi, along the Dead Sea shore, and at other sites, there were also a number of large storerooms and industrial complexes being excavated. They contained everything from loom weights to stone tools. A variety of goods were being produced there, perhaps for use by the Persian conscripts stationed at the many fortresses that were being built at the same time. There were signs of increased trade, particularly with Greece and areas under the Persian empire's control. Greek coins, delicate glass vessels, gold jewelry, and beautiful pottery in vibrant colors and a range of shapes were found in tombs in Jerusalem as well as in digs at sites just outside the city. A merchant class was clearly emerging.

All this signaled a burst of creativity and commercial activity that hadn't been seen in Jerusalem since the destruction of the First Temple, the archaeologists concluded. Even so, it didn't change the fact that Jerusalem remained small and poor relative to what it had been a century earlier. Some scholars even argued that such a Jerusalem, with its relatively limited economic means and demographic picture, simply couldn't support a project as elaborate as building a temple. Others questioned how the Persian period could have sustained the kind of literary activity Bible scholars had traditionally associated with the era.

The limitation of the Ezra and Nehemiah books was that they seemed to portray a Yehud that existed in a vacuum. Indeed, the heart of the religious reform that the two men pushed required a turn inward. The strict ban on intermarriage was designed to cut the people off from any outsiders, even those who worshipped Yahweh and had seen themselves up until that time as valued members of the Israelite community. As the Passover holiday to commemorate the exodus from Egypt is celebrated by the returning exiles, Ezra describes the children of the captivity as having separated themselves "from the filthiness of the nations of the land." That sort of separation is also the requirement for participating in the ceremony that Nehemiah describes in which the heads of the various Judean households make a covenant with God publicly pledging to live by the rules of the Torah as they have been instructed by Ezra. And the Book of Nehemiah closes with an act that most seems to symbolize this turn inward, the celebration of the sabbath. "And it came to pass that, when the gates of Jerusalem began to be dark before the sabbath, I commanded that the doors be shut," writes Nehemiah, "and commanded that they should not be opened until after the sabbath." Nehemiah assigns some of his servants to guard the gates, and the merchants who turn up to sell their wares are forcefully turned away. The gates remain locked, the new Israel has literally cut itself off from its neighbors.

That was the mistake many of the earlier scholars had made too, treating Yehud as if it had been isolated from the broader forces affecting the region. The archaeological record now argues for a different interpretation, linking Yehud's fate to events taking place in the larger Persian empire. Building a temple to Yahweh wasn't a unique privilege given only to the Judeans. The restoration of religious cults and the rebuilding of temples of various groups that had been oppressed by the Babylonians were a consistent feature of Persian policy, designed in part to insure greater loyalty among the empire's new subjects. These projects were often partially financed by money from imperial coffers, and it's likely that both Ezra's and Nehemiah's return to Jerusalem and their subsequent building plans had all been approved and partially financed by the royal court.

There was also a very interesting phenomenon taking place right outside Jerusalem that was never mentioned in the Bible or in Persian written records but that became evident as archaeological surveys spread from Jerusalem to surrounding areas. One of the places that had seen a dramatic rise in its population in the decades following the return of the exiles to Jerusalem was the nearby village of Modiin, nestled among the Judean mountains. In the years that the Greeks ruled Palestine, it would play an especially important role in Jewish history. Modiin was the base for the second-century Jewish uprising commonly called the Revolt of the Maccabees. The Maccabees' capture of Jerusalem and rededication of the temple (164 B.C.E.) is celebrated to this day in the Jewish holiday of Hannukah.

But that was still a long way off. At the time of the Persians, Modiin was just starting to emerge in importance, experiencing a large demographic surge. Historians studying the settlement patterns have been able to show that at the time Modiin was expanding, areas farther out declined in population, indicating that many of the people had decided to move to Modiin. These were fellow Judeans, who could have chosen to live right inside Jerusalem. But such a move would have required severing ties with their neighbors and their foreign-born wives and children, as well as with the looser style of worship that they had enjoyed up until then. So instead they lived in Modiin, right on the border of Jerusalem but not formally under the city's administrative, religious, or political control. Those who did so rejected Ezra and Nehemiah's narrow definition of the new Israel. Despite the attempt to impose new religious restrictions, many historians now believe, these Judeans remained key economic backers behind Jerusalem's expansion. Ezra and Nehemiah marginalized them and their beliefs, and attempted to outlaw the way that they practiced their religion. Nonetheless, their ties to Jerusalem continued. They didn't feel comfortable living there, but they sent money, celebrated festivals there, offered sacrifices at the temple, and made pilgrimages on holidays. Ezra and Nehemiah had tried to shut the gates of Jerusalem, but from the beginning the new Israel was always larger than Yehud.

Over the years, a phenomenon similar to the one occurring among researchers of Yehud's development during the Persian era started to take place in Dead Sea Scrolls scholarship as well. The traditional interpretation of the scrolls was that a Jewish separatist sect known as the Essenes, composed of a group of men living in monastic isolation in the desert, had written the scrolls and then hidden them in the caves surrounding Qumran, the site of their living and working quarters. The Essenes, so the theory went, wanted to protect the scrolls from the approaching Roman army, which had just put down a revolt in Jerusalem and was now marching into the Judean desert to conquer any remaining pockets of resistance. That view, almost uniformly accepted since its promulgation by the site's first excavators, has given way in recent years to very different ideas. Just as Yehud's history is now seen as reflecting larger forces at work in the Persian empire, Qumran is now being incorporated into the broader social and economic changes taking place in the Roman empire.

In the 1950s, shortly after the discovery of the scrolls, a group of archaeologists from Jerusalem led by Father Roland de Vaux began excavating the ancient ruins at Qumran. The archaeologists, many of them, like Father de Vaux, monks associated with the Dominican École Biblique et Archéologique in Jerusalem, saw something similar to their own lives. They argued that the main building was a monastery occupied by the Essenes. De Vaux also suggested that the different structures around the site were used for various activities by the sect. There was a room for meetings of the community and for eating communal meals, ritual baths, even a "scriptorium," where the scribes wrote and copied the scrolls. One of the key pieces of evidence for De Vaux's theory was the fact that the pottery found in the caves containing the scrolls was identical to pottery found at Qumran itself.

From the beginning, there were problems with the picture of a group of apolitical scribes living in the desert completely untouched by the upheaval going on in Jerusalem as the Romans sent more soldiers there to put down the Jewish Revolt in 68 C.E. At Masada, the desert fortress built by King Herod that served as the last bastion of Jewish resistance to the Romans, several documents similar to the ones found at Qumran had also been discovered. That seemed further indication that at least some of the literature at Qumran reflected broader currents in Jewish religious thought, rather than the views of some extremist group cut off from the mainstream. This idea was rejected at first by the majority of scholars, who still adhered to the idea of Qumran's isolation, but over the years a group of archaeologists began to question De Vaux's interpretation of Qumran.

The result in recent years has been a proliferation of theories about how the site was used. In July 1997 an international congress about the scrolls was held at the Israel Museum in Jerusalem, where the scrolls under Israel's control are housed, to celebrate the fiftieth anniversary of their discovery. In just a few short days, the Qumran ruins were described by various speakers as an isolated religious retreat, a trading post along an important commercial route, a military fortress, a rustic villa, a hostel for travelers, a wealthy manor house belonging to aristocrats close to King Herod, and a quarantine station for sick pilgrims on the way to the temple in Jerusalem. Some of the scholars argued that many or all of the scrolls had been composed at Qumran, others said they reflected Jewish intellectual thought of the Second Temple period and had been brought to Qumran from Jerusalem. Estimates about the population living at Qumran ranged anywhere from under 50 to over 150. No one could agree whether all the people lived at the main building in Qumran or in tents and caves close to the site. Even the dates of the beginning and the end of the community were under challenge.

One of the speakers at the conference that week was Yizhar Hirschfeld, an archaeologist affiliated with Hebrew University in Jerusalem. In the small clique of Jerusalem archaeologists, Hirschfeld often finds himself in the center of controversy. He always takes his dog, named Doggy, with him to digs. The two ride around in Hirschfeld's jeep, Doggy's face hanging out the open window, as they travel in the desert. Sometimes Hirschfeld will lose track of time, returning to base camp late, profusely apologizing, with Doggy trailing behind him. He holds regular press conferences at his digs, always, it seems, coming up with a theory most likely to buck the conventional wisdom and generate newspaper headlines. At first he steered clear of the Dead Sea Scrolls debate. It wasn't his issue, he said, he was a specialist in the Byzantine period. Then he started excavating a Roman-era estate in Ramat Hanadiv, located just outside the town of Zicharon Ya'akov in northern Israel. During the Ramat Hanadiv dig, the excavators found many luxury items, including lamps and imported goods. Hirschfeld speculates that the owners, wealthy Jewish landowners who were close to King Herod and who received the house as a gift for their loyalty, abandoned the place at the beginning of the Jewish Revolt in 66 C.E. There were no signs of a violent destruction, Hirschfeld says, but excavators came across a large quantity of expensive home furnishings, as if the owners had left in haste. The site at Ramat Hanadiv dates to the same time as Qumran, and Hirschfeld says he sees striking similarities between the architectural styles used at both places. To test his theory, he has studied the plans of other country houses dating to the period of the Roman empire. This has led him to conclude that Qumran was not a unique site at all, but could be placed in the context of a pattern of settlement typical to Judea in the first century B.C.E.–first century C.E. time period.

Not just Ramat Hanadiv but a number of manor houses have recently been identified within the borders of Herod's kingdom of Judea, at places like Horvat Salit and Arorer. None of the sites is exactly like any of the others, although Hirschfeld says there is no reason they should be alike, since each owner brought his own individuality to bear on how the house was built. Still, the main buildings on all of the sites were built according to a similar plan, including a fortified tower and a residential area built around a central courtyard. All of them were large complexes, located on elevations that offered control of the nearby roads, and most contained developed water supply systems as well as agricultural installations. Most important, Hirschfeld argues, they were all destroyed or abandoned around the time of the Jewish uprising against the Romans.

Qumran shares the same features. Hirschfeld has long rejected De Vaux's notion that Qumran was off the beaten track. He points out that two ancient roads pass through Qumran and continue on to Ein Gedi. One connected Qumran with Jericho, the other served as the shortest route between Jerusalem and Qumran. Qumran's architectural plans match those of the other manor houses Hirschfeld has studied. The walls of the main building created a square courtyard with a massive tower in one corner. Remains inside the buildings at Qumran reveal that most of the buildings around the courtyard had both upper and lower floors, indicating a high level of economic status of the owners. The water supply system at the site, based on a network of reservoirs and pools, was able to hold a considerable quantity of water, but not an extraordinary amount for a house in an area with such a warm climate. The remains of stucco in the tower at Qumran and in other buildings at the site also indicate some level of wealth. Among the pottery finds are examples of fine ware and beautifully carved stone vessels, all signs of luxury that would have been out of place among a group of ascetic monks.

Not everyone shares Hirschfeld's conclusions, but his work is part of the new scholarship emerging about Judean society in the period before the anti-Roman revolts. By the time of King Herod's rule, in the late first century B.C.E., the Second Temple had developed into much more than a cultic and religious place; it had also become the center of a huge economic complex. Jerusalem's economy was dependent on the steady stream of pilgrims who came to pray and offer sacrifices there. Related services had sprung up to handle the pilgrims' many needs, and the city's elite, both the priests and the secular merchant and political class, were wealthier than ever before. This phenomenon of an economic boom wasn't occurring just in Jerusalem, but throughout the Roman holdings in the region.

At a Dead Sea Scrolls conference held in New York several months after the Jerusalem session, archaeology historian Neil Asher Silberman argued that there were strong connections between what was taking place among Jerusalem's priestly families and events in Greece and Turkey. New cultic and economic centers also emerged in the former Roman provinces of Achaea in Greece and Galatia in central Turkey, and along with them a group of leaders and businesspeople who profited from serving as mediators between the Roman empire and the locals. In Greece, archaeological excavations had turned up a number of large estates operated by wealthy and powerful local families during this period. The Israeli archaeologist Hirschfeld's work on manor houses in Judea indicates that a similar process took place in Palestine. The gift of an estate or land was the typical way to reward a loyal servant of the royal court. The ancient historian Josephus had also written about how King Herod gave land and estates to former military troops who served him loyally and to friends throughout his kingdom. The estates, with their large number of tenants, served as important sources of tax revenues. Not everyone benefited from the new economy, Silberman said. Many simply weren't able to take advantage of the opportunities created by the Roman occupation. They didn't have the right political connections to insure access to the additional markets that opened to goods and products. They weren't able to profit from the new methods of cultivation that were adopted by the estate owners. The disparity of wealth between the various social classes grew even more pronounced.

"While the Dead Sea Scrolls were being composed, edited, and collected in Judea, something, however one may want to characterize it, was going on in the streets of Jerusalem, Antioch, Corinth, and Rome," Silberman told the audience gathered at the New York Public Library one spring morning. "And that something sparked a certain kind of reaction." All these places experienced a wrenching economic dislocation. Large groups of priests, former religious and social leaders, and the growing peasant class were either excluded from the new wealth or refused for whatever reason to cooperate with the Romans and their local representatives. Alienated from the mainstream, left out of the economic boom, these people became increasingly radical, developing ideologies and movements that called for a return to the past and a stricter adherence to traditional mores. They were the ones who would form the backbone of the spate of anti-Roman revolts that took place throughout the empire, including in Jerusalem. Archaeologists studying the Persian era had argued that the genius of the Bible's writers was that Ezra and Nehemiah were remembered not as imperial collaborators, but as the saviors of Judaism. Now historians like Silberman were asking similar questions about the historians active in the first century C.E. Perhaps Josephus's genius had been to present the Jewish revolt as the fault of a small group of outcast radicals rather than the product of a larger societal phenomenon. Assuming that the writers of the Dead Sea Scrolls were Essenes rather than disgruntled members of the Jewish mainstream now seemed too simplistic in light of all the new archaeological and historical evidence. Even if one accepted the traditional idea that the people living at Qumran were Essenes, it no longer seemed possible to keep the rebels' camp at Masada and the religious group's base at Qumran entirely separate, as Josephus had tried to do. "Has anyone ever asked what kinds of families or neighborhoods the people of the scrolls came from?" asked Silberman, drawing a laugh from the audience.

It certainly isn't a question that usually gets asked at the Shrine of the Book, built in the heart of the Israel Museum's courtyard to house the scrolls in Israel's possession. Its distinctive white dome gleams against the background of the hills of Jerusalem. A few weeks after the scrolls conference in Jerusalem has ended, things are back to normal at the museum. The scholars are gone, the tables heavy with wine and finger food packed away. The museum is filled with student groups running boisterously through the main courtyard. Some mothers sit in the shade of the trees on benches, baby carriages parked next to them. Tourists with maps wander through the gardens peeking out between the buildings. Inside the Shrine of the Book, it is a quiet morning. The museum's curators have mounted an exhibition trying to re-create a day in the life of the Essenes, or what can be gleaned about their lifestyle from the few written sources that exist. The exhibition consists primarily of small finds, the remains of daily life in the desert. There are nails that fell out of sandals found on the paths leading from the Qumran ruins to the caves nearby, as well as a mattock head that was used to create a primitive outdoor toilet. Accompanying the artifacts are neatly printed quotes from the works of Flavius Josephus, whose books about the Jewish revolt against the Romans are our main source of information about the Essenes.

This morning, most of the guides lead their charges through the exhibition quickly, reiterating what is on the exhibition's signs and heading directly for the scrolls. But one tour guide, taking a small group of American teenagers around the building, offers a new approach. "We have tried to show how the [Essenes'] way of life reflected their concept of separation," the guide reads from the introduction posted at the entrance to the exhibition. The students appear to be uninterested, just one more stop on their two-week tour of Israel. But then the guide points out all the finds that seem to contradict the very idea of separation. He gets excited over the smallest item, and slowly the students do too. Their personal conversations stop, and soon only the guide's voice, filled with enthusiasm, can be heard in the exhibition hall. He points out the combs that were found still with the remains of lice on them, and talks about what it was like to live in the Judea of that time period. He stops the group at the case containing the wornout pair of sandals and the nails that fell out of them that the archaeologists carefully collected. "Everyone wore the same kind of sandals, whether they lived in the desert or in Jerusalem," the guide says. When he gets to the picture of the ritual baths, called mikva'ot, he talks about how important immersion in these baths was to all levels of Judean society, how there were baths found inside the homes of wealthy aristocrats in Jerusalem as well as in the desert at Qumran. "Too often we're asked to look at what separates us," the guide says, "but often you can look at the same finds and see what the people all had in common."

Until only recently, what linked Ezra's time with that of the writers of the scrolls, continuing up to our own era, was that all read essentially the same Hebrew Bible. Various religious denominations had determined what books to include in their canon along the way, and the composition and number of sacred collections varied widely, ranging from the Jewish canon, with thirty-nine books, up to the Ethiopian Orthodox canon, with eighty-one books. Nonetheless, there was a sense that it had all started from a single source — the book that Ezra read that week in Jerusalem upon his return from Babylon. In the Ezra-Nehemiah records, the text is called the Law of Moses, the Law of God, or just the Law. But Jewish tradition to this day holds that Ezra read a copy of the Pentateuch, upon which the Masoretic text of the Bible is based. This text is the standard Hebrew Bible today, taking its name from the group of scribes, called the Masoretes, who worked in the city of Tiberias on the Sea of Galilee during the tenth century c.e. Their transcription was the oldest version of the Bible found until the discovery of the Dead Sea Scrolls. Orthodox Judaism insists that this Bible had not varied in its literary form since Moses' time. Most Bible scholars, however, accept what is called the documentary hypothesis of the Bible's development, the result of biblical scholarship done in the nineteenth century. This theory, most closely associated with the work of a German Protestant scholar named Julius Wellhausen, argues that there were four separate strands of the Bible written by different people at different times that were later brought together and edited by a single editor, or redactor. In the 150 or so years since this idea was first formulated, the theory hasn't evolved very much. But one of the changes that is now widely accepted by many scholars is that this final editor was Ezra, and that the text we use today is probably very close to the one he read aloud after his return to Jerusalem. The Talmud, the book of Jewish oral law compiled around 220 c.e., reinforces this notion of Ezra as the ultimate Torah scholar. "Had Moses not preceded him," it is written about Ezra in Tractate Sanhedrin, "Ezra would have been worthy of having the Torah given through him."

The latest Dead Sea Scrolls scholarship challenges the idea that Ezra's book is what we read today when we open the Bible. Eugene Ulrich, a professor of Hebrew scriptures at the University of Notre Dame, has been working on publishing the 127 biblical scrolls that were discovered at Qumran. He and the other scholars working with him have begun to believe that what links the Bible as we know it with the Law read by Ezra is not the final product so much as the process involved in its creation.

The scribes who copied the different books of the Bible stored at Qumran had been faithful overall to the material and the tradition they inherited. But they also "creatively expanded and reshaped [the Bible] to fit the new circumstances and the new needs that the successive communities experienced through the vicissitudes of history," Ulrich wrote in one piece outlining his ideas. In order to do this, they incorporated new material that they felt might clarify or sharpen some point for the people reading it. Ulrich attributes this to the scribes' belief not only in the importance of transmitting the Bible, but in making sure it remained relevant. This resulted in the appearance of regular new literary editions of the Bible. Current events, whether in the political, economic, or social realm, provided the catalyst for each new version.

Ulrich's Dead Sea Scrolls research has demonstrated that in the centuries after Ezra supposedly finished editing the Bible, there was still no agreed-upon list among the many religious groups of which works were considered Scriptures and which were outside the canon. Ulrich also argues that individual texts themselves were still changing as well. By his count, the Qumran scrolls include at least four editions of the books of Exodus and Numbers, a wide variety of Deuteronomy volumes, and two or more versions of Psalms, and he suspects there were even more editions that haven't survived. Many of the scholars studying the biblical scrolls speculate that the only thing that stopped this process of continual updating was a threat to Judaism itself, perhaps in 70 C.E., when the Romans destroyed the Second Temple, or even in 135, when the Second Jewish Revolt was crushed by the Romans and the Jews were expelled from Jerusalem. "Ezra may in fact have compiled a form of the Torah, but the Bible kept on growing long after Ezra's time," Ulrich says.

At the July 1997 Dead Sea Scrolls conference in Jerusalem, scholars presented papers on every possible aspect of modern scrolls research. There were talks about carbon-dating the scrolls, scientific studies of the composition of ancient ink, and the latest on DNA examinations of animal skin parchments, all recent techniques that are helping make significant scholarly advances. There was even a panel discussion about the scrolls in pop culture. Ezra and Nehemiah were never directly mentioned then or at the many other exhibitions and congresses celebrating the scrolls' discovery that were held in New York, London, and even Jordan throughout the rest of 1997. But Eugene Ulrich isn't alone among the many people who attended these various celebrations in seeing the connection between the latest in scrolls research and events taking place in Persian Palestine in the fifth century B.C.E.

A few months after the major scrolls celebration, Philip Davies has come to Jerusalem to speak at Hebrew University about the Damascus Document, which describes the rituals and rules of a Jewish sect. The Damascus Document was first discovered in Cairo in 1896 in the genizah, a storage room for sacred texts that are torn or worn-out and can no longer be used, of the Ben Ezra synagogue. Fifty years later, scholars examining some of the documents from Qumran found the same text among the Dead Sea Scrolls. But there is no consensus about who wrote it, Essenes or some other Jewish sect that existed at the same time. Davies sees the document as very similar in outlook to some of the ideas put forth in the Books of Ezra and Nehemiah. The members of the so-called Damascus community, who got their name from scholars because of the numerous references to that city in the document, had apparently separated from the mainstream and regarded themselves as the true Israel. This idea is what most fascinates Davies, a theme that he sees running from Ezra straight into our own times. In each generation, it seems, there were many competing approaches to Judaism, with each group considering itself the authentic link to the historical Israelite community, the guardians of the true interpretation of the Torah, and seeking to cut others out.

Davies' curiosity about Ezra and Nehemiah stems from his work covering the period when the Dead Sea Scrolls were written. "I had expected to find unity, one Judaism, since that is how later rabbinic tradition portrays it," Davies says one day in the lobby of the Jerusalem hotel where he is staying during the conference. "But it turned out that there were many Judaisms competing with each other. Even the priests who controlled the temple were not recognized by all Israelites as a centralized religious authority."

These are the same concerns that marked the Persian period, Davies argues. In the Bible, the Books of Ezra and Nehemiah promote the idea that the reform implemented by these men created a single Judaism, the one true Israel. Davies sees enormous diversity here too, arguing that the religion practiced by most Judeans of this time was essentially polytheistic. By the second century B.C.E., the Maccabees came to power from their base in Modiin, and the Judeans who had been cast outside the gates of Jerusalem by Ezra and Nehemiah as foreigners were now considered no different than the descendants of those who had returned from Babylon. In fact, the former outsiders were now in power, and they did just what Ezra and Nehemiah had done before them, promoting the idea that they alone represented the real Israel. The Maccabees fought not only against the Greeks but against any fellow Jews who wanted to adopt the values and practices of the Hellenists.

A few days before his talk in Jerusalem, Davies drives down to Tel Aviv, to meet with professors and graduate students in a seminar given by the university's archaeology department. There is quite a bit of tension in the small conference room when Davies, dressed in a white oxford cloth shirt and black pants, begins to speak. Israel Finkelstein, the head of the archaeology department, is one of the few Israeli archaeology professors who actually requires that his students read Davies' most famous book, *In Search of "Ancient Israel."* The book has been extremely controversial because it was among the first to argue in cogent, accessible terms that the Bible had been mainly written, not just edited, in the Persian era and perhaps even later. This attacked the traditional idea that the Bible's writers had recorded many events immediately after they happened. "The Bible is not completely unhistorical," Davies tells the students and professors near the end of his talk, "but it is largely unhistorical." Later he will expand on the idea.

"For every historical battle there is also a fictional miracle," he writes me a few months after his visit to Israel. "Whether the Bible is fictionalized history or historicized fiction is a matter of taste. It is a blend of both, and the argument is over the proportions and the extent to which history or fiction is in control."

In Tel Aviv, Davies tells the archaeology seminar participants that he sees the Bible's greatness as a religious history, the ultimate proof of its veracity being the existence of Judaism. "To be a modern Jew," argues Davies, "is to also be associated with that history, to take it as your own." But modern Israelis have a different history, he goes on to say. "Israel is the land in which Israelis live, and the land to whose history they belong." They should focus on uncovering the past of the land that they now live on, including the histories of all the land's previous inhabitants, whether Jewish or not. Religious Jews, as well as secular Jews who don't live in Israel, simply can't and don't belong to this enterprise in the same way, Davies concludes. Archaeology and the Bible tell the stories — and histories — of two different Israels.

After Davies finishes speaking, several of the professors begin to question some of his ideas. They challenge his theories about the late dating for biblical Hebrew and offer archaeological data to try to refute his idea that the Bible should not be seen as a historical record. The moment for real debate passes. No one takes him up on his most disturbing and provocative point. Davies seems to be arguing not only that these stories can't be reconciled but that one has to choose sides, and determine which Israel to belong to.

Yizhar Hirschfeld has already chosen sides. "I want to take Qumran back for the Jews," the archaeologist says one morning at the site in the desert where he is digging. The statement seems to place him among all the others interested in trying to create yet another exclusive new Israel. But he says he objects to efforts by earlier scholars to effectively place Qumran outside the currents of Jewish history. "I see Qumran as reflecting the diversity of Jewish thought at the time," he tells me.

Six months have passed since his controversial speech at the scrolls conference arguing that Qumran was a Judean manor, and Hirschfeld is finally back in the desert. He has continued to speak about the archaeology of Qumran at small gatherings around Israel, and is in the final stages of editing a scholarly article outlining his ideas. But January is digging season in the desert, and Hirschfeld's other work can wait. In the brief winter season of rain, Jerusalem's stone houses are impossible to warm and the city looks gray and somber. But in Ein Gedi, just twenty minutes away from Jerusalem along the modern road running to the Dead Sea, it feels like summer. We have just climbed to the top of a cliff on a narrow path. A mile below us is the ancient village of Ein Gedi, where Hirschfeld has been excavating a beautiful Byzantine-era synagogue. Hirschfeld, dressed in shorts, T-shirt, and hiking boots, sets out breakfast. There are boiled eggs, a thick white yogurt drink called eshel, and sandwiches. Four ibex clamber along the sides of the cliff. The sulfur haze rises above the Dead Sea, casting an incandescent light. In the distance, the pink and purple mountains of Moab glower, shoots of green burst from the brown sandy hills below, and the palm trees set on the edge of the azure sea sway slightly in the breeze.

During the digging in Ein Gedi, Hirschfeld began excavating what he now calls the Essene village located on this hilltop. The village consists of twenty-two cell-like structures built of roughly hewn stones as well as two pools located near a spring that had been hidden by overgrown cane and vegetation. The cells have beaten-earth floors and probably had roofs of palm fronds; each was big enough for one person to occupy. Pottery remains, all simple jugs and plates, were found in each cell. There are also three larger structures that Hirschfeld believes served as cooking and communal areas. Based on his findings at the site and a new interpretation of some of the traditional historical material about the era, Hirschfeld is arguing that this was the more likely home for an ascetic sect like the Essenes than a place like Qumran. Virtually no other archaeologist agrees with this particular idea, and there is some grumbling about how Hirschfeld, in his knack for creating headlines, has already arranged for a dramatic hilltop press conference complete with a hike up the mountain to view the site a few weeks from now.

"What went on in the desert was always directly connected to Jerusalem and intellectual and political events there," says Hirschfeld, wedging a battered coffeepot in between some stones and building a small pyramid out of charcoal beneath it. "The Jewish mainstream has always been wider than people like to think."

The latest archaeological work in the desert seems to support this idea. The desert did serve as a place of refuge. According to biblical tradition, David, not yet a king, came here to escape the wrath of his patron King Saul, who rightfully suspected that the young warrior intended to challenge his throne. The prophets Jeremiah and Elijah, as well as John the Baptist and Jesus of Nazareth, all spent time in the desert, and the hills around Ein Gedi are honeycombed with small caves that served as retreats for hermits and monks, eccentrics and thinkers. Archaeologists digging here have discovered archives, letters, and scrolls indicating that during the course of hundreds of years and many revolts against various empires, the desert also served as the administrative center for governments-in-exile that wanted to stay close to Jerusalem and political events taking place there.

To this day, one of the most interesting finds is the discovery in 1962 of a cache of personal documents belonging to a woman named Babatha. They show that just sixty years after the Essenes were supposedly living in isolation at Qumran, the area around the Dead Sea was clearly not barren. Babatha's documents were discovered during an expedition led by Yigael Yadin, who also excavated at Masada and Megiddo. In a cave near where Hirschfeld is now digging in Ein Gedi, archaeologists found documents left by Jews fleeing the Roman army at the end of the Second Jewish Revolt, which lasted from 132 to 135 C.E. Babatha's documents were overshadowed by the discovery in the same cave of letters from the leader of the revolt, Simon bar Kochba, to two of his lieutenants. But it is her documents, as well as the jewelry box, frying pan, and other personal items Babatha had taken pains to hide, that have shed the most important light on everyday life in Israel in the early second century C.E. The documents indicate that Jews and non-Jews conducted business together — Nabateans, Romans, Greeks, and Jews all sign or appear as principals in the documents, including loan agreements, bills of sale, and business contracts. The picture of Jewish life as somehow separate and ethnically isolated from what was happening in the rest of the Roman empire, as it is portrayed in rabbinic literature such as the Mishnah and Talmud, is not reflected at all in the archive. Babatha's world was one in which Jews lived peacefully with their neighbors, observing traditional Jewish customs and laws, but within the framework of local mores. Babatha had a whole network of contacts that extended even beyond Judea's borders.

In the 1950s, the American writer Edmund Wilson came to the desert to write about the discovery of the Dead Sea Scrolls. "The landscape of the Dead Sea wilderness is monotonous, subduing and dreadful," Wilson wrote later about his drive from Jerusalem deep into the desert on the way to Qumran. "This country is completely impersonal. It is a landscape without physiognomy: no faces of gods or men, no bodies of recumbent animals, are suggested by the shapes of the hills. 'Nothing but monotheism could possibly come out of this,' said one of my companions."

Monotheism came out of the desert, then existed there side by side with the remains of wayside religious shrines, places of cultural interaction where many gods were worshipped by travelers making their way in caravans from one end of the desert to the other. Trading routes crisscrossed the sands, connecting Jerusalem and the desert not just to each other, but to large cities and commercial centers located across the Middle East. Babatha, and others like her, saw their destinies linked not just to their own neighborhoods but to the world beyond. In the Bible, Jerusalem is the city on the hill, the place of glory and redemption; the desert is a place of wandering, harsh, stark, and uncompromising. One of the central themes of the Bible involves the journey from the desert to Jerusalem, the long trek from tribe to nation. The two places exist on opposite sides of the biblical world.

On the hills of Ein Gedi, things look different. Here the Bible can be seen in all its vastness and complexity, outside the narrow confines of any one religious group or political dogma. This is the true Israel, one able to encompass a rich diversity, that sees its history as part of the wider mainstream. On the drive back to Jerusalem, there is a brief moment of grace in the landscape. At the turn of a hill, the browns of Ein Gedi suddenly give way to a burst of color. All of a sudden the desert seems to run right into Jerusalem's purple and gold mountains. It is a vivid reminder of the desert's refusal to stay confined to the margins, and of the Bible's inexorable journey back to the center of things.

Notes on Sources

⁂

Much of the information in this book is based on my visits to archaeological sites in the Middle East and extensive interviews with archaeologists, historians, and Bible scholars. Many of the people I interviewed shared unpublished material and works in progress with me. They also have published extensively, and I benefited enormously from their work. Given the sheer number of books that exist on the Bible and Near Eastern archaeology, it would be impossible to read all of them, but I tried to consult what are considered the major works. It would be far too unwieldy to cite here everything I read, but I've listed below the books and articles that I found most useful and upon which I drew extensively in my own writing. All Bible quotes are from the Jewish Publication Society of America's *The Holy Scriptures* (Philadelphia, 1955). *The Anchor Bible Dictionary* (New York, 1992) is an indispensable reference work for anyone interested in the Bible. Amihai Mazar's *Archaeology of the Land of the Bible* (New York, 1990), Amnon Ben-Tor's *The Archaeology of Ancient Israel* (Tel Aviv, 1992), Ephraim Stern's *The New Encyclopedia of Archaeological Excavations in the Holy Land* (Jerusalem, 1993), and Thomas Levy's *The Archaeology of Society in the Holy Land* (London, 1995) offer comprehensive, detailed examinations of the archaeology and history of ancient Israel and some of her neighbors. Hershel Shanks's *Ancient Israel: A Short History from Abraham to the Roman Destruction of the Temple* (Washington, 1988) is a well-written collection of essays that address the key periods for Bible lovers. Shanks also publishes the invaluable *Biblical Archaeology Review,* a monthly magazine that contains articles about digs by the leading archaeologists in the region written in ways a lay person can comprehend. *Near Eastern Archaeology,* the monthly magazine of the American Schools of Oriental Research, is a more technical journal but also useful for following archaeological developments and debates. *The Annual of the Department of Antiquities of Jordan* is a tremendous resource about the many excavations going on in that country.

Introduction   The View from Nebo

The history of Nebo cannot be written without relying on *Mount Nebo: New Archaeological Excavations, 1967–1997,* by Michele Piccirillo and Eugenio Alliata (Jerusalem, 1998). I found this book indispensable in my reconstruction of exploration at the site. The quotes by the explorers of the site are from Piccirillo's fascinating chapter in the volume, "The Exploration of Nebo." The quotes from Piccirillo are from the author's 1999 interview with him.

Bruce Routledge was interviewed by the author in 1998. The quotes are from his speech at the 1998 conference in Philadelphia, which the author attended.

The author attended the Israel Exploration Society's 1998 annual meeting in Jerusalem. The author attended Israel Finkelstein's speech, from which his quote is drawn.

The author interviewed Philip Davies in Jerusalem and in Tel Aviv in 1998.

Israel Finkelstein's quote appears in an article he wrote, "Pots and People Revisited: Ethnic Boundaries in the Iron Age I," in *The Archaeology of Israel: Constructing the Past, Interpreting the Present,* edited by Neil Asher Silberman and David Small (Sheffield, 1997).

Paula Wapnish and Brian Hesse sent me a number of their studies and papers about animal bones at sites around the Middle East. They gave me an advance copy of a forthcoming article, "Pig Use and Abuse in the Ancient Levant: Ethnoreligious Boundary Building with Swine," that was very useful. The Gösta Ahlström quote appears in that article. Their article "Can Pig Remains Be Used for Ethnic Diagnosis in the Ancient Near East?" in the Silberman and Small volume, sets forth in a popular style what they call their "Pig Principles."

There are a number of helpful articles that discussed the issue of archaeology and ideology in the same book, including pieces by Amos Elon, Yaacov Shavit, William Dever, and Neil Asher Silberman. Silberman's *Digging for God & Country: Exploration, Archaeology, and the Secret Struggle for the Holy Land, 1799–1917*

(New York, 1982) remains the classic text about the political and religious motives behind archaeological exploration in the Middle East. Silberman recounts the history of American biblical archaeology in "Whose Game Is It Anyway? The Political and Social Transformations of American Biblical Archaeology," a chapter in *Archaeology Under Fire: Nationalism, Politics and Heritage in the Eastern Mediterranean and Middle East,* edited by Lynn Meskell (London, 1998). Another good history of biblical archaeology is John R. Bartlett's article "What Has Archaeology to Do with the Bible — Or Vice Versa?" in *Archaeology & Biblical Interpretation* (London, 1997).

Kamal Salibi discussed his theories about why the Bible took place in Saudi Arabia with me during an interview in Amman and in his book *The Historicity of Biblical Israel* (Amman, 1998). I visited Nebo in 1998.

James L. Kugel's work *The Bible as It Was* (Cambridge, 1997) contributed enormously to my understanding of how ancient biblical interpretation worked. Richard Elliott Friedman's *Who Wrote the Bible?* (New York, 1987) is an immensely readable and important account of the history of nineteenth-century biblical scholarship and the way it continues to influence how we think about the Bible.

Chapter 1   Genesis: Abraham's Odyssey

The information about folklore associated with Abraham around the region is based on material contained in *Abraham's Odyssey,* a documentary film directed by Yehuda Yaniv. Information about the academic debates surrounding the dating of Abraham comes from the author's personal interviews with Bible scholars Ronald Hendel, Kyle McCarter Jr., and Richard Elliott Friedman in 1998. *Biblical Archaeology Review* and *Bible Review* ran a number of articles about the Ebla discoveries and subsequent controversies, including "Ebla and the Bible — What's Left (If Anything)?" by Alan Millard, *Bible Review,* April 1992. The James L. Kugel quotation is from *The Bible as It Was* (Cambridge, 1997). All the information about the making of the *Abraham's Odyssey* documentary came from the author's personal interviews with Yaniv in 1998. Information about the Bab edh-Dhra' and Numeira sites is based on the author's personal interview with R. Thomas Schaub, as well as excavation reports Schaub and Walter Rast published in the *New Encyclopedia of Archaeological Excavations*. A more popular study of their finds was published in *Biblical Archaeology Review,* "Has Sodom and Gomorrah Been Found?" September/October 1980, page 26.

David Ilan shared an unpublished copy of a lecture he gave called "The Archaeology of Immigration: A Case Study from the Middle Bronze Age in the Levant," and gave the author a tour of the Tel Dan finds at the Skirball Museum. His article "The Dawn of Internationalism — the Middle Bronze Age" appears in *The Archaeology of Society in the Holy Land.*

The material about the Hebron dig is based on the author's personal interview with Avi Ofer and an excavation report he published in Hebrew in *Qadmoniot* 22 (1989). Ofer's article in English, "All the Hill Country of Judah: From a Settlement Fringe to a Prosperous Monarchy," offers a detailed look at his survey of the Judean hills region that appeared in *From Nomadism to Monarchy: Archaeological and Historical Aspects of Early Israel,* edited by Israel Finkelstein and Nadav Na'aman (Jerusalem, 1994). The author interviewed Ofer in 1999.

Information about the debate among Bible scholars regarding the dating of the patriarchal stories and the way they evolved over time is from the author's personal interviews with Kyle McCarter, Ronald Hendel, Oded Lipschits, and Steven Fine in 1998. McCarter sets out many of his arguments in a wonderful chapter about Abraham in *Ancient Israel: A Short History.* Hendel was kind enough to send an advance copy of his article about the patriarchal age that was published in a revised edition of the same book.

The section about modern-day Hebron and the way Jewish and Arab residents deal with the past is based on numerous reporting trips to the city and personal interviews by the author. The interview with Hebron's mayor, Mustafa Abdel Nabi Natsheh, was conducted on behalf of the author by Khaled Abu Toameh in 1999.

The history of the Cave of the Patriarchs' changing architectural styles is compiled in an article about Israeli exploration at the site by Nancy Miller, "Patriarchal Burial Site Explored for First Time in 700 Years," which ran in the May/June 1985 edition of *Biblical Archaeology Review.* Steven Fine sent me a draft of his unpublished paper "Between Beth She'arim and Eden: The Cave of Makhpelah in Rabbinic Literature," which describes many of the legends associated with Abraham's burial site from the Second Temple period.

Chapter 2   Exodus: Pharaoh Speaks

The confusions in the text of Exodus and the various scholarly theories that might explain them are discussed both in Nahum M. Sarna's *Exploring Exodus: The Origins of Biblical Israel* (New York, 1986), a traditional, well-written treatment of Exodus, and in *Moses: A Life,* by Jonathan Kirsch (New York, 1998).

The ways in which the Egyptians view their past is discussed in Neil Asher Silberman's *Between Past and Present: Archaeology, Ideology, and Nationalism in the Modern Middle East* (New York, 1989). More recent information is based on the author's 1998 interviews with Zahi Hawass, Kent Weeks, and officials at the Cairo Museum. Egyptian attitudes toward the Hyksos are detailed in Eliezer Oren's article "The Hyksos Enigma — Introductory Overview," which appeared in the book he edited, *The Hyksos: New Historical and Archaeological Perspectives* (Philadelphia, 1998).

The author visited the Cairo Museum in 1998.

The quotes from Hawass are all from the author's interview with him. Hawass provided the author with information about the workmen's community at Giza contained in an unpublished manuscript that he is writing called *The Giza Pyramids: Mysteries Revealed.*

Mansour Radwan was interviewed by the author at the Giza cemetery.

Mark Lehner was interviewed by the author in 1998. His annual excavation reports were published by the Oriental Institute in Chicago, whose press assistant kindly collected and sent them to me. The National Geographic Society provided me with a transcript of their program *Who Built the Pyramids?*, in which they re-created how the ancients baked bread.

The information about what was found at Deir el-Medineh and Pi-Ramesse is based on author interviews with Hawass, Lehner, and Weeks. Mark Lehner's *The Complete Pyramids* (London, 1997) is a beautifully illustrated study of all of Egypt's pyramids. A popular article about the Deir el-Medineh finds, "Pharaoh's Workers: How the Israelites Lived in Egypt," by Leonard and Barbara Lesko, was published in the January/February 1999 issue of *Biblical Archaeology Review.*

K. A. Kitchen's *Pharaoh Triumphant: The Life and Times of Ramesses II* (Cairo, 1982) is an interesting biography of one of ancient Egypt's most important leaders.

Weeks was interviewed in his office in Cairo. Douglas Preston wrote an excellent article about the discovery of the KV5 tomb called "All the King's Sons" that appeared in *The New Yorker* in 1996. Weeks chronicles his discovery of the KV5 tomb and its significance in *The Lost Tomb* (New York, 1998).

The information about the making of *The Prince of Egypt* is based on the author's interview with producer Penney Finkelman Cox. My *Wall Street Journal* colleague Bruce Orwall helped me navigate the bureaucracy at Dream-Works.

The changing views of Moses are chronicled in Kirsch's biography of Moses and in *Moses the Egyptian: The Memory of Egypt in Western Monotheism,* by Jan Assmann (Cambridge, 1997). Assmann also kindly answered written questions posed by the author.

Exodus: The Egyptian Evidence, edited by Ernest S. Frerichs and Leonard H. Lesko (Winona Lake, 1997), is still one of the only works to look at Exodus from the perspective of Egypt and the Egyptians. Jill Kamil demonstrates in *The Ancient Egyptians: Life in the Old Kingdom* (Cairo, 1984) the hold ancient Egypt's history continued to exert on the country throughout the ages.

Itzhaq Beit-Arieh and Eliezer Oren were interviewed by the author about their work in the Sinai desert. Beit-Arieh also wrote a popular article, "Fifteen Years in Sinai," that ran in the July/August 1984 issue of *Biblical Archaeology Review* and presents his findings and those of other Israeli archaeologists who explored that territory before the peace agreement was signed with Egypt. Ze'ev

Meshel's ideas about Bedouin customs having precedents in the biblical text are included in the article.

Chapter 3   The New Canaanites

I owe the opening sentence in the chapter to a paraphrase of the clever title of one of the lectures in a seminar run by Hershel Shanks's Biblical Archaeology Society about the debate over the origins of the Israelites. The lectures in the book based on the seminar, *The Rise of Ancient Israel,* by Hershel Shanks, William G. Dever, Baruch Halpern, and P. Kyle McCarter Jr. (Washington, 1992) are all excellent, informative, and to the point.

Ze'ev Herzog's research about Canaanite cities appears in Hebrew in a lecture he gave at a conference on "New Directions in the Archaeology of the Land of Israel," held at Bar-Ilan University on June 3, 1999, and in English in his book *Archaeology of the City: Urban Planning in Ancient Israel and Its Social Implications* (Tel Aviv, 1997). Herzog was also interviewed in Tel Aviv in 1998 by the author.

Amnon Ben-Tor spoke extensively with the author about his work at Hazor and also gave me a tour of the site in 1998. Several articles he wrote were particularly helpful, including "The Yigael Yadin Memorial Excavations at Hazor: 1990–93: Aims and Preliminary Results," which is included in the Silberman and Small book, *The Archaeology of Israel,* and "Season of 1991: Introduction," in the *Israel Exploration Journal* 42 (1992). He also wrote a two-part series on Hazor that was published in the March/April 1999 and May/June 1999 issues of *Biblical Archaeology Review.* Susan Niditch shows how the ancient Israelites and Canaanites worshipped in *Ancient Israelite Religion* (New York, 1997).

Paula Wapnish's analysis of the bones at Megiddo and other sites around the region is based on the author's interview with her. She and her husband, Brian Hesse, have written many interesting and helpful articles on the topic. "Can Pig Remains Be Used for Ethnic Diagnosis in the Ancient Near East?" was published in the Silberman and Small collection. She sent me copies of "Urbanization and the Organization of Animal Production at Tell Jemmeh in the Middle Bronze Age Levant," *Journal of Near Eastern Studies* 47:2, and "Faunal Remains from Tel Dan: Perspectives on Animal Production at a Village, Urban and Ritual Center," *Archaeozoologia* 4:2.

Ronny Reich was interviewed by the author in Jerusalem in 1998 and also took me through his site. The information and quotes about Elad's aims in the City of David are based on the author's interview with Elad official Yigal Naveh, also in 1998.

Jalal Kazzouh was interviewed in 1998 in Nablus by the author and also gave me a tour of the site and the archaeology department at An-Najah University.

Marwan Abu Khalaf's quotes are from an interview with the author in Jerusalem in 1997. Albert Glock laid out his aims for Palestinian archaeology in an article published after his death, "Archaeology as Cultural Survival: The Future of the Palestinian Past," *Journal of Palestine Studies,* Spring 1994. Similar themes are raised by the Palestinian historian Beshara B. Doumani in "Rediscovering Ottoman Palestine: Writing Palestinians Into History," in the *Journal of Palestine Studies,* Winter 1992.

Khaled Nashef was interviewed a number of times during 1998 in Bir Zeit by the author. He gave me a tour of the Khirbet Bir Zeit site and arranged for his students to discuss with me their vision of Palestinian archaeology at his office at the university. The quotes from his student Nail Jelal are from that interview. Hamdan Taha, the head of the Palestinian Department of Antiquities, was interviewed by the author in his office in Ramallah. He provided me with his 1996 paper, "Two Years of Archaeology in Palestine," which sums up the official Palestinian governmental viewpoint about what archaeology has accomplished.

All That Remains: The Palestinian Villages Occupied and Depopulated by Israel in 1948, edited by Walid Khalidi (Washington, 1992), offers a good example of the kind of alternative archaeological narrative the Palestinians hope to provide. Khalidi also discussed his ideas in an interview with the author in Cambridge, Massachusetts.

The archaeologist Robert Schick translated an article in Arabic by Khaled Nashef that ran in the February 8, 1999, issue of the Jerusalem-based Arabic newspaper *Al-Quds* that was helpful in understanding Palestinian resentments of foreign-run archaeology excavations, "Palestinian Archaeology . . . in French and Italian." I also learned about the politics of Palestinian archaeology from interviews with John Worrell and Uzi Baram. Baram sent me a copy of his paper "Entangled Objects from the Palestinian Past: Archaeological Perspectives for the Ottoman Period, 1800–1900," which touched on some of these issues.

The theories of Israelite settlement in Canaan are well-covered ground. Ann E. Killebrew's 1998 Hebrew University dissertation *Ceramic Craft and Technology During the Late Bronze and Early Iron Ages: The Relationship Between Pottery Technology, Style, and Cultural Diversity* helped me understand both the potential and the problems in using pottery to establish ethnicity in ancient times.

The classic archaeological treatise about the Israelite presence in Canaan remains Israel Finkelstein's book in Hebrew *The Archaeology of the Israelite Settlement* (Jerusalem, 1988). Nadav Na'aman offers a fascinating summary of the scholarly work that's been done and his theories about Israelite settlement in his article "The 'Conquest of Canaan' in the Book of Joshua and in History," which was published in the *From Nomadism to Monarchy* volume. The quotes from Finkelstein are based on an interview the author conducted in his Tel Aviv office in 1997. Adam Zertal was interviewed a number of times by the author in 1998 and allowed me to participate in one of his Friday surveys. Articles by

Larry Herr and Adam Zertal that discuss some of the similarities in finds at their excavations in Israel and Jordan, and the implications for reconstructing the history of Israelite settlement, appear in the volume *Mediterranean Peoples in Transition: 13th–10th Century B.C.E.*, edited by Seymour Gitin, Amihai Mazar, and Ephraim Stern (Jerusalem, 1998).

The history of the search for Ebal is based on the author's interviews with Zertal. He has also written about his work at Ebal for *Biblical Archaeology Review* (January/February 1985). An entire issue of *Tel Aviv* is devoted to a preliminary final excavation report written by Zertal and his team that helped me understand the site and its finds. Zertal also continues to publish installments in his monumental *Survey of Har Menashe* (in Hebrew, Haifa) every few years. The quotes from Shuki Levin come from a 1998 visit with the author and Zertal to Mount Ebal.

Chapter 4   In Search of David and Solomon

Meron Benvenisti first pointed out the misunderstood history of the Tower of David museum in his wonderful book *City of Stone: The Hidden History of Jerusalem* (Berkeley, 1996).

A collection of articles that first raised some of the major issues surrounding the scholarship on David and Solomon and the dating of the gates at Megiddo and Gezer ran in *Bulletin of the American School of Oriental Research,* number 277/278 (1990). David Ussishkin was one of the earliest to raise the question about the Megiddo gate's dating in "Was the Solomonic City Gate at Megiddo Built by King Solomon?" *BASOR* 239. *The Origins of the Ancient Israelite States,* edited by Volkmar Fritz and Philip R. Davies (Sheffield, 1996), raises key issues about dating and the united monarchy. Yigael Yadin wrote a number of articles outlining his thoughts about the Megiddo gate beginning in 1958.

Levant devoted much of its 1998 year to the debate between Israel Finkelstein and Amihai Mazar over the dating of Megiddo and Finkelstein's efforts to lower the chronology of key tenth-century sites. "The Archaeology of the United Monarchy: An Alternative View," by Finkelstein, ran in *Levant* 28; "Iron Age Chronology: A Reply to I. Finkelstein" appeared in *Levant* 29. The article that caused so much ire among other archaeologists was Finkelstein's final piece, "Bible Archaeology or the Archaeology of Palestine in the Iron Age: A Rejoinder," in *Levant* 30.

The quotes attributed to Finkelstein are from the author's personal interviews with him in 1998. He and David Ussishkin gave me a tour of the site at Megiddo in the summer of 1998. Neil Asher Silberman, who was present and interviewed during this same visit, also provided me with a copy of the lecture he gave from which his quotation about looking in the mirror is taken.

Israel Finkelstein describes what Judah and Israel looked like in the tenth century B.C.E. in his article "State Formation in Israel and Judah: A Contrast in Context, a Contrast in Trajectory," in *Near Eastern Archaeology* 62:1 (1999). Adam Zertal's survey results in Israel and Avi Ofer's results in the Judean hills are also described in articles they wrote in the Finkelstein and Na'aman *From Nomadism to Monarchy* volume.

The key texts written by members of what is referred to now as the Copenhagen School are Philip R. Davies' *In Search of "Ancient Israel"* (Sheffield, 1992) and Thomas Thompson's *Early History of the Israelite People from the Written and Archaeological Sources* (Leiden, 1992). *The Invention of Ancient Israel: The Silencing of Palestinian History,* by Keith W. Whitelam (London, 1996), is often at the center of heated debate about the politics of the past. *Can a History of Israel Be Written?* edited by Lester L. Grabbe (Sheffield, 1997), is a collection of essays written by scholars who share varying degrees of skepticism about the historicity of the Bible. William Dever is the most prominent critic of the Copenhagen School and a prolific writer. He sent me a number of papers that helped me understand his opposition to the group's work. Particularly helpful was his contribution to D. V. Edelman's *The Fabric of History: Text, Artifact and Israel's Past* (Sheffield, 1991). He was also interviewed by the author a number of times. J. M. Miller's article "Is It Possible to Write a History of Israel Without Relying on the Hebrew Bible?" in the same Edelman volume, was also useful.

I interviewed Thomas Thompson and Niels Lemche during a 1998 visit to Copenhagen and also corresponded with them.

Joshua Schwartz was interviewed at Bar-Ilan by the author in 1998. He invited me to attend both Lemche's lecture to the Bar-Ilan students and a private luncheon held for him and Israeli archaeologists. The quotations from Dever are from an interview the author conducted with him in Philadelphia in 1998.

Michael Niemann's ideas about David's and Solomon's being classic Middle Eastern chieftains is presented most clearly in his article "The Socio-Political Shadow Cast by the Biblical Solomon," in *The Age of Solomon: Scholarship at the Turn of the Millennium* (Leiden, 1997). Nadav Na'aman's article in the same volume is an insightful examination of the sources that might have been used to compose the text and how to date them. Na'aman was interviewed in Tel Aviv in 1998 by the author.

Ann Killebrew and Silberman are the sources for the information about the script and multimedia presentation they are working on; Killebrew provided me with a draft of their project proposal.

Chapter 5   The Divided Monarchy: The Near East Rising

Judah's development into a state is described in detail in *Scribes and Schools in Monarchic Judah: A Socio-Archaeological Approach,* by David W. Jamieson-Drake

(Sheffield, 1991). R. Kletter's "The Inscribed Weights of the Kingdom of Judah," *Tel Aviv* 18 (1991), was also useful in understanding state formation in Judah. Israel Finkelstein has written a number of papers and given lectures on the topic, and he provided me with copies of his work. I found "Israel vs. Judah in Biblical Times: Origins, Material Culture and Socio-Political Formations," a 1997 speech given at Hebrew University in Jerusalem, and an expanded version of the same talk in Hebrew, to be particularly useful.

There are a growing number of books and articles that give excellent overviews of the time period. William Dever's article "Social Structure in Palestine in the Iron 2 Period on the Eve of Destruction" and John S. Holladay Jr. on "The Kingdoms of Israel and Judah: Political and Economic Centralization in the Iron IIA-B (ca. 1000–750 B.C.E.)," in Levy's *The Archaeology of Society* volume, are both good resources.

The material about Moab's history is drawn from a number of studies, particularly the one by J. M. Miller, "Early Monarchy in Moab," that appeared in *Early Edom and Moab: The Beginning of the Iron Age in Southern Jordan,* edited by Piotr Bienkowski (Sheffield, 1992). Randall Younker's ideas about Moabite state formation are laid out most clearly in his article "Moabite Social Structure," which ran in *Biblical Archaeologist* 60:4 (1997).

Finkelstein shared his ideas about Omride architecture with me in a number of interviews in 1998 and 1999 and also sent a copy of a speech he gave at the Archaeology and Bible conference held at the University of Pennsylvania in November 1998 called "Omride Architecture: The Rise of the National States in the Iron Age: Archaeology and Text." The author attended the conference.

Norma Franklin was kind enough to share the results of her study of the mason marks at Megiddo and other sites with me in a personal interview in 1999.

There is a growing body of work about ancient propaganda. Keith Whitelam wrote an early and interesting article in the September 1986 *Biblical Archaeologist* called "The Symbols of Power: Aspects of Royal Propaganda in the United Monarchy." Peter Feinman touched on the topic in his 1998 presentation to the annual meeting of the American Schools of Oriental Research called "Nebo: Why North Moab Was Important to Israel — Claiming the Past to Legitimate the Present." Feinman provided the author with a copy of the speech. Nadav Na'aman also gets into the topic in "King Mesha and the Foundation of the Moabite Monarchy," in *Israel Exploration Journal* 47 (1997).

The reconstruction of Hazael's Aram owes a large debt to the work of Benjamin Mazar and his "The Aramaean Empire and Its Relations with Israel," *Biblical Archaeologist* 25. Na'aman has continued in the same tradition and has added considerably to the body of information available about Hazael. I rely on a number of his works in this chapter, including "Hazael of 'Amqi and

Hadadezer of Beth-rehob," *Ugarit-Forschungen* 27 (1995); "Sources and Composition in the History of David," in *The Origin of the Ancient Israelite States,* edited by V. Fritz and P. R. Davies (Sheffield, 1996); "Sources and Composition in the History of Solomon," in the *Age of Solomon;* and "Historical and Literary Notes on the Excavations of Tel Jezreel," in *Tel Aviv* 24 (1997). W. T. Pitard's book *Ancient Damascus* (Winona Lake, 1987) provides a picture of what Syria under Hazael might have looked like. Also useful was "Hazael's Booty Inscriptions," an article by I. Eph'al and J. Naveh in *Israel Exploration Journal* 39.

The information about the finds at Tel Jezreel is based on preliminary reports published by the excavators: "Excavations at Tel Jezreel 1990–91 Preliminary Report," *Tel Aviv* 19 (1992); "Excavations at Tel Jezreel 1992–93 Second Preliminary Report," *Levant* 26; and "Excavations at Tel Jezreel 1994–96 Third Preliminary Report," *Tel Aviv* 24 (1998). O. Zimhoni makes some comparisons of the pottery in Jezreel and Megiddo in "Clues from the Enclosure Fills: Pre-Omride Settlement at Tel Jezreel," *Tel Aviv* 24 (1998). An excellent piece that combines biblical and archaeological scholarship is "Tel Jezreel and the Dynasty of Omri," by H. G. M. Williamson, in the *Palestine Exploration Quarterly* 128 (1996).

Rami Arav, one of the excavators of Bethsaida, was interviewed several times by the author. *Bethsaida: A City by the North Shore of the Sea of Galilee,* edited by Rami Arav and Richard A. Freund (Kirksville, 1995), contains a number of interesting studies about the finds there. Arav also sent a copy of his article "Bethsaida Revealed," which ran in *Eretz* 63, March/April 1999 and contains a new look at the history of the Geshurites. The quote by Finkelstein about Hazael's presence in Hazor is from an unpublished paper he sent me, "Hazor and the North in the Iron Age: A Low Chronology Perspective," and from personal interviews with the author.

The significance of the Dan Stela is discussed in A. Biran and J. Naveh's "An Aramaic Stele Fragment from Tel Dan," *Israel Exploration Journal* 43, and "The Tel Dan Inscription: A New Fragment," *Israel Exploration Journal* 45.

Chapter 6   Babylonian Exile: The Ones Who Stayed Home

Hans M. Barstad recounts biblical scholarship about the idea of Judah's being empty after the exile in his monograph *The Myth of the Empty Land* (Oslo, 1996). The changing attitudes toward the exile period are summed up in a book edited by Lester L. Grabbe called *Leading Captivity Captive: "The Exile" as History and Ideology* (Sheffield, 1998). Grabbe was also interviewed by the author in 1998 and sent an unpublished paper, "Israel's Historical Reality After the Exile," which expands upon his ideas about the exile period. *Post-Exilic Palestine: An Archaeological Report,* a monograph by Saul S. Weinberg, was published in 1968 by the Israel Academy of Sciences and Humanities and is still useful for understanding what the state of knowledge about the period was until only recently.

The information about the finds at the City of David are from the author's personal interview in 1998 with Jane Cahill, who supervised the dig at the site, and with Dan Bahat, who is heading a current excavation there. The quotes from Yigal Naveh of Elad come from the author's personal interview in 1998. Speculation about what Jerusalem looked like before, during, and after the exile, as well as a report about the City of David dig by Cahill and David Tarler, can be found in the articles and reports contained in *Ancient Jerusalem Revealed* (Jerusalem, 1994).

Jeffrey Zorn gave me a tour of the Mizpah site in the summer of 1998 and provided me with a copy of a speech he gave setting out his ideas about life inside Judah during the Babylonian period called "New-Old Discoveries at Biblical Mizpah of Benjamin: The Recovery of Jewish Life in Israel During the Exile." He has written extensively about the site. The most helpful articles were "Mizpah: Newly Discovered Stratum Reveals Judah's Other Capital," in the September/October 1997 issue of *Biblical Archaeology Review,* and a series of pieces about the finds at the site that ran in *Tel Aviv* 20 (1993), *Tel Aviv* 22 (1995), and *Tel Aviv* 23 (1996). Zorn, Joseph Yellin, and John Hayes wrote about the stamp impressions found at the site in the *Israel Exploration Journal,* volume 44, 1994.

The information about Oded Lipschits's research is based on a number of interviews with him in 1998 by the author as well as speeches he gave at archaeology seminars. Lipschits kindly gave me a copy of his unpublished Ph.D. thesis in Hebrew, *The "Yehud" Province Under Babylonian Rule, 586–539 B.C.E.: Historic Reality and Historiographic Conceptions* (January 1997, submitted to Tel Aviv University), which provided a wealth of information about archaeological and biblical scholarship about the period. The material about the 1998 conference is from the collection of abstracts of papers given there and personal interviews with Lipschits. He sent me an unpublished paper setting forth his theories about Nebuchadnezzar's policies called "Nebuchadrezzar's [*sic*] Policy in Hattu-Land and the Fate of the Kingdom of Judah." The quote attributed to Ephraim Stern is from Stern's paper at the 1998 conference.

The material about the exhibits at the Babylonian Jewry Heritage Center is from the author's personal observations during a 1998 visit. Oded Bustenay was interviewed by the author.

Gabriel Barkay and the author visited the Ketef Hinnom site together in 1998. Barkay's article about the site, "Excavations at Ketef Hinnom in Jerusalem," appears in *Ancient Jerusalem Revealed.*

John Worrell, an American archaeologist working in the West Bank, first told me about the dig at Khirbet Shuweykeh and the political controversy over efforts to do a joint Israeli-Palestinian dig there and at Mizpah.

Chapter 7   Lot's Children: What Really Happened to the Ammonites

The archaeologists associated with the Madaba Plains Project file regular reports about their findings that appear in the *Annual of the Department of Antiquities of Jordan*. These reports were extremely helpful to me in reconstructing what they found and the evolution of their ideas. The Andrews University reference librarian tracked down and sent me preliminary reports written by the excavators about the Madaba Plains Project that appeared in the Spring 1996 and Autumn 1997 volumes of *Andrews University Seminary Studies*. Larry Herr sent me a draft of the 1998 preliminary report before it was published that was extremely helpful in my reconstruction of events. Rami Khouri's *Jordan Antiquity* newsletter has published extensively about the results of the digs at Hisban and Umayri. Larry Herr, Oystein LaBianca, Douglas Clark, and Larry Gerarty were all interviewed by the author a number of times and gave me a tour of their sites in 1998. Most of the information in the chapter is based on these interviews and their reports. Herr wrote a popular article about his Umayri finds called "What Ever Happened to the Ammonites?" that appeared in the November/December 1993 issue of *Biblical Archaeology Review*. Herr's articles in the Department of Antiquities' *Annual* outlining his theories about Umayri's fate under the Persians and the winepresses discovered in the surrounding area were invaluable.

LaBianca's "hardiness structures" were presented in a paper, "A Hardy People: Local Responses to Environmental, Socio-political and Economic Uncertainties in Jordan through the Millennia," to the Seventh International Conference on the History and Archaeology of Jordan, at the University of Copenhagen in June 1998, which the author attended. LaBianca provided me with a written copy for use in my research. Some of the team's ideas about the connections between the ancient Ammonites and modern Jordanians are contained in the book *Ancient Ammonites & Modern Arabs: 5000 Years in the Madaba Plains of Jordan,* edited by Gloria A. London and Douglas R. Clark (Amman, 1997). It also summarizes the discoveries and ideas driving the Madaba Plains Project.

The author attended Dr. Osamah Abu-Qorah's speech at the Copenhagen conference; the quotes are from my notes.

Leen Fakhoury and Kathy Sullivan were interviewed in Amman in 1999 on behalf of the author by Ghadeer Taher, who provided transcripts of their conversations, from which the quotations are taken.

The author visited the Amman Citadel Museum and attended the ceremony celebrating thirty years of digging at Hisban in 1998. The quotes from Hisban's mayor Yousef Msalam al Awalda and Mafous Abdul Hafez are from the author's personal interviews with them during a visit to the site. Oystein LaBianca provided me with a draft of the lesson plans for the site called "Tall Hisban: Gateway to the Archaeology of Central Jordan," which were created by Asta Sakala LaBianca, Oystein LaBianca, and Mafous Abdul Hafez. *Hesban After 25 Years,* edited by David Merling and Lawrence T. Gerarty (Berrien Springs, 1994), has numerous articles about the dig and its findings.

The quote from Herr's report is taken from his article that appeared in the *Mediterranean Peoples in Transition* volume.

Chapter 8   Esau's Birthright: A New Look at the Edomites

The history of how scholars viewed Edom and Edom's relations with Judah are based on interviews by the author with Itzhaq Beit-Arieh and Piotr Bienkowski.

Edom's history is detailed in a number of works that have come out in recent years. *You Shall Not Abhor an Edomite for He Is Your Brother: Edom and Seir in History and Tradition,* edited by Diana Vikander Edelman (Atlanta, 1995); *Early Edom and Moab: The Beginning of the Iron Age in Southern Jordan,* edited by Piotr Bienkowski (Sheffield, 1992); and J. R. Bartlett's *Edom and the Edomites* (Sheffield, 1989) were the most helpful. Oystein LaBianca and Randall Younker authored a good overall summary of archaeology in Ammon, Moab, and Edom called "The Kingdoms of Ammon, Moab, and Edom: The Archaeology of Society in Late Bronze/Iron Age Transjordan (ca. 1400–500 B.C.E.)," in Levy's *Archaeology of Society* book. Israel Finkelstein and Piotr Bienkowski conducted a spirited debate about Edom's history and the implications for dating in the region that ran in *Levant* magazine, volume 24, in 1992.

The information about Edom's involvement in copper mining appears in a number of works. Finkelstein's article "Under the Empires: Arabs, Edomites and Judahites in the Late Iron Age II," in his book *Living on the Fringe: The Archaeology and History of the Negev, Sinai and Neighboring Regions in the Bronze and Iron Ages* (Sheffield, 1995), talks about the copper mining and the Arabian trade in the area. His article "Horvat Qitmit and the Southern Trade in the Late Iron Age II," which ran in *ZDPV* 108, was also of interest. E. A. Knauf and C. J. Lenzen write about the "Edomite Copper Industry" in *Studies in the History and Archaeology of Jordan III,* edited by Adnan Hadidi (Amman, 1987). Rami Khouri wrote a number of reports about mining in his *Jordan Antiquity* newsletter during 1998. Particularly helpful was his report called "Firing the Furnaces of Early Bronze Age Feinan," about a German team's re-creation of early copper smelting at the site. Dr. Andreas Hauptmann, from the German Mining Museum at Bochum, was interviewed by the author in 1999 and provided extensive detail about his findings. All quotes from him in the chapter are from this interview.

Assyria's transformation of the region is chronicled most notably in Israel Eph'al's *The Ancient Arabs: Nomads on the Borders of the Fertile Crescent, 9th–5th Centuries B.C.E.* (Jerusalem, 1982). Nadav Na'aman writes about Assyria's power in the region in "Israel, Edom and Egypt in the 10th century B.C.E.," in *Tel Aviv* 19 (1992).

Piotr Bienkowski was interviewed by the author in Copenhagen during the 1998 conference, and by e-mail throughout 1999. He has written extensively about Edom's history. Most helpful were "The Edomites: Archaeological Evidence from Transjordan," in the Edelman book *You Shall Not Abhor;* "The Beginning of the Iron Age in Southern Jordan: A Framework," in the *Early Edom and Moab* book, and a 1995 article, "The Architecture of Edom," that ran in *Studies in the History and Archaeology of Jordan 5.*

The material about Horvat Qitmit is based on a number of interviews with Itzhaq Beit-Arieh, who also gave the author a tour of Malhata in 1998. Beit-Arieh's book about the site, *Horvat Qitmit: An Edomite Shrine in the Biblical Negev* (Tel Aviv, 1995), was very helpful. "The Edomite Shrine at Horvat Qitmit in the Judean Negev: Preliminary Excavation Report" ran in *Tel Aviv* 18 (1991). He sent a copy of "The Excavations in Tel Malhata: A Preliminary Report," which appeared in Hebrew in the 1998 issue of *Qedmoniot.*

Rudolph Cohen's quotations are from an interview conducted in his office in Jerusalem in 1998 by the author.

The information about the parallels between the material in Buseirah and in Judah comes from an unpublished paper sent to the author by Bienkowski, "Buseirah and Judah: Stylistic Parallels in the Material Culture," by Bienkowski and Leonie Sedman.

Chapter 9   Return to the Promised Land

The history of scholarship about Ezra and Nehemiah is chronicled by Charles Carter in "The Changing Face of the Persian Period," in *Second Temple Studies,* edited by Philip Davies (Sheffield, 1991). His study about Yehud's archaeology and history, *The Emergence of Yehud in the Persian Period: A Social and Demographic Study* (Sheffield, 1999), is the most comprehensive to date about Yehud's history. The *Second Temple Studies* books, with volumes focusing on the Persian Period and the Temple Community in the Persian Period, give a good overview of the latest research. *Achaemenid Imperial Administration in Syria-Palestine and the Missions of Ezra and Nehemiah,* by Kenneth G. Hoglund (Atlanta, 1992), set Ezra and Nehemiah's missions and the events described in the Bible in the larger context of Persian imperial goals.

Scripture and Other Artifacts: Essays on the Bible and Archaeology in Honor of Philip J. King, edited by Michael D. Coogan, J. Cheryl Exum, and Lawrence E. Stager (Louisville, 1994), had helpful essays by Carol L. Meyers, Eric M. Meyers, and Ephraim Stern about Yehud's history.

The information about sixth-century B.C.E. archaeology in Jerusalem comes from an interview with Jane Cahill as well as her article in *Ancient Jerusalem Revealed.* She sent me a number of helpful reports about the City of David excavations, including "Excavations at the City of David, 1978–1985," which appeared in *Qedem* 30 (1990), and "Stratigraphical, Environmental and Other Reports," in *Qedem* 33.

The material about Modiin is from the author's interviews with Oded Lipschits and Shmuel Gibson, who gave me a tour of the site in 1998.

There is no shortage of books about the Dead Sea Scrolls. Edmund Wilson's *Israel and the Dead Sea Scrolls* (New York, 1954) remains a great read forty-five years later. Hershel Shanks's *The Mystery and Meaning of the Dead Sea Scrolls* (New York, 1998) was invaluable for its summary of the many controversies that still surround the scrolls.

The controversy over the interpretation of the Qumran finds is based on the author's interviews with Yizhar Hirschfeld and Jean-Baptiste Humbert. *Biblical Archaeology Review* has run a number of interesting articles presenting alternative theories about the site, including "The Enigma of Qumran," in the January/February 1998 issue. Hirschfeld gave a lecture to a group of archaeologists at Hebrew University in 1998 about his ideas about Qumran, which the author attended. He also provided me with an advance copy of a paper he was writing arguing the similarities in architectural style between Qumran and other early Roman manor houses called "Early Roman Manor Houses in Judaea and the Site of Khirbet Qumran."

The author attended the "Dead Sea Scrolls and the Future of the Past in the 21st Century" conference held April 1998 in New York City, where Neil Asher Silberman spoke; he provided a written copy of the speech, "The Politics of the Dead Sea Scrolls," for quotation in the book.

The author viewed the Israel Museum exhibition on the Essenes in the summer of 1998.

Richard Elliott Friedman's book *Who Wrote the Bible?* is the most cogent explanation of the documentary hypothesis and how it has evolved over the years.

Eugene Ulrich was interviewed by the author in 1999 and also sent a number of articles about how the Dead Sea Scrolls are changing the way we view the development of the Bible that were very useful, including "The Bible in the Making: The Scriptures at Qumran," "The Community of the Renewed Covenant," and "The Dead Sea Scrolls and the Biblical Text," which were part of the *Notre Dame Symposium on the Dead Sea Scrolls.*

The author attended Philip Davies' lectures at Hebrew University and at Tel Aviv University in 1998, interviewed him in Jerusalem, and corresponded with him by e-mail. The quote in the chapter is from an e-mail he sent me after his visit.

The material about Ein Gedi is based on the author's interviews with Yizhar Hirschfeld and a tour of the site, all during 1998. *Biblical Archaeology Review* ran an interesting article summarizing the Babatha letters, "Babatha's Story" by Anthony J. Saldarini, in the March/April 1998 issue. The Edmund Wilson quote is from his book *Israel and the Dead Sea Scrolls.*

Index

❧